PROMETHEUS IN THE NINETEENTH CENTURY
FROM MYTH TO SYMBOL

LEGENDA

LEGENDA, founded in 1995 by the European Humanities Research Centre of the University of Oxford, is now a joint imprint of the Modern Humanities Research Association and Maney Publishing. Titles range from medieval texts to contemporary cinema and form a widely comparative view of the modern humanities, including works on Arabic, Catalan, English, French, German, Greek, Italian, Portuguese, Russian, Spanish, and Yiddish literature. An Editorial Board of distinguished academic specialists works in collaboration with leading scholarly bodies such as the Society for French Studies and the British Comparative Literature Association.

MHRA

The Modern Humanities Research Association (MHRA) encourages and promotes advanced study and research in the field of the modern humanities, especially modern European languages and literature, including English, and also cinema. It also aims to break down the barriers between scholars working in different disciplines and to maintain the unity of humanistic scholarship in the face of increasing specialization. The Association fulfils this purpose primarily through the publication of journals, bibliographies, monographs and other aids to research.

Maney Publishing is one of the few remaining independent British academic publishers. Founded in 1900 the company has offices both in the UK, in Leeds and London, and in North America, in Philadelphia. Since 1945 Maney Publishing has worked closely with learned societies, their editors, authors, and members, in publishing academic books and journals to the highest traditional standards of materials and production.

STUDIES IN COMPARATIVE LITERATURE

Editorial Committee
Professor Stephen Bann, University of Bristol (Chairman)
Professor Duncan Large, University of Swansea
Dr Elinor Shaffer, School of Advanced Study, London

Studies in Comparative Literature are produced in close collaboration with the British Comparative Literature Association, and range widely across comparative and theoretical topics in literary and translation studies, accommodating research at the interface between different artistic media and between the humanities and the sciences.

PUBLISHED IN THIS SERIES

Prometheus in the Nineteenth Century

From Myth to Symbol

CAROLINE CORBEAU-PARSONS

LEGENDA

Studies in Comparative Literature 25
Modern Humanities Research Association and Maney Publishing
2013

Published by the
Modern Humanities Research Association and Maney Publishing
1 Carlton House Terrace
London SW1Y 5AF
United Kingdom

LEGENDA is an imprint of the
Modern Humanities Research Association and Maney Publishing

Maney Publishing is the trading name of W. S. Maney & Son Ltd,
whose registered office is at Suite 1C, Joseph's Well, Hanover Walk, Leeds LS3 1AB

ISBN 978-1-907975-52-3

First published 2013

Printed in Great Britain

Cover: 875 Design

Copy-Editor: Dr Susan Wharton

CONTENTS

❖

To Matt and Eléa

ACKNOWLEDGEMENTS

I am deeply grateful to Professor Léonée Ormond, my PhD supervisor, for sharing so generously her immense knowledge and passion, and for her continuous guidance and kindness.

I am also indebted to Professor John Stokes, the late Professor Yoram Bar-David, Professor Edith Hall and Margaret Reynolds for their valuable advice and insight. At the Watts Gallery I wish to thank Richard Jefferies, its former curator, for sharing his expertise with so much passion, Julia Dudkiewicz, and Perdita Hunt for her continuous support over the years. I am also very grateful to Clare Rogan and Rob Lancefield of the Davison Art Centre. Tim Davenport, Dr Carol Jacobi, the Hon. Sandra de Laszlo, Richard Ormond and Dr Alison Smith have all helped along the way. Special thanks go to Dr Elinor Shaffer, Dr Graham Nelson and Dr Susan Wharton for their judicious remarks, guidance, and friendly support while this book was in preparation.

I also wish to acknowledge the AHRC, without whose support this project would not have seen the light.

Last but not least, this book would not have been possible without my friends and family and their unfailing love and support.

C.C.-P., London, January 2013

LIST OF ILLUSTRATIONS

INTRODUCTION

Contemporary perception of the Prometheus figure is paradoxical: it is based on a latent fascination so great that Gaston Bachelard named what is increasingly considered as one of the most important complexes in psychology the 'Prometheus complex', that is, 'all those tendencies which impel us to know as much as our fathers, more than our fathers, as much as our teachers, more than our teachers'.[1] As Bachelard also put it, pondering on the fascination of lighting a fire, 'the child wishes to do what his father does, but far away from his father's presence and so like a little Prometheus he steals some matches'.[2] However, in spite of the apparent similarity of the Prometheus complex with the Oedipus complex, Bachelard insists on the fact that the sexual parameter linked to the Prometheus complex is not as direct or strong as that linked to the Oedipus complex, and suggests that 'the Prometheus complex is the Oedipus complex of the life of the intellect'.[3]

The effect of the Prometheus myth on the human psyche surely derives from the fact that it draws its evocative power from two elemental forces endowed with symbolic functions: fire, and the notion of transgression. This might explain the development of mixed attitudes towards, and fascination with, the Prometheus figure. He brought fire to mankind: fire of life and creation, flame of knowledge and civilization; but at the same time, Prometheus's gift is an original infringement, and a threat to the order of creation. Prometheus is the benefactor of mankind, but he is also, par excellence, the one 'who plays with fire', and who is punished alongside his beloved creatures for doing so. It is revealing that the adjective 'promethean', depending on the language used, can apply to both an unethical and a courageous act.

Given the cultural and symbolic importance of the Prometheus myth in Western civilization, it is surprising how few studies have been devoted to it. Raymond Trousson, in the first edition of *Le Thème de Prométhée dans la littérature européenne*,[4] makes the same statement. After his detailed and near-comprehensive inventory of treatments of the theme, literature researchers may have felt that another study would be redundant. However, in 1972, Jacqueline Duchemin also made an important contribution to the study of the myth, adopting a different approach from Trousson's thematology: that of comparative mythology. I am much indebted to these two essential studies, as I am to Louis Séchan's brief but fundamental *Le Mythe de Prométhée*.[5] Unfortunately, at the time of writing, none of these three works has been translated into English. All translated quotations from these works are therefore my own, as are all quotations from French material used. The work of Raymond Trousson in particular will frequently be quoted at length.

This book is based on a PhD thesis completed in 2005 at King's College London, and it is encouraging that since then several scholars have devoted studies to the myth. Paul Bertagnolli, in particular, devoted a remarkable work to Romantic representations of the myth in music, which closely examines the sources on which these are based.[6] The scope of the present book is more wide-ranging and goes beyond the period analysed by Paul Bertagnolli, whilst focusing on interpretations of the myth that lead to the Symbolist period, but in many instances I shall refer to his invaluable study for more in-depth musical analyses. Carol Dougherty published a concise introduction to the Prometheus myth, aimed more at an undergraduate audience, which also highlights a resurgence of interest in the myth.[7]

However essential the first four studies above mentioned are, the subject, aim, and method of this work are very different. Séchan concentrates on the origins of the myth, whereas Trousson and Duchemin focus on the general evolution of the myth throughout literary history. Trousson opted for a monumental and quasi-encyclopaedic inventory of the occurrences of the myth, whereas Duchemin adopted what for her was the clearest way of emphasizing the orientation the Prometheus myth took, that is, a succession of essays. Thus, with two different approaches, their primary concern was the progression of the mythical material from a historical perspective. This latter aspect is crucial to consider the protean aspect of the myth, and constitutes the frame of the present book, but unlike Trousson's and Duchemin's studies, it does not aim to be a history of the Prometheus myth as such. Its starting point is the observation that, for Symbolism, Prometheus represented a prism in which the arts and a great number of ideals converged, as was also the case with Orpheus and Salome. Whereas many valuable studies have been devoted to the two latter characters, the Symbolist Prometheus has so far been neglected. This book is therefore an attempt to research this particular treatment of the mythological character and its sources.

In terms of construction and methodology, other studies of mythological figures have been a great source of inspiration, and in particular *Orpheus in the Nineteenth Century*,[8] by Dorothy Kosinski, The *Sappho History*,[9] by Margaret Reynolds, and *Pandora's Box*,[10] by Dora and Erwin Panofsky. *Pygmalion and Galatea: the History of a Narrative in English Literature*,[11] by Essaka Joshua, was also a point of reference, notably for the structure of the first section. Wider studies not exclusively devoted to Prometheus, but which put his figure into new perspectives, also proved stimulating. A notably valuable work was a short but insightful book by Dominique Lecourt, entitled *Prométhée, Faust, Frankenstein, fondements imaginaires de l'éthique*,[12] which outlines the extent of Prometheus's influence in the arts. *The Sin of Knowledge, Ancient Themes and Modern Variations*,[13] by Theodore Ziolkowski, examines the figures of Prometheus and Faust in a discerning way, and adds to this comparison the study of Adam. As can be seen from those two titles, the combined study of Prometheus, Faust, and Adam is a favourite one,[14] which has been expertly achieved by others, and on which I shall therefore not linger. For similar reasons, I shall not examine at length the parallels established between Satan and Prometheus.[15] Both rebel against a god, but whereas Prometheus's motivation is philanthropic, Satan's is purely egotistic. As Trousson pointed out, Aeschylus's Prometheus rebels against a 'moment' of Zeus's reign, Zeus being perfectible, whilst Satan, in his opposition to the perfect God of Christianity, was bound to embody Evil.[16] Satan was not perceived as a hero until the Romantic period, when God, as creator, was blamed for the existence of evil. But even then, Elizabeth Barrett Browning, in the preface to her translation of *Prometheus Unbound*, underlined the intrinsic difference between Satan and Prometheus: 'Satan suffered from his ambition, Prometheus from his humanity; Satan for himself; Prometheus for mankind; Satan dared peril which he had not weighed; Prometheus devoted himself to sorrows which he had foreknown. "Better to rule in hell", said Satan; "better to serve this rock", said Prometheus'.[17] Rather than examining the Prometheus figure exclusively through the scope and theme of transgression, which is the underlying link between the Titan, Faust, Satan and Adam, we shall consider all the nuances brought to Prometheus's persona thanks to the evolution of the mythical material. Rather than isolating and separating elements from the myth, we shall try to grasp its essential protean quality.

The present work was first intended as a study of artistic and cultural projections onto the Prometheus figure, questioning why such a phenomenon occurred at the end of the nineteenth century. Because Symbolism succeeds Romanticism and stems from it, the core of this study starts with Goethe, with whom the perception of the Prometheus myth radically changed, paving the way for its Romantic and Symbolist interpretations. With one of the pillars of Symbolism being the dream of a fusion between the arts, a methodological choice was made to consider and evaluate the Prometheus figure in literature and art, as well as in music. To use the image of the prism again, a study of the subject would have been incomplete or unfaithful to the Symbolist spirit had it not envisaged all the rays converging on Prometheus, especially at a time when communications between the arts and artists were so numerous. For the same reason I decided to take into account most of Symbolist Europe: England, France, Belgium and Germany. It will be seen that the musical, literary, and pictorial treatments of Prometheus are rarely all present in the same section. Hence the dominance of literature and history of art in the first section, a clear literary and musical dominance in the second, and the supremacy of cultural and pictorial studies in the last two sections. This division is not a methodological choice, but a reflection of the loose chronological frame given to this study in order to follow the evolution of the Prometheus figure, since composers, poets, writers and painters were not necessarily inspired by the Prometheus subject at the same time.

It should be noted that Prometheus was used as an allegory for the progress of science and materialism, especially when the industrial revolution came into full bloom. This allegory, based on the symbolic power of fire, should not be confused with the way in which late eighteenth- and nineteenth-century artists made a symbol of Prometheus. An allegory is based on a reduction process, from an abstract idea to a conventional and fixed image, whereas a symbol is by essence open and bound to evolve. The meaning and the form taken by this allegory of Prometheus have never changed, even if its users varied from Positivists to Russian Socialists. Prometheus extolled the omnipotence of science and industry, becoming a Stak-hanovian model for workers in the early twentieth century. With recent advances in genetics, it is interesting to note that this interpretation of Prometheus prevails nowadays, the adjective 'promethean', in most European languages, being applied to scientists 'playing with fire', with unlimited and potentially dangerous scientific powers. Phrased differently, the adjective is applied to modern Frankensteins, the superior power transgressed being ethics rather than God. We shall have to bear in mind that such an interpretation of Prometheus exists, but because it is antagonistic to Symbolist interpretations, we shall not examine its various uses.[18]

One of the first difficulties arising from the study of Prometheus is its reliance on the notion of myth, which needs to be clarified. The numerous definitions (ethnological, psychoanalytical, anthropological, and so on) ascribed to the myth are indeed confusing. The common use of the word myth, referring to an object or an individual which is a product of the imagination, or whose actual existence is not verifiable, is largely responsible for such confusion. An examination of the etymology of the word does not necessarily clear up these difficulties. The Greek origin of 'myth', *mythos*, which means 'speech', seems to be inevitably coupled with *logos* (rational speech), an association which falsifies the value of the myth. Unfortunately, through this opposition, the myth soon becomes a narrative relying on imagination, and therefore devoid of truth, when compared with an expression of rationality. Resorting to etymology is therefore particularly misleading, as one of the specific qualities of myth is to be a unifying cultural element, recognized by society as true. A myth is a narrative of sacred origin, which relates events as they might have happened in an indeterminate time in the past. Because of its oral and indefinite origins, the myth is not the product of an individual. It has a collective ownership, and it is created by this group. This explains why a myth is in essence protean: it evolves throughout history, depending on mentalities, on cultural, moral, and religious values. We shall see that a myth can be ignored or can fall into oblivion for a period of time, before being revived by a society which will project itself onto it. It could be said that man, like Prometheus, shapes myths to his own image, and that a society measures itself through them. Another essential element concerning myths is that turning to them is also a questioning of origins, since, as Mircea Eliade put it, 'we must never forget that one of the essential functions of the myth is its provision of an opening into the Great Time, a periodic re-entry into Time primordial'.[19] We shall come back to some of the specific qualities linked to myths in Part III, Chapter 1, especially in an examination of the value which nineteenth-century artists imputed to myths. However, in the nineteenth-century context of the *mal du siècle* (world-weariness), one of the reasons why a strong interest was shown in myths was that 'the modern world — in crisis ever since its profound break with Christianity– is in quest of a new myth, which alone could enable it to draw upon fresh spiritual resources and renew its creative powers'.[20] The nineteenth-century interest in myths expressed above all a need for the sacred.

To understand the originality of nineteenth-century interpretations of the Prometheus myth, I decided, in an introductory chapter, to examine its history briefly, from the beginnings to the nineteenth century: the origins of the myth, and the constitution of what we shall call Prometheus's persona, the fortune of Prometheus from Antiquity to Christianity, and the crucial period of the Renaissance, during which a rediscovery of the Prometheus figure was witnessed.

We shall see that, until the time of Johann Wolfgang von Goethe and *Sturm und Drang*, interpretations of Prometheus largely relied on this impetus brought into being by the Renaissance.

The second chapter opens with Goethe and the *Sturm und Drang*. Even though Goethe's tremendously influential poem 'Prometheus' dates from 1774, and his dramatic fragment bearing the same title from 1773, it would have been a methodological mistake to separate the study of these works from that of Romanticism. Goethe may not have been a Romantic, but to a certain extent he defined and shaped Romanticism, especially during his *Sturm und Drang* period. This is particularly true of the treatment of Prometheus, since its nineteenth-century interpretations rely on the turning point derived from the work of Goethe, on the new light that he cast on the Titan. After this study, and that of the musical pieces inspired by Goethe, we shall examine the Romantic appropriation of the Prometheus figure, by Byron and Shelley, and by Hugo and Balzac, who both identified the type of the artist with Prometheus.

Chapter Three will explore the Symbolist understanding of the Prometheus myth. In a first contextual section, in the absence of a precise definition of Symbolism, I shall attempt to show that it was not a movement but a spirit, essentially characterized by a crisis of faith which encompassed Aestheticism and Decadence. This will lead us to draw a map of Symbolist Europe, outlining the variations taken by Symbolism depending on the various cultural, political, and religious climates. Finally, we shall examine the Symbolist apprehension of the myth. In the two following sections, we shall consider how Prometheus was used in two different ways by Symbolists as an answer to this crisis of faith. First, we shall see that in Germany, following the 'twilight of the gods', Prometheus because a symbol for the start of a new era, that of mankind. In the last section, the focus will be on Prometheus at the heart of the Symbolist syncretism, particularly in France and in Belgium, where the religious crisis was especially strong.

In a final chapter, after my attempt to situate Prometheus within the Symbolist constellation, I shall examine the main projections that were made onto the Prometheus figure, through a study of the artistic works devoted to the Titan. The first two sections will appear as developments and illustrations of the previous chapter, with a study of Gustave Moreau and of the variations on the German vitalist Prometheus. In the third section, we shall examine one of the most original masks taken by Prometheus, in England, where a cross-fertilization of the Prometheus myth by the Pygmalion myth occurred. In the fourth and final section, we shall study the apotheosis of Prometheus in the last Symbolist generation, with František Kupka and Alexander Scriabin.

Notes to the Introduction

1. Gaston Bachelard, *Psychoanalysis of Fire* (Boston: Beacon Press, 1964), p. 12.
2. Ibid., p. 11.
3. Ibid., p. 11.
4. Raymond Trousson, *Le Thème de Prométhée dans la littérature européenne* (Geneva: Droz, 1964, repr. 2001).

5. Louis Séchan, *Le Mythe de Prométhée* (Paris: PUF, 1951, repr. 1985).

6. Paul Bertagnolli, *Prometheus in Music: Representations of the Myth in the Romantic Era* (Aldershot: Ashgate, 2007).

7. Carol Dougherty, *Prometheus* (London: Routledge, 2005).

8. Dorothy Kosinski, *Orpheus in Nineteenth Century Symbolism* (London: U.M.I Research Press, 1989).

9. Margaret Reynolds, *The Sappho History* (Basingstoke: Palgrave Macmillan, 2003).

10. Dora and Erwin Panofsky, *Pandora's Box: The Changing Aspects of a Mythical Symbol* (New York: Bollinger Foundation, 1962).

11. Essaka Joshua, *Pygmalion and Galatea: the History of a Narrative in English Literature* (Aldershot: Ashgate, 2001).

12. Dominique Lecourt, *Prométhée, Faust, Frankenstein, Fondements imaginaires de l'éthique* (Paris: Livre de poche, 1996).

13. Theodore Ziolkowski, *The Sin of Knowledge, Ancient Themes and Modern Variations* (Princeton: Princeton University Press, 2000).

14. See also Timothy Richard Wutrich, *Prometheus and Faust: The Promethean Revolt in Drama from Classical Antiquity to Goethe* (Westport, CN: Greenwood, 1995).

15. Prometheus has been confused with Lucifer, from the Latin 'lucem ferre', to bring or bear light. See R.J. Zwi Werblowsky, *Lucifer and Prometheus, a Study of Milton's Satan* (London: Routledge, 1999), which is particularly insightful. Raymond Trousson has demonstrated that the parallel between Satan and Prometheus is based on a simplification and intellectual shortcut (Trousson, pp. 66; 96–97; 208–09).

16. *Trousson*, pp. 96–97.

17. Elizabeth Barrett Browning, *The Poetical Works with Two Prose Essays* (London: Oxford University Press, 1951), p. 139.

18. See Ziolkowski, 'The Proletarization of Prometheus', in *The Sin of Knowledge*, pp. 111–48.

19. Mircea Eliade, *Myths, Dreams and Mysteries*, trans. by Philip Mairet (London: Collins, 1968), p. 34.

20. Ibid., p. 25.

PART I

From the Beginnings to the Nineteenth Century

Man achieves a state of awareness in which he is no longer
trying to revenge himself on a tyrant he has created, and so is
no longer divided against himself.[1]

NORTHROP FRYE

Myth is essentially linked to language: transmitted through generations, it appears as the cultural and historical product par excellence. To understand the nineteenth-century interpretations of the Prometheus myth and the specificity of the changes that occurred at that time, especially during its final decades, it is necessary to examine briefly the way in which the Prometheus myth constituted itself through history, in order to underline the evolution and consistency of Prometheus as a figure. However, given that our study is leading to the nineteenth century and notably to Symbolism, we shall concentrate on elements of the myth's history that are essential to the understanding of this period and its artistic development. We shall therefore leave aside centuries during which the myth, or Prometheus's persona, did not evolve in a way that would have influenced its nineteenth-century interpretations. Similarly, we shall leave aside or only briefly mention great literary figures such as Jean-Jacques Rousseau, if their treatment of the subject did not have further repercussions, or modify the general shape of the myth. To make an exhaustive account of all the treatments of the Prometheus myth in history would be an impossible task, but Raymond Trousson, in his seminal work,[2] makes a detailed survey to which one can refer for specific information about the evolution of the Prometheus theme from antiquity.

In order to clarify the origins of the Prometheus myth, I shall turn to the work of Martin Day,[3] whose approach to myths will be most useful for our purpose. Day distinguishes three different levels in the constitution of myths: first, at their roots, the archaic myth, which essentially relies on oral tradition; the intermediate myth, the product of a 'highly conscious artist, dominated by aesthetic impulses and intent upon neat, attractive telling of a good story'[4] and lastly the derivative myth, which will be our main concern.

CHAPTER 1

'Archaic' and 'Intermediate' Myths, or The Primitive Constitution of the Prometheus Myth

Etymology and 'Archaic' Myth

Prometheus in Greek means 'the fore-thinker', a man with 'foresight'. The name derives from the Indo-European root 'man', extended to 'man-dh', a semanteme containing the idea of thought, wisdom, and reflection. In this respect, Prometheus is opposed to his brother Epimetheus ('hindsight'), the clumsy character who does not think until after the event. The two brothers are so antithetical that Karl Kérényi named Epimetheus 'Prometheus' left hand'.[5] They are so closely linked in the first accounts of the myth that Kérényi assumed that originally there was a unique hybrid being, Epimetheus-Prometheus, a creature similar to Plato's androgyne which supposedly engendered mankind. Plato, in his *Protagoras*,[6] revived the complementary brothers, relating how Epimetheus was assigned to endow living things with assets for survival, forgetting to keep anything for mankind, thus forcing Prometheus to steal fire from Hephaestus and wisdom from Athena to give it to them.[7] As we can see, the mere etymology of 'Prometheus' plunges us into the myth itself. Louis Séchan[8] and Jacqueline Duchemin[9] fully explore the possible origins of Prometheus through the method of comparative mythology. In the present study, we shall attempt to throw light on the main traits of Prometheus, those that conditioned his later evolution as a persona. Even though, as Jacqueline Duchemin puts it, we might find the origin of Prometheus three millenia before our era in Sumero-Babylonian accounts,[10] we shall concentrate on the Greek sources of the myth, that is, on what Martin Day terms the 'archaic' myth.

The son of the Titan Iapetus and Klymene, Prometheus is traditionally presented as the brother of Menoetius, Atlas, and Epimetheus. When Iapetus led the war against the Olympian gods, only Prometheus and Epimetheus, amongst his sons, sided with the Olympians. According to Wilamowitz,[11] there were originally two different Prometheus figures. On the one side, the Ionian-Attic Promethos, founder of Kodride, husband of Asia or Hesione, who was worshipped in Athens during the Prometheia. Promethos was venerated during the torchlight run, which celebrated the god or daemon of ceramics (not the fire-giver). He was the patron deity of potters in Athens. Such a craft implying the mastery of fire, he was soon associated with Hephaestus, considered in that region as his youngest brother, beside whom he had an altar in the Academy with Athena (patroness of the arts and crafts). It is he who was said to have aided Zeus to get over a terrible headache by splitting his skull in two in order to give birth to Athena, and also to have shaped Pandora, before creating all human beings. In no sense does he steal fire from Zeus to aid men: he is not his enemy and does not incur celestial punishment. As Louis Séchan notes,[12] these features belong to the second Prometheus, the Boeotian-Locrian one, whose name eventually predominated. He was Hesiod's Prometheus, who also partly inspired Aeschylus.

Prometheus's duality was to be of great importance, as it determined the two facets that would influence the evolution of his persona: Prometheus *plasticator* and Prometheus the fire-giver. Let us now consider the 'intermediate' myth of Prometheus, through the accounts of Hesiod and Aeschylus, who both crucially shaped this persona.

The Constitution of Prometheus's Persona through the Intermediate Myth

Prometheus the Fire-Giver

Hesiod in the *Theogony* (lines 507–16)[13] relates that in Mekone, where gods and mortals used to meet during the golden age, Prometheus, who wanted to trick Zeus, carved up an ox for the feast, and divided it into two portions. He covered the best pieces with the ox's gut, and decorated the bones with enticing white fat. Then, when the Titan asked Zeus to choose between the two portions, the god naturally pointed to the inferior one. Furious at having been tricked, Zeus forbade mankind from receiving the gift of fire, therefore indirectly punishing Prometheus. However, the account does not end here. Determined to ensure that men would benefit from a civilized life, Prometheus stole fire in a fennel stalk and gave it to men. As a punishment, Zeus sent the first woman amongst them, created by Hephaestus and attractively dressed by Athena, whilst Prometheus was chained to a pillar to endure perpetual torture. Each day, an eagle was to tear out his liver, which would regrow every night to let the bird devour it anew. A point of note, in the *Theogony*, is the mention of Epimetheus, associated with Pandora, who in this work is not yet given a name. Epimetheus, not Prometheus, is referred to as the one to blame for 'the unhappiness of men eating bread, by being the first to receive under his roof the virgin formed by Zeus' (lines 512–14).

The persona of Prometheus in *Works and Days*[14] is very different, the Titan being presented by Hesiod as the one responsible for man's misery. As Theodore Ziolkowski puts it, whereas 'in the *Theogony*, Prometheus appears midway in the divine genealogy as a god cast out for reasons described in lavish detail, in the human context of *Works and Days*, in contrast, he stands at the beginning of human history as the source of man's grief and misery'.[15] Prometheus is punished for being a trickster and breaking the law. Far from being the benefactor of mankind, he is to blame for its fall. In the words of Zeus:

> Son of Iapetos, clever above all others, you are pleased at having stolen fire and
> outwitted me — a great calamity both for yourself and for men to come. To set

against the fire I shall give them an affliction in which they will all delight as they embrace their own misfortune.[16] (lines 55–59)

Such a contrast between the two works might be explained by the nature of *Works and Days*, a moral poem addressed to Hesiod's brother, Perses, who was in need of guidance in this regard. The focus of the poem, which deals mainly with Pandora, is also an element of explanation for the shift in Prometheus's persona. Because he is responsible for the existence of Pandora, he is also consequently responsible for the misery following her arrival on Earth.

In any case, we can see that Prometheus's characteristic role as the benefactor of mankind does not derive from Hesiod. The specific quality of the Titan which Hesiod emphasized through the gift of fire was trickery. Aeschylus took the opposite view from Hesiod on the Prometheus myth: where Hesiod emphasized the loss of the golden age, he saw the Titan as the initiator of progress.

Prometheus the Rebel

> Chez Hésiode, l'être humain était étroitement assujetti aux dieux; dans le *Prométhée*, il se forge un destin.[17]

Although artistic depictions of Prometheus flourished during the sixth century, Prometheus did not inspire many writers, and, in spite of a few comic treatments of the myth, detailed by Jacqueline Duchemin,[18] this period did not determine the evolution of the Prometheus myth. Far greater was the influence of Aeschylus on the treatment of the myth and the development of Prometheus as a persona. Prior to writing the influential *Prometheus Unbound*, Aeschylus had written another play entitled *Prometheus the Firelighter*. This satyr play was probably performed in 472 BC, the same year as the *Persians*, which led Jacqueline Duchemin to assume that because 'the first play the Prometheus legend inspired Aeschylus to write was not a tragedy, but a satyr play, [...] one could therefore be tempted to think that he was the first to treat the subject in a tragic way, and that he certainly did so at the end of his life',[19] an appealing but not necessarily convincing hypothesis. However, the work that determined the evolution of the myth was *Prometheus Bound*. Before examining the play itself and its impact on the constitution of the Prometheus myth, we should note that *Prometheus Bound* remains problematic, for three main reasons.

Firstly, even though it has been attributed to Aeschylus since the third century BC, scholars still dispute the authenticity of *Prometheus Bound*.[20] Apart from the fact that its style is more prosaic than others of Aeschylus's works, and that it presents staging issues that may not have been solvable in his lifetime, this debate is sustained by the fact that Aeschylus, a man of strong faith, truly believed in the justice of Zeus and in universal harmony. *The Suppliants*, the *Orestia*, or the *Persians* all demonstrate a coincidence between Zeus and *Ananke* (the Aeschylean concept of destiny or necessity, deprived of the concept of determinism). Since Aeschylus believed in an absolute justice, the appearance of Zeus as a tyrant in *Prometheus Bound* is difficult to justify in the light of the depiction of the god in his other plays. Nonetheless, if we agree with Trousson that law could not be on both sides in Aeschylus's thought, 'from now on, the divine order could only [...] be conceived as an evolution; [...]

gods, like men, are constantly evolving, and learn justice'.[21] From that perspective, Aeschylus was not entirely critical of the gods, but simply underlined their journey towards pure and absolute justice. This point leads to the second problematic aspect of *Prometheus Bound*: its situation within Aeschylus's trilogy.

Although the evolution of Zeus as a character could be understood as his progression as a benevolent and forgiving god,[22] this assumption is difficult to verify, as only fragments of the two other plays constituting the supposed Prometheia remain. Therefore we cannot exactly determine the nature of the link between *Prometheus Bound*, *Prometheus Unbound* (Prometheus Lyomenos) and *Prometheus the Fire-Bringer* (Prometheus Porphyros), also ascribed to Aeschylus in antiquity. It was long believed that *Prometheus Bound* was the first play of the trilogy, *Prometheus Unbound* the second, and *Prometheus the Fire-Bringer* the final one, but a few critics, among them Martin L. West, have suggested that *Prometheus the Fire-Bringer* could be the first play.[23] As a result of the two issues mentioned above, we are unable to establish, both for religious and stylistic reasons, whether *Prometheus Bound* came early or late within Aeschylus's production. We shall therefore limit our observation to the reception and perception of the works and will postulate, like the readers of the nineteenth century, that Aeschylus was the author of *Prometheus Bound*, a work that was part of a trilogy.

In *Prometheus Bound*, the angle from which Prometheus is viewed is radically different from that of Hesiod. The trickery at Mekone is not mentioned, and the only responsibility of Prometheus is the gift of fire to mankind, an act that took up only nine lines in the *Theogony*. As Theodore Ziolkowski notes, 'nor does Aeschylus refer to Pandora or Epimetheus; Prometheus alone must pay the penalty for his crime'.[24] The shift of focus in the myth is not without consequences: Prometheus's act of rebellion against Zeus takes a new significance, as the god is referred to as a 'new god' (line 439) without much legitimacy (having killed his father Kronos) who governs as a 'tyrant' (line 10). The opposition of the Titan, in this context, means much more than pure trickery, and appears as a conflict of values. Although Zeus does not appear on stage, the identity of his henchmen is telling: they are *Kratos* and *Bia*, Strength and Violence, the two pillars of tyranny. The change in Zeus's image entails a revaluation of Prometheus and his theft. In *Prometheus Bound*, the Titan is no longer motivated by his intention to trick Zeus, but by his love for mankind. In the first act of the play, Prometheus is told:

> Each changing hour will bring successive pain to rack
> Your body; and no man yet born shall set you free.
> Your kindness to the human race has earned you this.[25]

Trickery is not the end of his actions. Prometheus is certainly the victim of his hubris in *Prometheus Bound* (the word *authadia*, 'wilful stubbornness', is omnipresent in the play), but nobility is attached to his character. Twice in the play, in lines 11 and 28, his 'philanthropic turn' is mentioned. Indeed, in Aeschylus's play, he is the true saviour of mankind, since, in lines 232–33, Prometheus informs the chorus that Zeus intended to eradicate mankind from the Earth. Only the Titan attempted to save them from death. In this context, the theft of fire takes a new significance, as Prometheus remarks:

> I am harnessed in this torturing clamp. For I am he
> Who hunted out the source of fire, and stole it, packed
> In pith of a dry fennel-stalk. And fire has proved
> For men a teacher in every art, their grand resource.
> That was the sin for which I now pay the full price,
> Bared to the winds of heaven, bound and crucified.[26]

Even at this early stage in the evolution of the myth, fire becomes the symbol for knowledge, the arts and sciences, which are the means of civilization. Therefore, by bringing fire to mankind, Prometheus appears as the great educator of men, as a sort of spiritual father. Before his intervention, as well as being brutish, men had no proper conscience.

> Mindless, I gave them mind and reason [...]
> In those days, they had eyes, but sight was meaningless
> Heard sounds, but could not listen; all their length of life
> They passed like shapes in dreams, confused and purposeless.[27]

According to Aeschylus, Prometheus is responsible for the awakening of conscience in men. The playwright also strongly emphasizes another of the Titan's gifts to men, their 'blind hopes' (line 250). Such a gift could be considered as a curse, but is in fact very meaningful. Prometheus claims that, by this gift, he delivered men from their obsession with death. As Trousson notes,[28] he preserved them from the feeling of absurdity, and 'gave them the illusion of the value of dynamism and action, together with the ambition to be free'. Aeschylus depicts this gift, which at the outset seems anything but a present, as one of the main traits of man.

Another key element brought out by Aeschylus's tragedy — wherein resides the dramatic aspect of the play — is Prometheus's secret. Prometheus 'the forethinker' knows the possible destiny of Zeus. He reveals that he 'Shall yet be needed by the Lord of Immortals to disclose the new design, tell him who it is/ Shall rob him of his power and his glory.' Prometheus adds, 'Nor shall I cower under his fierce threats, or tell this secret,/ Until he free me from these brutal bonds/ And consent to compensate me for his outrage.'[29]

Later in the play, Zeus sends Hermes to enquire into this secret, crucial to the action of *Prometheus Bound*, since the main character of the play is totally motionless. The secret, which is that the child that Zeus will have with Thetis will overthrow him, will be of tremendous importance to the further development of the myth. Zeus's offspring, named Demogorgon by Shelley, will be the precondition for Prometheus's and mankind's liberation in the Romantic play.

This analysis of Aeschylus's play was elementary, but its aim was to highlight its contribution to the constitution of the myth. We now have to examine a final major trait of Prometheus's persona, which also appeared in Ancient Greece at a later stage.

Prometheus Plasticator

The Athenians, though fascinated by Prometheus, did not represent him as the creator of mankind. Louis Séchan explains this apparent paradox by assuming that the people of Athens were probably even more attached to the idea of the city's autochthony than to Prometheus.[30] In *Prometheus Bound*, we see that, through the gift of the fire of knowledge, Prometheus appears as a spiritual father for mankind. But this trait of Prometheus was soon to take a literal significance in the myth. Prometheus's role as a creator was to become as important as his role as a fire-bringer. It is not the purpose of this study to analyse all the ancient texts referring to Prometheus as a creator,[31] but we should mention that Aesop[32] was the first to depict Prometheus in that function. We then have to wait for fourth-century comedies by Philemon[33] and Menander[34] to see Prometheus forming men and animals from earth. Menander approves of Prometheus's suffering since, in his view, the creator of woman is to blame for the gods' resentment.

Jacqueline Duchemin put forward the theory that the origin of Prometheus *plasticator* might be found in Sumero-Babylonian pantheons.[35] However, she also mentions that Prometheus's predecessor was not a god of fire.[36] The fortune of this aspect of Prometheus owes much to the Roman world, which was particularly influenced by it. For example, Hyginus's fable CXLII, 'Pandora', tells us that mankind was formed by Prometheus from silt, before Hephaestus created Pandora, who was brought to life by Athena. The first woman married Epimetheus, and gave birth to a daughter called Pyrrha. In *The Library* (I, 7,1), Apollodorus gives an account of the creation of men, modelled by Prometheus with earth and water. Many early texts deal with the creative aspect of Prometheus, without bringing new elements to the constitution of the Titan's persona. The roles of the other gods change in these accounts, without modifying the shape of the myth. However, we should mention the most important text in the transmission of the image of Prometheus as a creator. We know what influence Ovid's *Metamorphoses* had on countless generations of poets, and the myth of Prometheus *plasticator* was one of his legacies. His tale notably inspired, amongst others, Boccaccio and Goethe. The literary quality of Ovid's poem, more than the novelty of the mythological material, appears as the reason for such an impact. The famous passage on Prometheus is the following:

> Then man was made perhaps from seed divine
> Formed by the great Creator, so to found
> A better world, perhaps the new-made earth,
> So lately parted from the ethereal heavens,
> Kept still some essence of the kindred sky-
> Earth that Prometheus moulded, mixed with water,
> In likeness of the gods that govern the world-
> And while the other creatures on all fours
> Look downwards, man was made to hold his head
> Erect in majesty and see the sky,
> And raise his eyes to the bright stars above.
> Thus earth, once crude and featureless, now changed
> Put on the unknown form of humankind.[37]

The poetry of Ovid had a considerable effect upon the constitution of Prometheus's persona on an artistic level, even though the content of the myth itself did not undergo any major change.

Finally, an important influence on the evolution of the myth was that of Lucian of Samosata, who made use of it several times in order to give shape to his thoughts. Lucian had already used the Prometheus myth in *To a Man who Had Told Him: You are a Prometheus in Your Speeches*, in which he presents the Titan as the creator of mankind, and employs him as the key element of rhetorical games. Lucian compares himself to Prometheus, making a parallel between the material the Titan's creatures are made of — clay, and the quality of his words — fragile and crumbly. He also draws a parallel with Prometheus because the structure of his speech is based on a pre-existing model, like Prometheus with men. Lucian takes the various elements of the myth as paradigms, which he uses to give root to his rhetorical construction. However, more importantly for the evolution of the myth, *Prometheus or the Caucasus* goes further than a demonstration of Lucian's virtuoso skills. In spite of the comic tone of this text, its consequence and contribution to the myth is the idea that the gods are the creation of men. Lucian put forward the idea that the world would be useless without men, since gods would not know their happiness if mankind were not unhappy. Equally true is the fact that, without men, the gods would not be admired and worshipped. This is how the writer comes to the conclusion that men simply make gods become so, which is a crucial step both in the constitution and interpretation of the Prometheus myth, even though we shall have to wait for the end of the eighteenth century and Goethe to see it become a fundamental element. Nonetheless, during the constitutive phase of the myth, the evolution of Prometheus as a persona was not only linked to the way in which his actions were treated by these various writers, but also to his relationship with the other mythological characters surrounding him.

Prometheus's Auxiliaries

Athena and Hephaestus

Together with Prometheus, Athena and Hephaestus make up the trio of fire gods in Athens. The three most famous lampadedromies (torchlight processions) were to honour these three gods: the Panathenaes, the Hephaesteias, and the Prometheia, all named after them. Because of their association in the Academy, their roles in the Prometheus myth are sometimes interchangeable. We have seen[38] that in the primitive accounts of the Prometheus myth, the Titan was linked to the birth of Athena. However, this is not the only existing version of the birth of the goddess. Indeed, if in Euripides's *Ion*,[39] Prometheus is the one to deliver Athena from Zeus by splitting his skull into two, according to Pindar,[40] Hephaestus, not Prometheus, fills that role. However, apart from the name of the improvised midwife in this mythological account, its content is identical. This element of the myth is not the only link between Athena, Hephaestus and Prometheus.

In a way, Hephaestus seemed to be in competition with Prometheus. Excepting their confusion in the account of Athena's birth, these two figures also shared the paternity of men for a while. Because both were gods of fire, which in Athens links them to the crafts of pottery and ceramics, both were soon to be associated in the creation of mankind. In Greek mythology, since this type of creation seems invariably to be symbolically related to these two crafts, the evolution of the two gods as *plasticator* was not totally unexpected. However, as Marie Delcourt puts it,[41] whereas Hephaestus was originally a more powerful divinity in Greek cults, Prometheus, as a creative god, would have supplanted him. In the early accounts of the myth of Pandora, Prometheus is never clearly mentioned as her creator, as opposed to Hephaestus, who, since Hesiod, was traditionally regarded as her father. This attribution, as we know, was not to last. There is an undeniable kinship between Hephaestus and Prometheus, but, in spite of his great reluctance to comply, Hephaestus himself, in Aeschylus's *Prometheus Bound*, is in charge of the binding of Prometheus. This element reveals the essential difference between the two gods. Jacqueline Duchemin, quoting Georges Dumézil, emphasizes the crucial importance of the distinction, in mythology, between 'binding gods' (Zeus being one) and 'bound gods'.[42] Hephaestus and Prometheus respectively appear as the perfect embodiments of these two categories. Hephaestus, in Homer's *Odyssey*, makes Aphrodite and Ares prisoners, and in Plato's *Republic* (II, 378 d), he binds his own mother, Hera. This characteristic schism among Greek gods would therefore have limited the confusion between Hephaestus and Prometheus, and avoided their assimilation.

As far as Athena is concerned, we will leave aside her relationship to Hephaestus (so close that in certain accounts, she was referred to as his wife), to concentrate on her link to Prometheus. At that stage in the history of the myth, the symbolic importance Athena would have in its evolution was only being set up, but all the elements of their future association were already beginning to take root. Athena, in the Prometheus myth, is less important for what she represents as a goddess than for what she symbolizes on a higher level. Athena is the offspring of Zeus and Metis, but an unusual offspring, since Zeus devoured the goddess. This is no coincidence, since Metis symbolizes divine intelligence. The unexpected way Zeus gives birth to Athena is therefore as meaningful as Zeus's 'union' to Metis: she appears as the resurgence of the embodiment of divine intelligence. It explains why, in many accounts of the creation of Pandora, she is the one to breathe life into her, that is, to awaken her conscience and to give birth to her. This element, as we shall see, will be at the origin of the close association of Athena and Prometheus in later versions of the myth. However, it is now time to examine a character who, in association with Prometheus, constitutes one of the most famous mythological duos.

Pandora

Pandora, in Greek, means 'the present of all' (*Pantes*, 'all', *doron*, 'gift') , but appears as an ambivalent gift to men. At the beginning of the history of the Prometheus myth, she is almost always presented as part of a trio including the Titan and Epimetheus, and as such embodies the triumph of Zeus over Prometheus. The binding of Prometheus is not the sole punishment for his crime, since his chastisement is not directed exclusively towards the Titan. In Hesiod's *Works and Days*, the creation of Pandora by the Olympian gods aims first to upset Prometheus's plans for men, and second to make their destiny miserable (line 56 and following). Many of the Olympian gods take part in the creation of Pandora: Hephaestus gives her shape from clay, she inherits her grace from Aphrodite, whilst Athena teaches her crafts, adorns her and girds her loins. But the gift of the gods is meant to be the curse of men. From line 591 to line 612, Hesiod develops a long diatribe against women, this 'accursed crew'. Pandora is ambivalent on more than one level: both a curse and a gift, she is the 'present of all', being both the present of gods, as their creation, and the present of men, since they are its recipients. In the *Theogony*, Pandora's character, nameless in *Works and Days*, is much more developed than in Hesiod's previous work. She receives an extra 'gift' from a god, Hermes, who transmits deceitfulness to her, together with the art of lying. Adorned in that fashion, she is led to Epimetheus, who, despite his brother's warning, cannot resist his fascination with Pandora. As soon as she arrives on Earth, she opens the jar[43] containing all the ills of the world and men are plunged into misery. Only Hope remains under the lid. Hesiod's conclusion, after the account of the Pandora episode, makes clear the fact that she is the punishment for Prometheus's crime towards Zeus: 'There is no way to escape Zeus' schemes'. Prometheus tried to help men, and they are punished for it. In Hesiod's text, how and where Pandora found the jar is not revealed, but scholars[44] agree that it was probably in the possession of Epimetheus, who himself opens the jar in a few early accounts of the myth.[45]

If we take into account Karl Kérényi's interpretation of the relationship between the two brothers, Pandora's role is even more interesting.[46] If Prometheus and Epimetheus, in early accounts of the Prometheus myth, are but the two opposite poles of a primordial being, it might explain why Epimetheus is irremediably attracted to her, whereas Prometheus desperately warns his brother against her. Their antagonistic feelings of attraction/repulsion would therefore be the reflection of the bipolarity of this single being as perceived by Kérényi. When Epimetheus begins to disappear from versions of the Prometheus myth, this duality of feelings for Pandora is carried by Prometheus alone, and becomes ambivalent, as we shall see in the next chapter when studying Goethe's unfinished play *Prometheus*.[47] Another interpretation of Pandora's value as a character is that of Raymond Trousson,[48] based on Guarducci's theories. According to him, the myth of Pandora, as an original myth, is a food myth, the equivalent of which can be found in every civilization: 'a quarrel between demons and gods around a foodstuff providing immortality is usually at the basis of original myths. The gods, who succeed in winning this good, are stolen by the demons. Thus, a god dressed up like a woman or a goddess comes to the enemy, and, by guile, manages to take the object of contention back. Then a war starts between the two groups, in which the demons are eventually defeated. From this legendary complex, the feature referring to Pandora is the expedition of the transvestite god, or the goddess, amongst the enemies.'[49] From that perspective, the strong link between the Prometheus myth and that of Pandora would be reinforced by the fact that both were fundamental myths, that of Prometheus as a creation myth, and that of Pandora as a food, and therefore original myth. This might explain why, as we shall see, the fortune of the myth of Pandora was also bound to be of great significance. Having briefly cast light on how the Prometheus myth and its corollary were constituted during Antiquity, we now must consider what happened to the pagan myth at the dawn of Christianity.

Notes to Chapter 1

1. Northrop Frye, 'Prometheus: The Romantic Revolutionary', in *A Study of English Romanticism* (Brighton: Harvester Press, 1968), p. 110.
2. Trousson, *Le Thème de Prométhée dans la littérature européenne* (Geneva: Droz, 1964, repr. 2001).
3. Martin Day, *The Many Meanings of Myth* (Lanham: University Press of America 1984).
4. Ibid., p. 5.
5. Karl Kérényi, *Mythologie des grecs* (Paris: Payot, 1952), and Carl Gustav Jung, Karl Kérényi, and Paul Radin, *Le Fripon divin*, trans. by Arthur Reiss (Geneva: Georg, 1958).
6. Plato, *Protagoras*, trans. by C. C. W. Taylor (Oxford: Oxford University Press, 2009)320c8–322d5, pp. 16–24.
7. The story of Prometheus is used in the dialogue by the sophist Protagoras in an attempt to prove to Socrates that virtue can be taught. He explains that civic wisdom, Zeus's attribute, was not granted to mankind, but that Zeus endowed Hermes with the mission of distributing justice and shame among them. Protagoras thus argues that the story illustrates why wisdom about architecture and medicine is only understood by very few, whereas the understanding of politics and justice is more widespread.
8. Louis Séchan, *Le Mythe de Prométhée* (Paris: PUF, 1951, repr. 1985).
9. Jacqueline Duchemin, *Prométhée, histoire du mythe, de ses origines orientales à ses incarnations modernes* (Paris: Les Belles Lettres, 2000).
10. Ibid., pp. 33–44.
11. Ulrich von Wilamowitz-Moellendorff, *Aischylos Interpretationen* (Berlin: Weidmann, 1914), p. 138.
12. Séchan, *Le Mythe de Prométhée*, p. 13.
13. Hesiod, *Theogony* and *Work and Days*, trans. by M. L. West (Oxford: Oxford University Press, 2008), p. 18.
14. Ibid., pp. 35–61.
15. Ziolkowski, *The Sin of Knowledge*, p. 29.
16. Hesiod, *Theogony* and *Work and Days*, p. 38.
17. Trousson, p. 51: 'For Hesiod, the human being was strictly subject to the gods; in *Prometheus*, he created a destiny for himself'.
18. Duchemin, pp. 88–95.
19. Ibid., p. 87.
20. See Mark Griffith, *The Authenticity of Prometheus Bound* (Cambridge: Cambridge University Press, 1977), pp. 1–7; M. Hadas, *A History of Greek Literature*, p. 81; D.W. Lucas, *The Greek Tragic Poets*, 2nd edn (London: Cohen and West, 1959), p. 91; G. Norwood, *Greek Tragedy*, 4th edn (London: Methuen, 1948), pp. 91–92; Louis Séchan, *Le Mythe de Prométhée*, p. 23; M. Delcourt, *Eschyle*, p. 63; Trousson, pp. 42–43.
21. Trousson, p. 42.
22. Phillip Vellacott, in his introduction to *Prometheus Bound* (London: Penguin Classics, 1961), p. 9, states that 'There can be little doubt that by the end of the trilogy Zeus himself abandoned the use of force and opened negotiations with Prometheus, who then told him of the prophecy concerning the sea-nymph Thetis; that Heracles [Hercules], with the permission of Zeus, set Prometheus free, perhaps first shooting the eagle with his bow; that the centaur Chiron, longing for death in the agonies of the wound Heracles had inflicted, was allowed to lose his immortality and descend to Hades, thus 'taking on himself the pains of Prometheus' in fulfilment of prophecy; and that the final settlement recognized the supremacy of Zeus, the right of the human race to exist and develop, and the superiority of reason to violence.'
23. Martin L. West, *Studies in Aeschylus* (Stuttgart: Teubner, 1990), Mark Griffith, *The Authenticity of the Prometheus Bound*; C.J. Herington, *The Author of the Prometheus Bound* (Austin: University of Texas Press, 1970).
24. Ziolkowski, *The Sin of Knowledge*, p. 36.
25. Aeschylus, *Prometheus Bound*, trans. by Philip Vellacott (New York: Penguin Classics, 1961), p. 21. The authoritative edition of the original text remains that of Mark Griffith (Cambridge: Cambridge University Press, 1983).

26. Ibid., p. 24.

27. Ibid., p. 34.

28. Trousson, p. 48.

29. Aeschylus, *Prometheus Bound*, trans. by Philip Vellacott (New York: Penguin Classics, 1961), p. 26.

30. Séchan, p. 33. See also, on the figure of the artisan, Françoise Frontisi-Ducroux, *Dédale: mythologie de l'artisan en Grèce ancienne* (Paris: F. Maspero, 1975).

31. For instance, Aesop, *Fabulae*, 124, *Prometheus and Men*; Apollodorus, *Library*, I, 7; Horace, *Odes*, I, 16; Hyginus, *De Astronomia*, II, 15; Ovid, *Metamorphoses*, I, 78–83; Juvenal, *Satires*, XIV, 35; IV, 133–34; Lucian, *Works*, I, 3 and 11–17.

32. *Fabulae*, 155 and 183.

33. Philemon, *Fragmenta*, trans. by F. Dübner (Paris: Didot, not dated), III.

34. Menander, *Works*, ed. and trans. by W. G. Arnott (Cambridge, MA: Harvard University Press, 2000). On the interplay between myths in ancient Greece and the ancient Near East, see Martin West's *The East Face of Helicon*, new edn (Oxford: Clarendon Press, 1999) and Walter Burkert, *The Orientalising Revolution*, new edition (Cambridge, MA: Harvard University Press, 1995).

35. Duchemin, p. 20.

36. See Duchemin, pp. 20–21.

37. Ovid, *Metamorphoses*, I, trans. by A.D. Melville (Oxford: Oxford University Press, 1986), p. 3.

38. See above, p. 9 (16).

39. Euripides, *Ion*, 454 and following.

40. Pindar, *Olympics*, VII, 35.

41. Marie Delcourt, *Hephaistos ou la Légende du Magicien* (Paris: Université de Liège-Belles Lettres, 1957), pp. 156–57.

42. Duchemin, p. 55.

43. In Hesiod's text, it is a jar, not a box.

44. Louis Séchan, *Pandora, l'Eve grecque* (Paris: Bulletin de l'Association Guillaume Budé, XXIII, 1929), p. 12; Georges Dumézil, *Le Festin d'immortalité* (Paris, 1924), p. 98.

45. Babrios, *Fable 58*, and Philodemus, *De Pietate*.

46. See above, p. 15, note 23.

47. Johann Wolfang von Goethe, *Early Verse Drama and Prose Plays*, ed. by Cyrus Hamlin and Frank Ryder, trans. by Robert M. Browning, Michael Hamburger, Cyrus Hamlin, and Frank Ryder (New York: Suhrkamp, 1988).

48. Trousson, p. 31.

49. Ibid., p. 31.

CHAPTER 2

From Antiquity to Christianity

A Christianized Prometheus, or the Legend within the Myth

Countless nineteenth- and twentieth-century commentators have noted the clear parallel drawn between Jesus Christ and Prometheus by the Fathers of the Church. Such a parallel was not striking for their time, since many contemporary works of art were based on it. However, finding grounds to assert its accuracy at the beginning of Christianity is a much more complex task, in spite of the confident assertions of generations of commentators. The still-widespread belief that Prometheus, according to the Fathers of the Church, was a prefiguration of Jesus Christ relies on a dubious interpretation and conflation of works by Tertullian.

To give one of the most conspicuous examples, the nineteenth-century French intellectual Edgar Quinet, in the preface to his *Prométhée* (1838),[1] quoted two phrases, which he attributed to Tertullian, to justify the idea that his conception of Prometheus was shared by the Greek and Latin apologists, namely: 'Hic est verus Prometheus, Deus omnipotens blasphemiis lancinatus', and 'crucibus Caucasorum'. Yet these words do not figure anywhere in Tertullian's works.

In his *Apology* (XVIII, 2), having mentioned great pagan men who had deserved to have presentiments about the Christian God, he states, '(Hic enim est verus Prometheus), qui saeculum certis temporum dispositionibus et exitibus ordinavit'.[2] Thus, it appears that instead of establishing a parallel between Jesus Christ and Prometheus, Tertullian is suggesting that Prometheus, compared to God, is an impostor. The second passage is in *Adversus Marcionem*[3] (I, I, 3), when Tertullian describes his enemy Marcion's hostile country, Pontus. The passage is worth quoting in full: 'nihil illic nisi feritas calet illa scilicet quae fabulas scenis dedit, de sacrifiis Taurorum et amoribus Colchorum, et crucibus Caucasorum. Sed nihil tam barbarum ac triste apud Pontum quem quod illic Marcion natus est, Scytha tetrior, Hamaxobio instabilior, Massageta inhumanior, Amazone audacior, nubilo obscurior, hieme frigidior, gelu fragilior, Istro fallacior, Caucaso abruptior. Quidni? Penes quem verus Prometheus Deus omnipotens blasphemies lancinatur'.[4] Thus, in *Adversus Marcionem*, Tertullian again rejects any type of parallel between Prometheus and Jesus Christ, and presents Prometheus as a fraud compared to God, 'the true Prometheus'. The quality of Prometheus to which Tertullian refers here cannot be his rebellious side, but may be his creative power, or, more plausibly, because Tertullian uses Prometheus's name as a category, the quality contained in its etymology: 'the forethinker'. In any case, what was presented as undeniable evidence of the existence of a 'Prometheus Christus' at the beginning of Christianity, when analysed in its context, tends to prove the contrary.

Edgar Quinet was not alone in making this mistake. Trousson[5] attempted a census of the various critics who sustained or contributed to spreading such a false statement about the interpretation of Prometheus at the beginning of Christianity. We shall limit ourselves to a few examples restricted to the nineteenth century and the Symbolist period in order to show how such a misinterpretation could continue to develop in modern criticism. Trousson suggested that, because of his great influence, Quinet was the first to propagate this interpretation of the Prometheus myth. As well as quoting the authority of Tertullian, he wrote that 'a commentator of Aeschylus, the Englishman Stanley, noted that the Fathers of Christianity took it upon themselves to interpret in that way the Prometheus figure, a long time before I did. [...] They often compared the torture of the Caucasus with the Passion of Calvary, thus making Prometheus a Christ before Christ. Among these authorities, that of Tertullian is especially striking'.[6] Even more striking is the fact that, while Thomas Stanley duly compared the intensity of the suffering of Jesus Christ and the Titan, the only authority that he quoted was that of Tertullian. Henceforth, because of the unchallenged authority of all the Fathers of the Church (even though only the distorted passage from Tertullian could be quoted), together with those of Thomas Stanley and Edgar Quinet, commentators took for granted that, since the origins of Christianity, Prometheus and Jesus Christ had been associated. Thus A. Nicolas stated that 'the double persona of the Messiah, both triumphant and a victim, can be found in the drama *Prometheus Bound*, which could be called *Waiting for the liberator*'.[7] During the second half of the nineteenth century, references to the Fathers of the Church became ever bolder. In 1913, F. Polderman put forward the idea that the link established between the tortures of the Caucasus and Calvary was no more than 'a poetical commonplace since Tertullian'.[8] These examples, taken from amongst many others which seemed to multiply until the publication of Trousson's work in 1964, reveal the awesome phenomenon of criticism feeding upon itself. However, if there was indeed no ground for identifying Prometheus with Jesus Christ in patristic literature, and however astonishing the legend around Tertullian's distorted quotation might be, we cannot entirely reject the value of the commentaries which arose from it.[9] Indeed, we must never neglect the aspect of reception, and, as we shall be led to examine in a further chapter, this legend had a strong impact on nineteenth-century artists. It could even be argued that, even if the association between Jesus Christ and Prometheus had not been made by critics by mistake, it would have influenced Romanticism, and, consequently, Symbolism, being in the *air du temps*. Nevertheless, having examined the supposed status of Prometheus at the beginning of Christianity, we must now study what was really made of the Titan at that time.

Prometheus, Euhemerism and Pagan Presentiments

At the very beginning of the Christian era, there was no evolution of the Prometheus myth, as the early Fathers of the Church did not attempt to link the myth to the Bible. As we have seen, Tertullian did not attempt to link Prometheus and Jesus Christ, and it is understandable that no early Father would have done so. Indeed, at a time when Christianity was barely established and still comparatively fragile as a religion, such a parallel would have had threatening implications. The dangers involved in suggesting that Prometheus was a forerunner of Jesus Christ were considerable, as it would have involved the association of Zeus with the Christian God. If Prometheus truly rebelled against Zeus, a revolt by Jesus Christ against His Father, on the other hand, was absolutely inconceivable. Moreover, had the parallel been pushed further, Zeus, whimsical and fallible, had little in common with the Christian God. Trousson wonders rhetorically whether it would have been possible to make of Prometheus 'a precursor of Jesus Christ, a sort of prophet revolting against pagan beliefs, Fire coming to symbolize the true faith',[10] a question which he immediately answers in the negative: 'paganism was still very near, and we would have risked a return to idolatry'.[11] Prometheus was a powerful figure within paganism, and using him to strengthen the new religion would probably have weakened it. Myths were still structuring people's lives, and still represented a way of thinking, a system of values and cultural references.

The Christian apologists therefore attempted to highlight the absurd, even ridiculous, aspects of myths, and to show that they were nothing but distorted stories or historical facts. In order to do so, they judged the myth by Christian criteria, the most important being the notion of history. Jesus was a historical character, which gave him a tangible aspect, as opposed to mythical characters, who were presented as nothing more than fabulous creations and implausibilities. The first Christians, to weaken the influence of myths on other people, did not recognize myths and the new religion as two different systems, but exposed the irrelevance of the myths from a historical point of view. They invoked a way of thinking which was completely antithetical to the notion of myth. Indeed, as Mircea Eliade put it, 'we must never forget that one of the essential functions of the myth is in its provision of an opening into the Great Time, a periodic new-entry into Time primordial. This is shown by a tendency to a neglect of the present time, of what is called the "historic moment"'.[12]

The first Fathers of the Church therefore adopted the theory of Euhemerism[13] in order to counteract the tendency to return to myths, if not in the form of idol-worship, at least as a way of thinking. Thus they tried to rationalize the fantastic aspect of the Greek myths in order to show that if they had remote origins, they were nonetheless products of embellishment and human imagination. As Trousson put it, 'Generally, exegetes tackled [the Prometheus myth] with [...] care, in order not to arouse contradiction and controversy. Christians themselves had to be shown the foundation of pagan beliefs and that the lack of religious value of these myths should be demonstrated to them. They were not to ignore Prometheus, but to bring him back to human dimensions, to present the myth as a banal historical fact, distorted by credulousness and superstition, sublimated by poetical imagination'.[14] In such a euhemerist perspective, one of the common 'human identities' that was lent to Prometheus was that of an Egyptian sage, who lived at the same time as Moses. Trousson provides an exhaustive analysis of the sources of this euhemerist interpretation of the Prometheus myth.[15]

Another interesting explanation of the 'identity' of Prometheus is that he was the inventor of statuary, a theory first put forward by Lactantius and redeveloped by Isidore of Seville three centuries later.[16] Therefore, one can see that the various mythological characteristics of the Titan, as the forethinker who rebels against the Olympian order as well as the creator of mankind, were accounted for by the Fathers of the Church. As Trousson noted, commenting on Lactantius's and Isidore's shared interpretation of Prometheus, it '[developed] a soothing doctrine which allowed [the Fathers] to clear up the potential doubts of lukewarm Christians concerning the excellence of their religion, and even [seduced] backward-looking pagans by demonstrating the absurdity of their beliefs'.[17]

Such explanations of the Prometheus myth coexisted along with theories of pagan presentiments, which, in a different way, allowed the myth to be funnelled into new ways of thinking. Indeed, before the fifth century, the power of myths — particularly influential ones such as the Prometheus myth — was still very strong, and another way of dealing with them was to recognize that there was some truth in the narratives which the Greeks constructed, but only because they were a partial revelation of the truth. This was aimed at enabling pagans to discover, in due time, the true religion. One of the most troubling aspects of the Prometheus myth, and one which conflicted with the theory of God's Creation, was the representation of Prometheus as the creator of mankind. Thus the theory was put forward that this element of the myth was in fact a confused, distorted and fragmentary revelation of the Creation.[18] From the dawn of Christianity to the fifth century, because of the double concern with showing people the implausibilities of myths as well as converting unbelievers, the Prometheus myth was tackled with great caution. The result of this attitude was that, although the Prometheus myth was not ignored by the Fathers of the Church, the interpretations of the myth did not evolve as such. Moreover, as noted earlier, there were no associations between the Titan and biblical characters.

From the fifth century AD, Christianity had nothing to fear from myths and pagan beliefs, and, from that point, a redevelopment of the Prometheus myth might perhaps have been witnessed. However, during the Middle Ages, Prometheus was one of the great absentees of literature, given that mythology was then being rediscovered and feeding the inspiration of many vernacular writers.[19] Pandora, on the other hand, was largely elaborated upon as a myth, possibly because in a euhemerist perspective, she was inevitably linked to Eve, who was also a 'negative' character. Given that Prometheus was largely ignored until the Renaissance, we now have to consider what was made of him at that time, notably in the pictorial field.

Notes to Chapter 2

1. Edgar Quinet, *Prométhée* (Paris, 1838)
2. Tertullian, *Apology; De Spectaculis*, trans. by T. R. Glover (London: Heinemann, 1966), '(For He is your true Prometheus!) — Who ordained to the course of the world, appointing the seasons, the one to follow the other'.
3. *Ante-Nicene Christian Library*, volume VII, trans. by Peter Holmes (Edinburgh: T. &T. Clark, 1868).
4. 'Nothing there has the glow of life, but that ferocity which has given to scenic plays their stories of the sacrifices of the Taurians, and the love of the Colchians, and the torments of the Caucasus. Nothing, however, in Pontus is so barbarous and sad as the fact that Marcion was born there, fouler than any Scythian, more roving than the waggon-life of the Samartian, more inhuman than the Massagete, more audacious than an Amazon, darker than the cloud, colder than its winter, more brittle than its ice, more deceitful than the Ister, more craggy than Caucasus. Nay more, the true Prometheus, Almighty God, is mangled by Marcion's blasphemies.', Ibid., p. 2.
5. Trousson, pp. 110–13.
6. Quoted by Trousson, p. 110.
7. Ibid., p. 111.
8. Ibid., p. 112.
9. Cf. Trousson, pp. 98–99, n. 24, and Duchemin, pp. 110–11, where both authors present as absurdities the attempts to establish links between the tortures of Prometheus and Jesus Christ. However 'superficial' and 'tasteless' (Duchemin, p. 111) they might be, their development in the nineteenth century is important from a historical point of view.
10. Trousson, p. 96.
11. Ibid., p. 96.
12. Mircea Eliade, *Myths, Dreams and Mysteries*, trans. by Philip Mairet (London: Collins, 1968), p. 34.
13. The word Euhemerism derives from the name of Euhemerus, a Greek philosopher from *c.* 300 AD, who believed that mythological gods were in fact deified mortals, whose deeds had been exaggerated.
14. Trousson, p. 101.
15. Ibid., p. 102, and note 30 on the same page.
16. Trousson, pp. 104–05.
17. Ibid., p. 105.
18. This was the theory put forward by Clement of Alexandria. Cf. Trousson, p. 105.
19. From the twelfth century, when vernacular romances appeared, myths were 'rediscovered' as a profuse and endless creative material, as Paul Renucci explains *in L'Aventure de l'humanisme européen au Moyen Age (XIVème-XVème siècle)* (Paris: Les Belles Lettres, 1953).

CHAPTER 3

Prometheus during the Renaissance and Beyond

The Revaluation of Prometheus

In spite of the general ignorance of Prometheus during the Middle Ages, one account of the myth, dating from the fourteenth century, undoubtedly influenced and gave shape to the interpretation of the Prometheus myth during the Renaissance: that of the humanist Giovanni Boccaccio. In the mid-fourteenth century, he was commissioned by Hugo, King of Cyprus, to compile an encyclopaedic work of classical myths and various legends, the *De Genealogia Deorum Gentilium*, in which an entire chapter, 'De Prometheo Japeti Filio, qui fecit Pandoram et genuit Ysidem et Deucalionem',[1] is devoted to Prometheus. Renaissance scholars had often gained their remarkable knowledge from compilations such as that of Boccaccio, not from first-hand literary sources. This is why the *Genealogy* was so influential. A second explanation lies in the originality of Boccaccio's thoughts on the Prometheus myth. The methodology of the *Genealogy* followed that of the traditional medieval hermeneutics, divided into literal, allegorical, moral, and analogical interpretations. For the first analysis, he relied on Ovid's account of the myth presenting Prometheus as the creator of mankind, as well as on a secondary account by Fulgentius,[2] in which Athena takes Prometheus to the sky, where he steals a spark from Apollo's chariot. If Boccaccio first presents the Prometheus myth as an attempt to explain divine creation, his interpretation of Prometheus himself is far more original, since he puts forward the idea that there are in fact two Prometheus figures. The first is Ovid's character Prometheus *plasticator*, or the distorted pagan image of the Creator, God Almighty. The second Prometheus is presented by Boccaccio as a wise man, an ascetic who had retreated to the Caucasus for years before teaching sciences and the art of living within society to his fellow men. Boccaccio's analysis, although euhemeristic in nature, is fascinating in the sense that his 'Prometheus duplex' is linked to a 'homo duplex'. Indeed, Boccaccio suggests that the first being made by Prometheus (in fact by God Almighty) was perfect, and did not need to be taught anything. However, this same man, after the Fall, became debased, justifying the intervention of the second Prometheus, who brought civilization and dragged men out of their natural state. We can see how this interpretation of the Prometheus myth appears as resolutely humanistic, inasmuch as it emphasizes man's perfectibility, and the possibility of fulfilment in spite of, or over and above, original sin. As Trousson states, '[man's] individuality eventually asserts itself and his ability to create is compared, although deferentially, to that of the Almighty'.[3] Boccaccio's humanistic interpretation of the Prometheus myth truly paved the way for a revaluation of Prometheus at the Renaissance, when Humanism blossomed. It is also important to note that according to Boccaccio, the notion of Prometheus's guilt disappeared, since he retreats to the Caucasus of his own free will. Therefore, Boccaccio analyses 'the eagle [...] [as] the symbol of the 'high considerations' which torment the solitary searcher'.[4]

Among the great humanist thinkers who were directly influenced by Boccaccio were Marsilio Ficino and Giovanni Pico della Mirandola, who developed similar interpretations of the myth,[5] whilst differing in their conclusions. Indeed, both men, like Boccaccio, saw Prometheus as the benefactor of mankind, in the sense that he endowed them with the various techniques and knowledge which enabled them to survive and to found civilization. According to Ficino, Prometheus represented a superior spiritual power, as opposed to Epimetheus, who embodied instincts and the natural state, on the side of bestiality. In this respect, Ficino also presents the duality of man, already highlighted by Boccaccio, in a different light.

However, Ficino and Pico developed an interesting aspect of the Prometheus myth when putting forward the idea that thanks to Prometheus, man, with his spiritual and natural sides, became 'a go-between between Earth and Heaven, between contemplation and action'.[6] The knowledge that man received from Prometheus allowed them, to quote Ficino's famous phrase, to become God on Earth: 'est utique Deus in Terris'.[7] It is at that point that the views of Pico and Ficino diverge. According to Pico, man can glorify himself for the nobility of his position, and for his striving towards the spiritual world, whereas according to Ficino, that same position is tragic, since man is ineluctably bound to his material existence. In other words, man is condemned to contemplate the spiritual world without being able to reach it. What is particularly thought-provoking in the interpretations of Ficino and Pico della Mirandola, fed by Boccaccio, is that for the first time since Aeschylus, the value of Prometheus's sacrifice is at stake. Even for Aeschylus, the focus of the myth was on the value of the Titan's act regarding Zeus and his power. When mankind was mentioned, it was to point out its indifference or ingratitude. But for the first time in the history of the myth, the implication of Prometheus's relationship with mankind is examined. He is no longer considered in a unilateral manner, as a trickster, a rebel, or a creator, and the focus of the myth shifts beyond the evaluation of his rebellion onto the beneficiary of his sacrifice, man. Other great humanists gave the same orientation to the myth: for Pomponazzi[8] and Erasmus,[9] Prometheus brings a nobility to the terrestrial life, the quest of knowledge giving meaning to human life, whereas for Francis Bacon,[10] the theft of fire represents the prerequisite for the development of tangible technical knowledge aiming at the improvement of the human condition. In parallel with this interpretation of the myth, there emerged one that would later have a tremendous influence on artists, notably in the nineteenth century. To analyse it, we have to go back to Boccaccio's time and look at the work of another precursor, Filippo Villani.

The Birth of the Titan as Artist

In the fourteenth century, the Florentine Filippo Villani wrote *Le vite d'uomini illustri fiorentini*[11] (*The Lives of Famous Florentine Men*), a study of individuals among which ranked two of the most celebrated artists of the time, Cimabue and his pupil Giotto. In one of his chapters, 'Di Giotto et altri dipintori fiorentini',[12] Villani praises artists such as Cimabue and Giotto, who understood and applied to their work the aesthetic principle of mimesis, the idea that art has to imitate Nature, and that artistic creation has to follow the model given by Creation itself. It is in this context that Villani conjures up the figure of Prometheus, putting forward the idea that during antiquity, it was thought that 'Prometeo pe' suoi ingegni e diligenza, aveva del limo della terra creato un uomo'.[13] Therefore, according to Villani, the Prometheus myth was an illustration of the power of the artist, who, through his creative power, rivals God, or, on another scale (the humanist concept of microcosm), is the god of his own realm. Villani's idea was not new, but the way in which he tackled the Prometheus myth represented a milestone in its interpretation. Indeed, as Trousson noted, 'it is not the banal application of the procedures of euhemerism any more, but the use of a symbol',[14] a symbol which would inspire many artists, especially in the nineteenth century.

Despite the revival of an interest in the Prometheus figure among humanists, especially during the Renaissance, few works were painted on the subject. However, a famous diptych by Piero di Cosimo, renowned for its mystery, echoed and perfectly illustrated Villani's interpretation of the myth. The diptych in question is entitled *Storie di Prometeo*,[15] dated 1515–1520. The first panel (Fig. 1.3.1) is in the Alte Pinakothek in Munich, and the second in the Musée des Beaux-Arts in Strasbourg.

In these two paintings, the focus Piero adopted centres on Prometheus *plasticator* and on the creation of men. However, Prometheus is not represented in Titanic dimensions, but as a rural craftsman with an apron, an appearance in total contrast with the beauty of Prometheus's statue, a version of Michelangelo's *David*. The mythical attributes of Prometheus are faded out to emphasize the figure of an artist who appears as human, and very possibly as a *mise en abyme* of the artist. The way in which the other elements of the myth are treated would tend to confirm this hypothesis. Indeed, the fact that some of the characters are depicted in courtesans' outfits is certainly not fortuitous. In the Munich panel, the left part of the painting is devoted to Epimetheus, Piero probably following here Boccaccio's *Genealogy*, in which he mentions that Epimetheus, and not Prometheus, first attempted to mould man from clay. In the top left corner of the painting, he is depicted as a monkey, still following Boccaccio's account, which mentions that such was Jupiter's punishment of Epimetheus for his initiative. The rest of the painting is devoted to Prometheus and his sculpture. A semi-circle starting from the bottom right corner of the painting and finishing in the second quarter of the painting, in the top left of the composition, depicts Athena taking Prometheus to the sky so that he can steal a spark from Apollo's chariot. On the left of the second panel, Prometheus is bringing his sculpture to life with the fire he stole from the Olympian gods, as shown in the

FIG. 1.3.1. Piero di Cosimo, *Storie di Prometeo*, 1515–20, Alte Pinakothek, Munich.
Photo: akg-images

upper centre of the panel. In the opposite corner, Prometheus is being bound to a tree by Hermes, dressed as a courtesan, while the eagle is waiting to start his work. In the middle, the figure of Epimetheus is represented again, accepting the Olympian gods' present, Pandora. In this respect, as Daniel Arasse notes, what is presented as a divine favour (Athena's offer to Prometheus to bring back anything he desires from Heaven, and Zeus's gift to Epimetheus, Pandora) to the two brothers is in both cases a poisoned chalice.[16] Given that, in this diptych, Piero used Prometheus as a symbol for the artist, along the same lines as Villani, and given that he chose to represent Prometheus's torturer, Hermes, as a courtesan, we might interpret his paintings as a representation of the dependence of artists on patrons. This is confirmed by the only account we have of Piero's life, by Vasari,[17] who depicted the painter as a wild and eccentric man who preferred nature and animals to the society of men. Piero di Cosimo's original interpretation of the Prometheus myth fully exploits the symbolic use of the Titan inaugurated by Villani, through a *mise en abyme* of the artist's figure. However, such an interpretation remained confined to the pictorial world of the time, possibly solely to this work by Piero. Another frequent treatment of the Prometheus myth which emerged during the Renaissance was the use of his main attribute, fire, as a metaphor for the suffering of passionate love, as found for example in the work of Ronsard; but such an interpretation falls outside the scope of the present study. We must now consider briefly the other pictorial interpretations made of the Prometheus myth during the Renaissance, as one in particular was to determine the representation of Prometheus for more than a century.

Origins of the 'Traditional' Representation of Prometheus

In 1548 and 1549, Titian painted a series of four paintings for Philip II of Spain, entitled 'The Four Condemned'. It depicted Ixion, Tantalus, Sisyphus, and Tityus. Of the four paintings, only two have survived, *Sisyphus*[18] and *Tityus*[19] (Fig. 1.3.2). The latter was traditionally thought to be a representation of Prometheus, and which became a great source of inspiration for subsequent painters. Tityus suffered the same punishment as Prometheus, since he was chained to sharp rocks and condemned to have his vitals preyed upon by a vulture to the end of time. However, unlike Prometheus, such punishment did not result from his love for mankind, but from having violated Latona.[20] Titian's depiction of Tityus is particularly striking since the painter, by focusing on the plasticity and muscularity of Tityus's naked body, emphasized the tension and unbearable suffering of his endless martyrdom. As Harold E. Wethey put it, 'it is indeed unexpected and astonishing that Titian, renowned for the seductive beauty of his feminine nudes and the gay abandon of his bacchanalian figures, should render so successfully the horror of eternal torture'.[21] The way in which Titian chose to depict Tityus may not be unrelated to the fact that he started working on 'The Four Condemned' not long after his return from a trip to Rome, where he had time to examine the work of Michelangelo,[22] and surely, to appreciate the muscular beauty of his male bodies. The confusion surrounding the identity of the martyr in Titian's painting can probably be explained by the fact that, in the *Odyssey,* Tityus was tormented by two vultures, whereas Titian only depicted one black eagle tearing Tityus's liver. Calvete de Estrella, the official chronicler of

FIG. 1.3.2. Titian, *Tityus*, 1548–49, Museo del Prado, Madrid.
Photo: akg-images / Erich Lessing

FIG. 1.3.3. Pieter Paul Rubens, *Prometheus Brings Fire to the Earth*, *c*.1636,
Museo del Prado, Madrid. Photo: akg–images / Erich Lessing

Philip II, who saw 'The Four Condemned' at Binche in 1549, thought that Tityus was in fact Prometheus, and for centuries the painting was often identified as such.[23] The composition of *Tityus*, which represents him lying on the rocks, writhing in pain with his head thrown back, deeply influenced later pictorial representations of Prometheus. Rubens's *Prometheus Bound* (1611–12),[24] which is usually considered the most famous painting of the Titan, clearly shows the influence of Titian.

An extra element of horror is present in the Rubens painting, where the eagle's talons, painted by Frans Snyders, are shown gripping Prometheus's forehead. One of the main additions to the composition of Titian's painting is the main attribute of Prometheus, his torch of fire, burning in the bottom left corner of the painting.

Rubens offered a very different vision of Prometheus in a design for Philip IV's Torre de la Parada at El Pardo.[25] A preparatory sketch kept at the Prado (Fig. 1.3.3) represents the Titan as a stout middle-aged bearded man carrying fire, closer to the traditional representations of Vulcan.[26]

The finished painting, also at the Prado, was executed by Jan Cossiers from Rubens's design.[27] The treatment of this aspect of the myth did not have an immediate iconographical impact, but it resurfaced in the nineteenth century.

The painter Jacob Jordaens, friend and occasional collaborator of Rubens, painted his own *Prometheus Bound* (c.1640)[28] almost thirty years after Rubens. It could be claimed that Jordaens was also influenced by Titian's *Tityus*, but if so, it was probably indirectly, through Rubens's painting. Indeed, the setting of Rubens's work, with the trees and the blue cloth thrown on the rock to which Prometheus is bound, seems to be almost identical. The posture of Prometheus is almost the same as in Titian's and Rubens's pictures, but Jordaens, instead of representing the Titan from a three-quarters perspective, chose to represent Prometheus in a frontal way. Jordaens's originality lies in his introduction of Hercules, about to kill the eagle with one of his arrows, in the top right corner of the painting. Thus a form of hope is introduced into the painting with the intimation that the suffering of Prometheus is coming to an end. Later, around 1660, Luca Giordano painted an admirable *Prometheus*,[29] which adopted a similar focus on the Titan, since he is once again depicted writhing with pain at the torture of the eagle, bound to his rock, and again, in a similar posture, his head back and his knees bent. Giordano interestingly chose to represent Prometheus standing, not lying, on the rock.[30] This, highlighted with remarkable chiaroscuro, endows the sinuous lines of Prometheus's body with remarkable grace and beauty, and adds even more drama to that scene of torture. Nicolas Sébastien Adam's Baroque masterpiece *Prometheus Bound*,[31] his reception piece at the French Academy, clearly derives from Giordano's painting, but emphasizes further the dramatic effect of the billowing drape.

Thus, if we examine the works that were directly or indirectly inspired by Titian's *Tityus*, we can see that over a century the pictorial representation of Prometheus did not radically evolve. The focus on Prometheus's punishment (and therefore on the theme of revolt) was shared by those artists, who opted for very similar compositions. This helped establish what we might call a traditional visual representation of Prometheus, which persisted throughout the centuries, but which would be abandoned by late eighteenth- and nineteenth-century artists.

Towards the Nineteenth Century

From the seventeenth until the end of the eighteenth century, changes to the Prometheus myth that influenced and led to nineteenth-century interpretations of the myth were rare. I shall therefore limit myself to a brief survey of what happened to the story of the myth.[32] In terms of novelty, a general stagnation of its treatment could be witnessed during the seventeenth century, with the exception of Calderón's *La Estatua de Prometeo*.[33] This play appeared as the superb synthesis of the Renaissance interpretations of the myth, whilst adding many symbolic and original elements to the myth, making the work very rich but also difficult to interpret. Calderón's play also illustrates a phenomenon which started to develop during the seventeenth century: the cross-fertilization of the Pygmalion and the Prometheus myths, which became fully developed in the nineteenth century. We shall return to Calderón's play and to that process in Part IV, Chapter 3.

The main interest in Prometheus during the seventeenth century came from philosophers. In 1669 Thomas Hobbes,[34] in particular, saw in the Titan the condemnable embodiment of political rebellion and democracy, since according to him, the only pure and true power was monarchy. The interpretation of Prometheus from a social perspective flourished during the Enlightenment. Diderot, along the lines of the Renaissance, considered him as the benefactor of mankind, since he brought knowledge to mortals; the eagle, in this context, was 'the emblem of deep meditation and loneliness'.[35] Jean-Jacques Rousseau, like Diderot, saw in Prometheus the initiator of civilization, but in his *Discours sur les Sciences et les Arts*,[36] he presented the Titan as the corruptor of mankind, as the one who took them away from their idyllic primitive state. At that stage in the evolution of the myth, Prometheus was not seen as a man, but solely as a god, or an image somehow separated from men. Only for Voltaire[37] and Wieland[38] did he represent the spirit of revolt: for Voltaire, Prometheus's human revolt is justified by the unfairness and evil of Jupiter,[39] and for Wieland, who takes the opposite view from Rousseau, Prometheus showed men that original sin did not damn mankind, but on the contrary put it on the path of progress and greatness. In this respect, those two thinkers paved the way for forthcoming interpretations of Prometheus.

One final interpretation of the myth, which also left its trace, should be mentioned: that of Anthony Ashley Cooper, third Earl of Shaftesbury. In his *Soliloquy, or Advice to an Author*, Shaftesbury praises the poet who can create from inner forms, and not through imitation, which leads him to say that 'Such a Poet is indeed a second maker, a just Prometheus under Jove'. The importance of Shaftesbury is that he was the first to widen the symbol of Prometheus as an artist to make him fully a creator, far beyond his role as a sculptor. He is still compared to Zeus [Jove] and is still subordinate to him, but as we shall see in the next chapter, Goethe was soon to push Prometheus's power even further.

New texts and new treatments of the myth were not the only decisive factors in the history of Prometheus. Translations, too, were decisive in casting new light on the Titan, and the turning point in the interpretation of the myth occurred shortly after the publication of a number of translations of *Prometheus Bound*. Greek theatre, until the final third of the eighteenth century, was little appreciated, as it was perceived — partly because of the lack of vernacular translations — as coarse and offensive, Aeschylus even more so. The first modern translation of *Prometheus Bound,* in 1754, was by M. Cesarotti, into Italian.[40] It was followed in 1770 by J. J. Le Franc de Pompignan's French version.[41] The first ever English translation of Aeschylus was *Prometheus Bound*, by T. Morell, in 1773.[42] The most influential by far, however, was that of Robert Potter, four years later. He translated all Aeschylus's tragedies,[43] which triggered a completely new perception of the playwright. His translation was followed by many others, and women in particular were particularly drawn to translating his plays. The most notable example of this phenomenon was Elizabeth Barrett Browning's translation of *Prometheus Bound* in 1833.[44]

Interestingly, Potter urged artists to use Aeschylus's plays, which in his view could be conjured up pictorially with great power. George Romney, who painted Potter's portrait, certainly felt enthused by his call. In a small preparatory ink drawing[45] and a cartoon executed in black chalk,[46] the artist presented a new vision of the Titan, full of physical tension — as dictated by the subject — but also deeply atmospheric.

Prometheus is shown lying down in profile to the left, being tied to his rock by Bia and Kratos, whose arched bodies, arms outstretched, form a wave which seems about to crush him. Prometheus's body and features, with Hephaestus looming over him, do not express pain so much as heroic resistance. His fellow artist John Flaxman described Romney's cartoons as 'examples of the sublime and terrible; at that time perfectly new in English art',[47] and he recommended that William Blake should engrave them. Romney could only dedicate his nights to his cartoons, having to work on his portrait commissions during the day. They were never developed into paintings, but their spontaneity display the burst of his creative energy. His *Prometheus Bound* influenced Flaxman himself, who represented the Titan being chained to a rock, standing between Kratos and Bia.[48] The powerful resistance of his Prometheus is indebted to Romney, but the composition of his design also draws on the traditional representation of Prometheus, as treated by Luca Giordano. Henry Fuseli, who was at the heart of an international community of artists in Rome, to which Romney and Flaxman belonged,[49] made a drawing of Prometheus as early as 1770–71.[50] Its composition is unlike any others, as it is the result of a 'five-point' game challenge, 'which involved placing dots in a random pattern on a sheet and joining these with the head and extremities of a drawn figure'.[51] Prometheus's figure is hunched, his back against the rock, his right palm up towards the eagle's head, knees to his chest. The contortion of his body emphasizes its physicality, and recalls Michelangelo's *ignudi*, which is surely deliberate: it is thought that the initials M.A.B. inscribed by Fuseli on Prometheus's rock denote <u>M</u>ichel<u>a</u>ngelo <u>B</u>uonarroti. As Martin Myrone noted, for Fuseli and artists in his Roman circle, 'the treatment of classical themes and physical forms both conformed to conventional ideas of high art, and exploded those ideals by matching the more expressive and extravagant forms of expression associated with novel concepts of the Sublime and "original genius"', the idea of which found its expression in the 'theme of confinement and heroic struggle'.[52] The Prometheus myth was thus bound to be favoured by this new current. The translations of Aeschylus mentioned above offered a fresh outlook on Prometheus and his rebellion, feeding into these new ideas and aesthetic. Although it is not known whether the young Goethe knew Fuseli's drawing in particular, he admired Fuseli's work, whose aesthetic of the sublime found an echo in his writings.

Notes to Chapter 3

1. Giovanni Boccaccio, *Genealogia deorum gentilium libri*, ed. by V. Romano (Bari: Laterza, 1951), book IV, Chapter XLIV.
2. Fulgentius, *Fabii Planciadis Fulgentii V.C. Opera*, ed. by Rudolf Helm (Leipzig, 1898; repr. Stuttgart, 1970).
3. Trousson, p. 131.
4. Ibid., p. 132.
5. *Marsilii Ficini, philosophi Platonici, medici atque theologij, omnium praestantissimi, opera...* , (Basel, 1561); Giovanni Pico della Mirandola, *De Hominis dignitate Heptaplus de ente et uno, e scritti vari*, ed. by Eugenio Garin, vol.I (Florence: Edizione Nazionale dei Classici del Pensiero Italiano, 1942).
6. Jacques Réattu, *Sous le signe de la révolution* (Paris: Musée de la Révolution Française, Actes Sud, 2000), p. 44.
7. Quoted by Trousson, p. 146.
8. Pietro Pomponazzi, *Libri quinque de fato, de libero arbitrio et de pradestinatione*, ed. by R. Lemay (Padua: Antenore, 1957).
9. Desiderius Erasmus, *Adagia, id est: Proverbiorum, paroemiarum et parabolarum omnium, quae apud Graecos, Latinos, Hebraeos, Arabos, etc. in usu fuerunt* ([Frankfurt a.M.]: Typis Wechelianis, Sumptibus Joannis Pressii, 1643).
10. Francis Bacon, 'De Sapientia Veterum Liber' in *The Works*, ed. by J. Spedding, R. L. Ellis, and D. D. Heath (London, 1889–1892).
11. Filippo Villani, *Le vite d'uomini illustri fiorentini*, annotated by Count Giammaria Mazzuchelli (Venice: Academico della Crusca, Pasquali, 1747).
12. 'On Giotto and other Florentine painters', ibid., pp. 80–82.
13. 'Prometheus, thanks to his talents and diligence, had created a man from the silt of the earth'. My translation. Quoted by Trousson, p. 144.
14. Ibid., p. 144.
15. Piero di Cosimo, *Storie di Prometeo*, 1515–20, oil on panel, 66 × 118.7 cm, Alte Pinakothek, Munich, and oil on panel, 64 × 116 cm, Musée de Beaux-Arts, Strasbourg.
16. Daniel Arasse, *Le Sujet dans le tableau* (Paris: Flammarion, 1997), p. 56.
17. Giorgio Vasari, *The Lives of the Artists*, trans. by Julia and Peter Bondanella (Oxford: Oxford University Press, 1998).
18. Titian, *Sisyphus*,1548–49, oil on canvas, 237 × 216 cm, Museo del Prado, Madrid.
19. Titian, *Tityus*, 1548–49, oil on canvas, 253 × 217 cm, Museo del Prado, Madrid.
20. *Odyssey*, XI, 779–94. The other literary sources of Tityus's story are Virgil, *Aeneid*, VI, 595–600, and Ovid, *Metamorphoses*, IV, 457–58.
21. Harold E. Wethey, *The Paintings of Titian*, vol. III: *The Mythological and Historical Paintings* (London: Phaidon, 1969), p. 61.
22. However, it is not known whether Titian had any knowledge of Michelangelo's own drawing of Tityus, which is very different in conception, and which is now part of the Queen's collection at Windsor Castle (Popham and Wilde, 1949, cat. N° 429). Paul de Saint-Victor, in *Les deux masques*, mentioned that Michelangelo, while sketching his first general designs for the Sistine Chapel, had made two drawings of Prometheus, the first one depicting him being tortured by the eagle on the threshold of a collapsing pagan temple, whereas in the second one, he is vertically crucified on a big oak (the tree of knowledge?). Unfortunately, these two drawings, which would have been important in the analysis of Prometheus in relation to Christianity, are now lost. Cf. Duchemin, pp. 117–18, and Séchan, Chapter I, note 100.

23. In 1566, the poet Mal-Lara, who was asked to write verses on Philip II's Titians, mentions *Prometheus* as well as *Tityus*. In 1776, when Ponz drew up the inventory of the Alcázar, he identified *Tityus* as *Prometheus*. Pedro de Madrazo, in 1843, and Wilhem Suida, in 1935, made the same mistake. Prints, made after Titian's painting, were entitled *Prometheus*. This is the case for those by Cornelius Cort (1566), 38 × 29 cm (examples in Madrid, Biblioteca del Palacio; Munich, Kupferstich-Kabinett; Paris, Bibliothèque Nationale), and Martino Rota (1570), after Cort. There is also a drawing of Tityus by Titian in the Louvre, from the collection of Mariette (inventory no. 5518), pen and bistre, 12.7 × 10.3 cm, formerly entitled *Prometheus*.

24. Pieter Paul Rubens, *Prometheus Bound* (1611–1612), oil on canvas, 244 × 210 cm, Philadelphia Museum of Art: The W. P. Wilstach Collection.

25. The hunting lodge was renovated by the architect Juan Gómez de Morain 1636, and Philip IV of Spain commissioned leading painters to decorate it.

26. Pieter Paul Rubens, *Prometheus Brings Fire to the Earth*, c. 1636, oil on panel, 25.7 × 16.6 cm, Museo del Prado, Madrid.

27. Jan Cossiers, *Prometheus Carrying Fire* (c.1636), oil on canvas, 182 × 113 cm, Museo del Prado, Madrid.

28. Jacob Jordaens, *Prometheus Bound* (c.1640), oil on canvas, 245 × 178 cm, Wallraf-Richartz Museum, Köln.

29. Luca Giordano, *Prometeo* (c.1660), Museum of Fine Arts, Budapest.

30. He may have been inspired by the Genoese painter Gioacchino Assereto (1600–1649), who also painted a standing Prometheus (oil on canvas, 83 × 69.5 cm, Musée de la Chartreuse, Douai) that focuses with intense, gruesome realism on the torture the Titan has to endure.

31. Nicolas Sébastien Adam, *Prométhée Enchaîné*, 1762, marble, 144 × 82.5 × 48 cm, Louvre, Paris.

32. See Trousson, pp. 195–300, for a detailed history of the myth during this period.

33. Pedro Calderón de la Barca, *La Estatua de Prometeo*, in *Obras completas*, I, ed. by A. Valbuena Briones (Madrid: Aguilar, 1959).

34. Thomas Hobbes, *Man and Citizen: 'De Homine' and 'De Cive'*, ed. by Bernard Gert, trans. by C. T. Wood and T. S. K. Scott-Craig (Indianapolis: Hackett 1991).

35. Quoted by Jacques Réattu, *Sous le signe de la Révolution*, p. 47.

36. Jean-Jacques Rousseau, *Discours sur l'origine de l'inégalité parmi les hommes — Discours sur les Sciences et les Arts*, ed. by Jacques Roger (Paris: Garnier Flammarion, 1995).

37. Voltaire, *Pandore*, in *Œuvres Complètes de Voltaire*, ed. by Ulla Kölving et al (Oxford: Voltaire Foundation, 1968-), volume 18C.

38. Christoph Martin Wieland, *Beiträge zur geheimen Geschichte des menschlichen Verstandes und Herzens*, and *Ueber die Von J.J.Rousseau vorgeschlagenen Versuche den Wahren Stand der Natur des Menschen*, in *Sämmtliche Werke*, 53 volumes (Leipzig: G.J. Göschen, 1818–1828).

39. On the contrary, for Christian thinkers such as Servandoni, Prometheus is the embodiment of the danger of the development of science, which makes man forget that he remains the creature of God. According to them, the only possible conclusion of the story of Prometheus is his reconciliation with Zeus. Cf. Trousson, pp. 275–76.

40. M. Cesarotti, *Prometeo legato, tragedia trasportata in versi Italiani* (Padua, 1754).

41. J. J. Le Franc de Pompignan, *Tragédies* (Paris, 1770).

42. T. Morell, *Aischulou Prometheus Desmotes. Cum Stanleiana versione, scholiis ... amplissimisque ... notis; quibus suas adjecit, necnon scholia de metro, ac Anglicanam interpretationem* (London, 1773).

43. Robert Potter, *The Tragedies of Aeschylus* (Norwich, 1777).

44. Lorna Hardwick and Eva Parisinou, *Translating Words, Translating Culture* (Bristol: Bristol Classical Press, 2000), pp. 31–36.

45. George Romney, *Prometheus Bound*, c. 1779–80, pencil, ink and wash on paper, 28 × 41 cm, private collection, reproduced in Martin Myrone, ed., *Gothic Nightmares: Fuseli, Blake and the Romantic Imagination* (London: Tate Publishing, 2006), p. 61.

46. George Romney, *Prometheus Bound*, c. 1779–80, black chalk on six sheets of laid paper, 100.5 × 126 cm, National Museums Liverpool, Walker Art Gallery.

47. Quoted by S. Spooner, *A Biographical History of the Fine Arts*, 4th edition, vol. II (New York: Leypoldt and Holt, 1867), p. 800.

48. John Flaxman, *Prometheus Bound*, 1794, pen and ink on paper, 27.5 × 36.3 cm, Royal Academy

of Arts, London, reproduced in Martin Myrone, ed., *Gothic Nightmares: Fuseli, Blake and the Romantic Imagination* (London: Tate Publishing, 2006), p. 64.

49. Romney returned to London in July 1775, after a stay of 18 months, whereas Flaxman was in Rome between 1787 and 1794.

50. Henry Fuseli, *Prometheus*, c. 1770–71, pencil and brown ink and brown wash on paper, 15 × 22.2 cm, Kunstmuseum Basel, Kupferstichkabinett, reproduced in Myrone, *Gothic Nightmares,* p. 58.

51. Ibid. p. 58.

52. Myrone, *Gothic Nightmares,* p. 53.

PART II

The Nineteenth-Century
Turning Point:
From Myth to Symbol

CHAPTER 1

Genius and Creation:
Johann Wolfgang von Goethe

In 1814, more than forty years after the 1773 *Prometheus* fragment, Goethe, reflecting on the importance of the Titan in his own life, drew a parallel between Prometheus and himself. He related that at a time when he was in search of his independence, his talent had appeared to him as 'the most reliable guarantee'[1] of it. Cherishing the thought that his entire existence would grow from this gift, 'This conception soon assumed a distinct form; the old mythological figure of Prometheus occurred to me, who, separated from the gods, peopled an entire world from his own work-shop. I clearly felt that a creation of importance could be produced only when its author isolated himself. My productions which had met so much applause were children of solitude.'[2]

It is not surprising to find such a parallel coming from Goethe's pen, since in his *Shakespeare Rede* (1771), he compared Shakespeare to Prometheus, because 'he created human beings in his image'.[3] Therefore, the comparison with the Titan being essentially based on an artistic level, it could explain why Goethe's 1773 drama, *Prometheus*, remained unfinished, and why he treated the Prometheus myth on three occasions. As we shall see, the impact of the *Prometheus* fragment, of *Pandora*, and above all of his poem 'Prometheus', marked the origin of the main turning-point in the history of the Prometheus myth.

The Two *Prometheus* and *Pandora*

The 1773 Dramatic Fragment

In 1773, the twenty-four-year-old Goethe began a play on the subject of Prometheus. Around 1770, the *Sturm und Drang* ('Storm and Stress') movement had appeared in Germany. For these young writers, poetry was no longer a matter of structure, metric rules, topoi and other conventions, but an attempt to give an account of individual experiences. 'Nature and Genius' became the key words for these young poets, who, against reason, based their creations on the passionate feeling of their hearts, perceived as a cosmic power. They praised the original unity between man and God, exalted freedom, and therefore assumed that genius made them creators. As Pierre Grappin puts it, 'poetry, which was a present from divine grace, becomes the conquest of man'.[4] In other words, the writers of the *Sturm und Drang* became the rivals of God. 'The original genius does not create from Nature' any more, 'but like Nature'.[5] Against this background, mythological characters were to take on a special significance for them. The young poets rejected any kind of allegorical interpretation of the classical pantheon so as to capture the intrinsic poetical value in each mythological figure. They gave these characters a new life, often identifying with them, and therefore 'haunting' them.[6] They saw in the ancient figures the pure type of mankind, and wanted to use this energy in their work. However, there was one major difference between the representation of mythological figures in Ancient Greece, and that in the works of the *Sturm und Drang*. Indeed, as Trousson puts it, paraphrasing F. Strich, '(Goethe) understood [...] that the Greeks' efforts had been the will to divinize the human being, and not to humanize the divine.'[7] In the context of Goethe's *Prometheus*, we may recall that the *Sturm and Drang* artists' interest in Prometheus came from their knowledge of the Earl of Shaftesbury's *Soliloquy, or Advice to an author* (1710), in which the philosopher had expressed the idea that poetry is superior to plastic arts, in that it creates non-existing objects and transcends the reproduction of models and the principle of imitation. As quoted at the end of the previous section, according to Shaftesbury, 'Such a poet is indeed a second maker, a just Prometheus under Jove'.[8] This English influence shows a community of thought between Germany and England, to which we shall return. The significance of Goethe's *Prometheus* fragment is complex, and the subject has been extensively discussed by literary critics. We shall therefore focus our examination of *Prometheus* on its significance within the context of the evolution of Prometheus as the pillar of a myth and as a persona.

In this work, which remained unfinished,[9] the depiction of the Titan appears as a legacy from the Ancients.[10] Prometheus being the creator of mankind and civilization, the first act is clearly focused on him as *plasticator*, and the second on Prometheus as the educator of mankind. Nonetheless, possibly because of Goethe's own identification with Prometheus, especially in the first act, the work appears as a milestone in the evolution of the myth.

> PROMETHEUS. I will not! Tell them that!
> And there's an end of it: I won't.
> Their will against mine.
> One against one —
> I'd call it even.[11]

These are the opening lines of Goethe's drama. *In medias res*, these words, spoken by Prometheus, enable us to note a major change in the interpretation of the Prometheus myth, and also to have a clear insight into Goethe's Titan's main characteristic. The power of Prometheus equals that of the gods, and this equality is dependent on his intelligence, his independence of mind, and his power of creation. Later in the drama , Prometheus, speaking to Athena, adds:

> What sort of claim
> Do the proud dwellers of Olympus
> Think they have upon my powers?
> They are mine and mine to use. (lines 128–31)

The powers mentioned here are referred to, in the immediate context (line 126), as 'creative powers'. Prometheus puts them forward as a part of his essence, something the gods 'cannot rob [him] of' (line 74). This power is reasserted later, when Prometheus claims:

> I too can think my goddess,
> And I too have power.[12] (lines 137–38)

Jacqueline Duchemin comments on these two lines: 'Here is the essential theme, the dominant — and domineering — trait of his (Goethe's) Prometheus, and himself. Borne off out of time by an intuition which makes him immediately perceive his own genius, he feels he is eternal like immortal beings.'[13] Surely, these lines, which imply the primacy of an inner form in the matter of creation, confirm the nature of Goethe's link with Prometheus: that of identification.

We should mention at this stage what Duchemin sees as 'revealing inconsistencies'[14] in the fragment. Prometheus, though presented as the creator of mankind, exchanges his condition for ours in the most famous lines of the play, which, as we shall see later, are very similar to the tone and style of the 1774 poem:

> What was the forge of my manhood
> If not almighty Time,
> My lord and yours?[15] (lines 29–31)

Duchemin sees in these three lines the spontaneity of a young poet totally identifying with his characters.[16] While not entirely disagreeing with this opinion, we have to bear in mind that, if Prometheus had not presented himself as a man (more precisely a 'Promethean man', as we shall see), his kingdom being the earth, his accusations towards the Olympian gods could well have backfired on him. Prometheus does not want to overthrow the gods to replace them: this is not the implication of his equality to them. If we take the measure of the change in Prometheus's persona, the main implication of this equality is that the original transgression, based on hubris in the primitive and intermediate myths, does not enter the equation any more. Pride is not a factor in Goethe's *Prometheus*.

The only supreme force Prometheus recognizes is Destiny,[17] and all Olympian gods have to submit themselves to this power. It is probably on this essential subordination that the equality between Prometheus and the other gods is founded in Goethe's fragment. This crucial aspect is introduced in the play by the omnipresent theme of the vassal/master relationship. If Goethe's Prometheus is so concerned with freedom, it is essentially because he had to conquer it. At the beginning of the play, Prometheus rejects any kind of negotiation with Mercury, the messenger of Zeus and the Olympian gods.

> Now leave me; I'll serve no vassal! (line 48)

Further on, Prometheus refuses 'To be their steward/ And to guard their heaven' (lines 68–69). However, we are informed that this has not always been the case. There is a reminder of the fact that Prometheus helped the Olympian gods get rid of the Titans (lines 139–50), when his character tells Athena that, for fear of what they could do, he '[bore] the burden they/ Made solemn show to place upon [his] shoulders'(lines 141–42).

It is useful here to draw a parallel between Aeschylus's Prometheus and that of Goethe. In *Prometheus Bound*, he refused to submit himself to the power of the god to whom he was once allied, and with whom he was once equal. In Goethe's fragment, the situation is very different: it appears that Prometheus was originally inferior to the gods, and in charge of their safety. Thus, in Jacqueline Duchemin's words, Goethe's Prometheus 'equals the personal gods with all the rush of his powerful will, aware of the superhuman value of human genius.'[18] The context in which Prometheus's persona is perceived is therefore different, and the actions of the Titan find legitimacy. One character in particular plays an important role in defining this aspect.

Although the link between the goddess Athena (Minerva in Goethe's text) and Prometheus was not established by Goethe,[19] this ancient association reaches its climax in his work.

> MINERVA: I honour my father,
> And I love you, Prometheus[20]

Of course, we must not interpret her words literally here, and we shall see why by examining the nature of her relationship with Prometheus. However, the link uniting the Titan and the goddess immediately appears as very close. In order to create mankind and Pandora, as well as to accomplish all his work for men, Goethe's Prometheus is helped by the goddess. Athena — especially after Aeschylus's *Eumenides* — personifies divine thought, a characteristic inherited from her mother Metis. This has a tremendous effect on the significance of the Prometheus myth. Whereas Athena was traditionally on her father's side, in Goethe's 1773 *Prometheus* the goddess gives her approval to the Titan. He at first rejects Minerva's help to give life to his creatures when she intervenes as the representative of Zeus, not wanting any form of alienation for his creatures, but Minerva eventually decides to give this power to Prometheus in her own name and to lead him to the source of life. In this very 'rallying' lies Prometheus's symbolic victory. Divine wisdom being on his side, his acts are perceived in a new light. From this point, Prometheus becomes a symbol of intelligence confronting an oppressive and arbitrary power.

This symbol is strengthened by the fact that Prometheus and Minerva seem to be one:

> PROMETHEUS: And you are to my spirit
> As it is to itself [...]
> And thus with you and me
> One in spirit always
> My love for you eternal![21]

Prometheus is a creator because Minerva endows him with the power to give life to his creatures. We have previously mentioned that the artist, according to Goethe, creates 'like Nature', which implies that he is driven by an inner form. Prometheus's relationship with Minerva, in this fragment, illustrates this: she, being the animative principle, had to be part of Prometheus. It leads Raymond Trousson to conclude that the 'animative power symbolized by her is thus in Prometheus himself, immanent and not transmitted, totally part of his own being'.[22] The nature of the association between Prometheus and the goddess also makes Goethe's point that one cannot create something great without isolating oneself. This is probably why Prometheus, in the fragment, does not want his 'kingdom', the earth, to be touched by the Olympian gods. A definite rupture is made with Heaven. The lines that follow emphasize this segmentation, and Prometheus's will to protect his creatures.

> Look down, oh Zeus,
> Upon my world. It lives,
> And I have shaped it in my likeness,
> A race to be like me,
> To suffer, weep, enjoy, to have its pleasure,
> And pay no heed to you —
> No more than I do.[23]

However, Prometheus's wish is not to create another world in which he could be another Zeus. From lines 92 to 97, Prometheus states that men are in fact images of himself:

> Here's my world, my all!
> Here I know who I am!
> Here- all my wishes
> Embodied in these figures,
> My spirit split in a thousand ways
> Yet whole in my beloved children.[24]

The world the Titan creates for mankind has to be based on freedom, sustained by the idea of equality. Epimetheus (line 84) accuses his brother of depriving his creatures of the happiness of harmony, precisely because Prometheus wants to protect them from the gods. Even though the fragment is incomplete, we may assume that the young Goethe had planned a reconciliation with the gods. Two facts confirm this assumption: the intervention by Epimetheus, and the final stage direction in the manuscript, which states that Athena returns once more in the name of the Olympian gods in order to find an agreement. The isolation preached by Goethe was therefore probably just the first stage in the process of creation. Such a conception of the artist and of creation is necessarily linked to an aesthetic. As Trousson remarks, 'Going by his creative power, Goethe doubles his existence with an essence, defines himself and rejects the submission to a personal divinity whose principle would be identical to the one that animates him. If the metaphysical revolt is unquestionably present in the fragment, nevertheless, it does not come first, but second: it is the result and not the origin of his conception of the poet.'[25] If the first act of the fragment essentially deals with this matter, the nature of the second act differs greatly. Whereas Prometheus was essentially seen as a creator in the first part of the play, in the second he is exclusively depicted as a legislator, the educator of mankind and founder of civilization. In the second act, the creation of Prometheus is mankind, not the poem, as was implied in the first act. As Trousson puts it, 'from the new hero created by Goethe, we come back to the traditional mythological hero'.[26] The attempts to explain this 'gap' between the two acts of *Prometheus* have been numerous, and we would agree with Trousson,[27] who reminds us that the young Goethe had read widely and was tormented by many questions. Fiery and enthusiastic as he was, the study of Prometheus led him to scatter his thoughts and to write spontaneously. This would probably provide a partial explanation for the relative heterogeneity of the play, and, most of all, for its incompleteness.

In the second act of *Prometheus*, Goethe expresses views on society which are clearly opposed to Rousseau's.[28] Whereas the latter, in an idealized state of Nature, had depicted the original man as good and corrupted only by society and civilization, Goethe believes in man and shows confidence in progress, without idealizing mankind. Prometheus himself notes:

> You've not belied your nature, my children.
> You're lazy and industrious,
> And gently cruel,
> Generously mean,
> Like all your brothers in this fate,
> Like all the beasts, and like the gods. (lines 316–21)

Man is animated by mixed feelings, and is by essence complex, according to Goethe, and this is what seems to make his richness. Yet again, because the fragment remains unfinished, we cannot exactly tell how mankind would have evolved in *Prometheus*, but the first fights between men have already started.

Another essential aspect of this second act is the relationship between Prometheus and his creature, Pandora. As we know, she was traditionally regarded as the creature who brings sin to earth, and who initiates the fall of man. In Goethe's *Prometheus*, her status is perfectly antithetical to this perception, since she is Prometheus's favourite creature. We are given this indication in the first act, when Prometheus, observing Pandora (a statue at that stage), says:

> And you, Pandora,
> Holy vessel of all gifts
> That please
> Under the wide sky
> On the endless earth (lines 175–79)

These lines reverse the tradition of the Pandora myth, in which the significance of her name, the 'present of all', is directed towards the destruction of mankind. Prometheus here does not love Pandora as a woman, but as a daughter. This is how he addresses her, and Pandora calls him 'father'. In the second act, we observe him telling Pandora about the secrets of life, love and death. Pandora witnesses Mira and Arbar's embrace, and, shocked by the strength of what she is unable to understand, she runs away in order to find her father. Prometheus then explains to Pandora the mystery of love through that of death:

> And still there comes a time when all is fulfilled,
> Everything we've longed for, dreamed or hoped
> Or feared, my beloved. And that time is death.[29]

She appears as a pure being, who brings only satisfaction to her creator and father, Prometheus. Pandora, who usually embodies the corruption of mankind, is a positive creature in *Prometheus*. This emphasizes the turning point in the evolution of the myth. Prometheus, though different in the first and second act of Goethe's play, is transfigured by this work. He seems to rebel, less against the god of gods, than against a form of passivity towards fate. Moreover, his antagonism to Zeus is not based on pride or hubris, because, in the face of Destiny, Prometheus and the gods are equal. Goethe's Prometheus is presented as a harbinger of freedom, and above all, as an artist with metaphysical concerns. More than the character of the second part of the play, whose function as a legislator and educator is directly inherited from mythology, Goethe's Prometheus distinguishes himself as a rebellious artist. This image is strengthened by the famous 1774 'Prometheus', intended as an opening to the third act of the play, which was never written. It therefore appears as a last word, and as the conclusion of the play.

The 1774 Poem

The seven-strophe ode Goethe composed in 1774[30] appears as the illustration of Prometheus's revolt against the Olympian gods, but takes another form and value from that expressed in the fragment. As Trousson remarks, 'in the fragment, Prometheus ignores the gods, in the ode, he destroys them'.[31] The ode, a tempestuous address to Zeus and the Olympian gods in the form of a lyrical outpouring, is the expression of Promethean revolt. Whereas Prometheus in the fragment wanted to avoid the gods, he now confronts them. Possibly more than the unfinished play, Goethe's ode was extremely influential in the nineteenth century, both in artistic and philosophical circles, as the poem was caught up in the turmoil of the 'pantheism quarrel'.

In 1775, Friedrich Jacobi published the poem Goethe had sent him, without his permission and without mentioning his name,[32] using the ode as an example of pure Spinozism. Jacobi did not publish his *Letters on Spinoza's Doctrine* until 1785, but was already keen to put forward his mystical and non-atheistical interpretation of the philosopher, an interpretation which would become dear to the hearts of most German Romantics. Goethe, however, did not approve of such an attempt to reduce his poetry to a philosophical idea. As Boyd notes, 'Goethe [...] showed resentment at the unauthorized publication, which, he believed, placed him in a false light'.[33] We must also be careful not to link the ode to a philosophical theory, an approach that limits and distorts its poetical impact. However, one major reason for the great influence of 'Prometheus' relates to Friedrich Nietzsche and Karl Marx, who perpetuated the powerful interest which it had already aroused. As will be seen in Part III, Chapter 2, they did not use the poem in order to adjust it to their theories, but rather as a starting point.

'Prometheus' appears as an appeal to Zeus to stop his despotic and cruel attitude in Prometheus's realm, that is Earth. From the first strophe, Zeus is referred to as inconsequential and therefore unfair, since he is compared to a child.

> Cover your heaven, Zeus,
> With cloudy vapors
> And like a boy beheading thistles
> Practice on oaks and mountain peaks
> Still you must leave
> My earth intact (lines 1–7)

The intensity of the call to Zeus is the measure of the gods' power, which is certainly not denied in the poem. However, what is withheld from them is their right to be worshipped, for they are represented as unjust and unable to feel pity. Prometheus challenges their privileges and their original right to be treated as gods. In the second strophe, they are called 'wretched' (line 12), and their coldness occupies the third strophe, in which Prometheus recalls that, as a child, 'not knowing where to turn' (line 22), he tried to find comfort from the gods,

> as if above there were
> An ear to hear my complaint,
> A heart like mine
> To take pity on the oppressed (lines 24–27).

But there is only a 'sleeper above' (line 36), since Zeus does not deign to look at men, in spite of the adoration of these 'Poor hopeful fools' (line 20). Zeus and the Olympian gods, with their coldness and harshness, are therefore totally opposed to Prometheus, whose 'holy and glowing heart' (line 32), 'Unaided, accomplish[ed] all' (line 33). The implication of such a statement is that men give the power they want to the gods. Mankind is responsible for it, because, by adoring the gods, by recognizing them, men actually make them powerful, make them gods.

As in the *Prometheus* dramatic fragment, Goethe recognizes only one supreme power, that of Destiny. But the assertion of this force is so spirited in the ode that the four lines expressing this thought were decisive. Forming as they do the climax of the poem, they contain decisive implications on the evolution of the Prometheus myth. Addressing Zeus, the Titan proclaims:

> Was it not omnipotent Time
> That forged me into manhood,
> And eternal Fate,
> My masters and yours? (lines 42–45)

We shall discuss later the 'manhood' of Prometheus in Goethe's work, but, for now, the recognition of Time and Fate as omnipotent relegates the gods to the rank of hollow idols. In the poem their order is destroyed to 'recreate' a world based on faith in mankind and its power. Prometheus's address to Zeus and the gods is not purely devastating: it ends in a cry of victory and an acceptance of mankind's condition.

> Or did you think perhaps
> That I should hate this life,
> Flee into deserts
> Because not all
> The blossoms of dream grew ripe? (lines 46–50)

The main trait of Prometheus's character as a creator appears here to have been replaced by rebellion. However, there is a consistency in Goethe's Prometheus from the dramatic fragment to the ode. Although the poem does not exactly deal with the figure of the creator, it deals with Prometheus's power of creation. As well as being a diatribe against Zeus and the Olympian gods, 'Prometheus' is an invitation to build something new in freedom. The poem has an undeniably performative value: Prometheus's language truly breaks the power of gods and builds new possibilities for men. As Trousson remarked, 'it is always in his power of creation that Prometheus founds his revolt and his challenge, it is from this certitude he draws his assurance.'[34] Prometheus's persona therefore remains coherent. Prometheus's revolt, as it appears in the ode, derives from the awakening of conscience to genius, an idea sustaining the entire dramatic fragment. It is true that, in the 'Prometheus' poem, this element is emphasized, and, to a certain extent, detached from its context. However, it is the consequence of the awareness of genius. Goethe does not depict two different Prometheus: 'In the drama, Prometheus fights for his independence. In the ode, he explains his faith. Since the theme of the creator had led Goethe to revolt, revolt leads him to define the very object of this revolt: the ode is a branching of his thought.'[35]

It remains to examine the main consequences of this poem and the *Prometheus* dramatic fragment within the evolution of the myth, but we can already perceive that the transformation Goethe introduced in Prometheus's persona relies mainly on his own identification with the Titan. It gave new life to Prometheus, thanks to its intense and powerful language and allowed the myth to reach another step. It is hard to know whether this achievement was in the spirit of the age, because the Prometheus myth had accumulated enough elements to take on a new significance, or whether it relied on the great individual Goethe was. Both factors probably had a role to play in the history of the myth. However, thanks to the injustice of the gods and their equal submission to Fate, the actions of Prometheus found legitimacy, and men gained their real freedom. Prometheus, with Goethe, had freed mankind from them. Before examining the transformation Goethe imparted to the Prometheus myth, we must mention the last work this myth inspired in him, more than thirty years after the *Prometheus* dramatic fragment and poem.

Pandora (1807–1808)

Pandora, a complex and unfinished drama, depicts a radically different Prometheus from that of 1773–1774. This could, of course, be explained by the fact that *Pandora* is a late work, far removed from the *Sturm and Drang* aesthetic. Another possible explanation could be the fact that *Pandora* only has very loose links with the Prometheus and Pandora myths, and seems to be much more part of a personal mythology. There are undeniably enlightening matters in *Pandora*, which have to be taken into account in the development of the Prometheus myth, but the fortune of this drama was not as great as the *Prometheus* drama, nor the ode, and its impact on the interpretation of the myth was minor. Therefore, we shall only consider its most important aspects for the transformation of the Prometheus myth.

In autumn 1807, Leopold von Seckendorf and Joseph Ludwig Stoll, editors of a new journal entitled *Prometheus*, asked Goethe for a short contribution: this was the unfinished *Pandora*. As early as July 1806, the name 'Pandora' had figured in Goethe's diary beside that of Frau von Levetzow. Goethe may well have identified her with Pandora, who, for him, was the embodiment of the Ideal. Nonetheless, in the drama, Pandora is not the central character. Late at night, a solitary and nostalgic character (Epimetheus) remembers his past and his youth, until a

young man, Phileros (Prometheus's son), interrupts him. The youth announces
to Epimetheus that he is deeply in love with a young girl whose name he does
not know. This evocation of love makes Epimetheus dream of his unspeakable
happiness with Pandora, a long time ago. She was his wife for a few months, and
then disappeared for ever, leaving her daughter Epimeleia (the symbol of sorrow)
behind, taking with her Elpore, the embodiment of Hope. When Epimetheus falls
asleep just before dawn, Prometheus appears, torch in hand, to urge the blacksmiths
to set to work. The Titan then praises his unending activity, the virtue of hard
work, and his physical strength. When asked by the shepherds to make musical
instruments and tools, Prometheus proudly rejects their enquiry, replying that
he only wants to make weapons. While Prometheus works, Elpore appears to
Epimetheus in his dreams, and promises him that Pandora will soon come back.
However, Epimetheus's dreams suddenly come to an end when Epimeleia arrives,
screaming, running away from Phileros. Overwhelmed by jealousy, the young man
has just killed a shepherd, and now tries to hit Epimeleia, accusing her of betrayal in
front of Epimetheus and his father, who violently rebukes Phileros for his actions.
Phileros leaves in haste to throw himself into the sea. Epimeleia, devastated, justifies
herself and explains the misunderstanding. In the dialogue that follows, Epimetheus
tells Prometheus the story of Pandora, the woman the mistrustful Prometheus
had himself rejected. The shepherds, to avenge the loss of their fellow, set fire to
Epimetheus's house. Epimeleia jumps in the fire to kill herself. Eos then emerges
from the sea to announce the imminent union of Phileros and Epimeleia, saved by
the will of the gods. The fragment ends here.

From this it will be seen that the Prometheus of *Pandora* and the coherent character
depicted by Goethe in 1773 and 1774 are clearly distinct, although the Titan is not
entirely unrecognizable. The character Goethe depicts in *Pandora* is essentially
pragmatic. As Lichtenberger puts it, he represents 'all that, in mankind, is a will
of power, all that strives towards taming the elements, conquering and exploiting
Nature, creating amongst men an organization, a hierarchy.'[36] Paradoxically, as a
result of such an approach to reality, Prometheus is plunged into immediate action,
in spite of the original meaning of his name, the forethinker. However, if we
take this comparison with the origins of the myth a little further, we can see that
Prometheus's persona, once again, is totally opposed to Epimetheus.[37] Yet the value
of this antagonism is different from that in primitive and intermediate versions
of the Prometheus myth. Indeed, the opposition of the two brothers in Goethe's
Pandora is not based on the traditional antithesis between foresight and hindsight
any more, but on their personae, which appear as complementary.

While Prometheus in *Pandora* praises the value of action, Epimetheus, on
the other hand, is nostalgic and dreamy. Epimetheus very much relies on his
imaginative power, of which the Prometheus of *Pandora* is deprived. Whereas
Prometheus only values human activity, Epimetheus is passive, fully accepting his
destiny. Because of Epimetheus's contemplative attitude, it has been said that the
ageing Goethe identified with his character, but it is difficult to agree with this
theory.[38] He does not have enough depth for the writer to identify fully with him.
On the other hand, although Prometheus is so unyielding that he almost appears

as an allegorical figure, Goethe probably felt close to certain traits of his character. In this respect, we might agree with Lichtenberger's assertion that 'the interview between the two brothers is in fact a dialogue between the two lobes of [Goethe's] brain'[39]. Such an explanation would be revealing of a new stage in the Prometheus myth itself. We outlined in the first part[40] of this work Karl Kérényi's theory about the duo Epimetheus-Prometheus: according to him the two brothers were, like Plato's androgyne, a single complete being divided into two. Though relevant and fruitful, this conception is difficult to reconcile with the primitive and intermediate myths. However, Goethe's depiction of the two brothers to a large extent backs up Kérényi's explanation. The construction, perpetuation and evolution of a myth relies on the understanding and interpretation of its components. Because men are in charge of this process, the shape a myth takes depends on history, but mainly on sociological and psychological factors. The collective unconscious is at stake when taking the evolution of a myth into account. An individual work can give valuable insight into the unconscious, and if Goethe's two *Prometheus* works were so influential, it is probably because they appeared as the expression of many elements present in the collective unconscious at a given time. On the other hand, *Pandora* being a very personal work with its own symbols and imagery, its influence on the Prometheus myth is practically indiscernible. That is, if we except the relationship between Prometheus and Epimetheus, which clearly derives from intermediate myths, and appears as the product of a long maturation. The opposition of the two brothers being based on something deeper than the foresight/hindsight antithesis, namely two conceptions of the world, the value this duo takes is decisive. According to the drafts Goethe left behind, he intended to reach a harmonious unity by the end of the play, and, inevitably, a balance between the brothers' two antagonistic conceptions of the world. After Goethe's *Pandora*, Epimetheus almost entirely disappeared from derivative works on the Prometheus myth. Does this mark the end of a phase within the Prometheus myth? Given that such a disappearance would logically entail the completion of Prometheus's persona, it is more fruitful to note that this event coincides with the humanization of Prometheus.

The Titan Becoming Man

Prometheus's humanization was certainly a natural event within the *dynamis* of the myth, as Jacqueline Duchemin remarked.[41] Goethe's partial identification with the Greek character, combined with his great talent, undeniably played a part in this turning-point. Moreover, his treatment of the Titan occurred at a favourable time. Works on Prometheus, as we have already noted, are countless, and it cannot be said that Prometheus's humanization was unheard of before Goethe. He possibly had precursors in his new perception and interpretation of Prometheus's persona, but Goethe was undoubtedly responsible for the Titan's great fortune once his status changed. Myths evolve thanks to a process of inheritance and individual creation, and from that point of view, one could say that Prometheus's humanization appeared as the result of a favourable conjunction of time and personal creation, that of Johann Wolfgang von Goethe.[42] The constitution and evolution of a myth is inevitably involved in time and history, and implies a series of metamorphoses. If myths appeal so much to men, it is surely because they are rooted in their origins, but also because they are perpetually renewed by each generation. Therefore, Prometheus's gain of manhood appears as the product of a natural process within the *dynamis* and dialectic at stake in the formation of the Prometheus myth. From a historical point of view, we must add that Goethe's ode influenced his contemporaries more than his *Prometheus* fragment did, since the latter was not published until 1833, sixty years after it was written in 1773, when Romanticism was already established. The fragment did not shape the Romantic interpretation of the Prometheus myth. However, the ode played an important part in this formation, and it is no coincidence that, within the poem itself, the lines most commented upon are the climactic:

> Was it not omnipotent Time
> That forged me into manhood,
> And eternal Fate,
> My masters and yours?[43]

They directly address Prometheus's manhood, a trait which was the main innovation of Goethe, and on which the turning-point of the Prometheus myth in the nineteenth century was based. We have already seen that the essential issue of the myth, in Goethe's works, shifts from that of Hesiod and Aeschylus, where the essential question was that of evil and its consequence, that is the transgression of divine power through hubris. The passage quoted above is enlightening when we take this aspect into account: because the Olympian gods have to submit to 'eternal Fate', as does Prometheus, and, because the real power comes from this immanent *Moira*, the notion of guilt based on pride becomes irrelevant. From then on, the focus of Goethe's *Prometheus* appears to be man's power of creation, which includes its condition of existence and Prometheus's fight for it. Indeed, these four lines emphasize this shift and show the humanization of Prometheus, who decided to change his condition for that of men. They also mark the birth of Promethean man, a notion to which we shall return later. Jacqueline Duchemin emphasized the inconsistency in these famous four lines by Goethe, which she imputed to his youth. This is the explanation she gives for the fact that Prometheus 'changes his condition for ours', since, in Goethe's poem, the Titan is also the creator of mankind. She questioned whether Goethe 'wanted it fully and consciously', whether 'he could not control his cry', and eventually favoured this second hypothesis. However, the matter may be more complex: although the ode was later placed at the end of the *Prometheus* fragment, as a climax and a conclusion to it, they were originally independent. Although the role of Prometheus as a sculptor and therefore tangible creator of mankind is largely elaborated upon in the play, we must not assume that the Prometheus depicted in the ode is identical to his dramatic counterpart. Even though Prometheus's power of creation is probably the most apparent aspect of his persona in the fragment, he is also described as the educator of mankind in the play, and that is a trait we must remember in the interpretation of the poem. In the passages related to Prometheus's creation of mankind, our reading must surely not be a literal one.

When the Titan, addressing the gods, pronounces the four famous lines, the meaning of 'manhood' must certainly not be restricted to the idea of a common biological nature. We have to interpret it as a condition shared by all men. When Prometheus evokes his childhood and the disappointment of his prayers addressed to the gods, in the third strophe of the ode, it appears that it is this deep feeling and not simply his nature which has led him to free himself from them.

> Once, too, a child,
> Not knowing where to turn,
> I raised bewildered eyes
> Up to the sun, as if above there were
> An ear to hear my complaint,
> A heart like mine
> To take pity on the oppressed.

Manhood, in this context, might be defined in relation to the gods' oppression, and also by what can be perceived as a common sensitivity. Men are defined in opposition to the coldness and cruelty of the gods. It is certainly on this basis that Prometheus identifies with men, whether he is their creator or not. Prometheus glorifies a special quality which he presents as the main attribute of mankind. This quality, to which he refers twice, is a 'glowing heart' (lines 10 and 32). In the first occurrence of this expression, it is attributed to Prometheus's 'kingdom', the earth (line 7), and, by extension, to men, its inhabitants. Further on, Prometheus uses exactly the same term to describe his own principal power:

> Did not my holy and glowing heart,
> Unaided, accomplish all? (lines 32–33)

The addition of the adjective 'holy' reminds us of Prometheus's divine nature, and therefore of a certain ascendance over men, but it is also clear that an identity exists between Prometheus and mankind, an identity which essentially relies on this quality of heart and feelings. The glow Prometheus presents as the pillar of his works, of which gods themselves are deprived, is also part of the essence of Man. It seems that Prometheus's essential sensitivity of heart is also his main legacy and gift to mankind, and this would explain why Prometheus claims his manhood. From this angle, it is interesting to observe that the original gift of fire is understood here in a metaphorical and symbolic way, since the heat of the flame is instilled in the human heart. In this context, the flame does not appear as a symbol of knowledge or of passionate love, but as another form of love, which would be a great generosity, in the sense of empathy for fellow men.

A second important expression in the poem gives us another indication of the way in which we have to interpret Prometheus's manhood. When, in the final strophe, he exclaims:

> Here I sit, forming men
> In my image,
> A race to resemble me:

we must probably not limit the meaning of 'forming' to the act of a sculptor; the following lines invite us to see Prometheus, in this last strophe, as the educator of mankind more than as its tangible creator:

> To suffer, to weep,
> To enjoy, to be glad,
> And never to heed you, like me!

Prometheus here refers to the emotional side of men, the one he is proud to share with them, as opposed to the passive indifference of the gods. We are reminded of the episode of the *Prometheus* Fragment in which Prometheus explains love and death to Pandora. If Prometheus 'forms' men, in the ode, this is probably as an educator, and a father, as was the case in the second act of the *Prometheus* fragment. Therefore, we do not see in Prometheus's claim to manhood an inconsistency of the young Goethe so much as the accomplishment of both the fragment and the ode in the coronation of the Promethean man. It is with this event that the nineteenth-century turning-point in the Prometheus myth is truly initiated.

As Trousson opined, 'creative talent frees the man of genius from the gods: he does not need them'.[44] This is probably Goethe's main legacy to the history of the Prometheus myth, and could serve as a definition of Promethean man. His trust in his own ability to create delivers him from the gods, and, more importantly, from his responsibility for the loss of the golden age and from his resulting guilt. Trousson pursues his analysis by stating that '[Prometheus] stopped trusting the [gods] the day he realized that the wisdom and power he attributed to them was only dependent on his own faith. From that day, he has known there was nothing they could do to him if he provided himself with the weapon of his belief; he is the master of earth and of his existence: so there is no reason to fear gods.'[45] The moment when Prometheus becomes aware that, to a certain extent, gods are the creation of his faith, appears as an act of liberation which coincides with the birth of Promethean man. Such a change in the perception of Prometheus, as we shall see later with Shelley, cannot but have an impact on the very conception of the world order. The Prometheus myth, in its content and interpretation, was about to change dramatically, and its very value was to appear in a new light. Goethe's interpretation of Prometheus evoked a strong reaction from his contemporaries, and it is now time to examine the works which were influenced by him.

Prometheus, Goethe, and Music

Goethe's interpretations of Prometheus did not only influence poets and writers of his time, but also musicians, and his work proved extremely stimulating for composers.[46] Beethoven's *The Creatures of Prometheus*, Op. 43, was composed at the suggestion of Salvatore Viganò, the court ballet master, whose libretto, now lost, was apparently based on eighteenth-century allegorical interpretations of the myth. Paul Bertagnolli, in his study of the Prometheus myth in music, devotes a whole chapter to Beethoven's ballet.[47] The atmosphere of the piece, however, also reflects Goethe's new interpretation. Beethoven and Goethe had a strong admiration for each other,[48] and Beethoven in particular was fascinated by Goethe's writings. There is no doubt he knew the ode when he composed *The Creatures of Prometheus*, which was premiered in March 1801 in Vienna's Burgtheater before the Empress

Maria Theresa, and he suitably emphasized the greatness and triumphant character of Prometheus, as shown by the outbursts of fortissimo and the dynamic syncopated rhythms of the overture. The final theme of the piece was later used by Beethoven in the finale of the *Eroica* Symphony, originally entitled *Bonaparte Symphony* by the composer. This is not fortuitous: there was a Romantic tradition associating Prometheus with Napoleon, which tends to prove that Beethoven's interpretation of the Titan was rooted in that of Goethe and his followers rather than in Viganò's sources. Since Trousson devoted a whole chapter to the parallel between Prometheus and Napoleon,[49] I shall not examine it at length, but I will nevertheless come back to that aspect when considering the Romantic interpretations of the myth.

The link between Goethe's ode and Beethoven's *Creatures of Prometheus* is not explicit, but Franz Schubert's lied 'Prometheus' is a setting of the ode. Schubert first made use of the subject in 1816, when he wrote a cantata entitled *Prometheus*,[50] for soloists, chorus and orchestra. Three years later, he set Goethe's ode to music and sent *Prometheus*,[51] together with other lieder, to the German poet, who famously returned the parcel unopened. Unfortunately we do not have Goethe's opinion of Schubert's lieder, but the lied itself gives us a very precise interpretation of Goethe's poem, a 'reading in music' which, besides its artistic quality and originality, is an interesting testimony of the reception of his ode.[52]

Even though we are dealing with two different media, to set a poem to music is in itself an interpretation of the original poem. Schubert did not limit himself to reproducing, through the musical medium, the general atmosphere of the poem: the different movements of the poem can be found in the lied, with all their contrasts and climaxes transposed into music, at the level of the phrase, as well as at the level of the word. Schubert made elaborate use of modulations and modes to express the evolution of the poem. There is neither an exposition nor a re-exposition of a theme in the poem, a choice which enabled Schubert to reflect as faithfully as could be the rise of Prometheus's words.

In a piano introduction, Schubert managed to express at once defiance and nobility, by combining the major mode, the allegro tempo, *forte*, and the dotted eighth note followed by a sixteenth, which here expresses an idea of dynamism and majesty (emphasized by the octaves in the left hand). However, when Prometheus starts his address to Zeus, Schubert uses the key of G minor for the five first verses evoking Zeus in his ethereal realm, which, associated with the *piano* nuance, introduces a certain stormy quality. Prometheus's interlocutor is highlighted by the melody, a fifth (G-D) stressing the name 'Zeus', the D being held for two and a half beats. This illustrates Schubert's use of contrasts in his lieder: from the sixth line, when Prometheus enjoins Zeus to 'leave /[His] earth intact', the major mode reappears in the firmness of a recitative. Interestingly, despite the fact that Goethe, in his poem, began another strophe, after 'Du mich beneidest', Schubert inscribed in the same movement the first two verses of the second strophe, ('Ich kenne nichts Ärmeres/ Unter der Sonn' als euch, Götter!'), two verses in which Prometheus carries on his diatribe against the Olympian gods. The composer again stressed a climactic and accusative word, 'euch', referring to the gods by means of a fifth (A-B flat), the B flat having a suspensive quality before the announcement of the accused name: 'Götter'. After a pause, the second strophe takes a contrasting mournful aspect to evoke the pathos of the 'Poor hopeful fools', the 'children and beggars'. The repetition of sixths followed by long descending phrases confers a plaintive coloration to those lines. Moreover, the slower tempo, and the harmonic writing of the passage, in the style of a chorale, express an almost religious recollection.

This passage contrasts greatly with the following strophe, which deals with Prometheus's evocation of his childhood. The tempo is doubled, and Schubert ascribed a lightness to this third strophe with alternating chords between the two hands, and tonal mobility. Schubert again emphasized the original rhythm of the poem by stressing melodically the words 'Ohr' (ear) and 'Herz' (heart) with two appoggiaturas in E♭. He thus managed to highlight in music Prometheus's sensitivity and humanity as opposed to Zeus's indifference and unfairness. After that strophe, which finishes *piano*, a pause prepares the biggest contrast in Schubert's lied.

The piano opens the fourth and most famous passage of Goethe's ode with two chords of the second inversion of a diminished seventh in C♯, fortissimo, Prometheus entering contra-tempo to start a violent ascending recitative. The tension thus starts accumulating. The second interrogation, based on the same harmonic proceeding at the accompaniment, is one tone higher.

The following musical phrase, *piano*, more melodic, and descending, expresses recollection again. This coincides with the last three lines of the fourth strophe, in which Prometheus expresses regrets about his past obedience to Zeus. However, in the penultimate bar of that phrase, the piano starts a conclusion *fortissimo* with a double-dotted quarter note followed by a sixteenth note, a type of rhythm previously associated with Prometheus. The restrained treatment of those lines allows Schubert to prepare for the climax of the ode. It is interesting to consider why Schubert did not maintain a defiant tone from the fourth strophe to the end of the ode, as could be done in a reading of the poem. The fourth strophe is opened by a steady accompaniment at the piano, fortissimo. Prometheus asks the first two questions in that strophe in the same manner, as in the ode, and twice answers them with a slightly descending recitative, ending pianissimo. Those two 'waves', as we might call them, announce the climax of the ode. Indeed, Schubert, like his contemporaries, was obviously deeply touched by verses 42 to 45 of the ode. In order to emphasize their importance, Schubert did not exploit the dotted eighth or double-dotted quarter note followed by a sixteenth note, but chose the greatest rhythmic and melodic stability. The melodic phrase, *fortissimo*, ascends very slowly, with an emphasis on the words 'geschmiedet' (forged), thanks to a fourth, on 'Zeit' (Time), with the same proceeding and interval, and, eventually, on 'meine Herrn' (my masters). The final pause of the strophe, which intervenes contra tempo, introduces an unexpected emphasis on 'und deine' (and yours). Through the melodic line, Schubert highlighted the most important words and ideas of the poem, and imposed an interpretation, a reading of the verses.

After this climax, Schubert does not attempt to maintain such intensity until the end of the poem. The fifth strophe contrasts with the previous one, as if to depict the sad option mentioned by Prometheus

> Or did you think perhaps
> That I should hate this life,
> Flee into deserts
> Because not all
> The blossoms of dream grew ripe?

The previous steadiness at the piano is broken by an alternation between the two hands, as well as by the *pianissimo*.

The final strophe, opened by the piano, combines different elements previously used by Schubert in order to transcribe Prometheus's triumph. Schubert uses the dynamism of the dotted eighth followed by a sixteenth note fortissimo with the stability of two quarter notes at the beginning of each bar (as he previously did with the four climactic verses). Schubert chose the majesty of C major, a chord fully exploited by Prometheus's singing, which relies strongly on the tonic and the dominant and has the characteristics of a march. Such is the spirit Schubert decided to ascribe to Prometheus's presentation and affirmation as a free creator. The composer rhythmically stressed the infinitive 'freuen sich' (to be glad). However, he also introduced one last contrast in a verse in the minor mode, related to Zeus, and whose realization could break his freedom: 'dein nicht zu achten', which Schubert repeated twice, before finishing on two triumphant chords, fortissimo, in a major key.

This brief analysis may enable us to delineate the main aspects of Schubert's interpretation of Goethe's poem. Besides the subtle transcription of the various movements of the ode, Schubert, through the musical medium, defined, combined and contrasted different moods ascribed to Prometheus and his address to Zeus. Thanks to the use of tonality and to a precise 'chiselling' of the melodic line, Schubert also created specific inflexions and stresses. This resulted in a musical 'reading', an interpretation of the ode in music. This evidence allows us to consider the impact of lines 42–45, and of the newly rediscovered Prometheus.

Such a gain in the history of the Prometheus myth would be limited neither to Germany, nor to continental Europe. Goethe's view of Prometheus was at the basis of the Romantic interpretation of the Prometheus myth, and was in the *air du temps*. Two giants of English poetry were about to give shape to the myth in an orientation similar to that of Goethe, and that in spite of their irreducible originality.

Notes to Chapter 1

1. Quoted in Dominique Lecourt, *Prométhée, Faust, Frankenstein. Fondements imaginaires de l'éthique* (Paris: Livre de poche, 1996).
2. *The Auto-biography of Goethe. Truth and Poetry: from my own life*, trans. by the Rev. A. J. W. Morrison, M.A., 2 vols (London: Henry G. Bohn, 1849), II. p. 38.
3. James Boyd, *Notes to Goethe's Poems*, I (1749–1786), (Oxford: Blackwell, 1944), p. 76.
4. Pierre Grappin, *La Théorie du génie dans le préclassicisme allemand* (Paris: PUF 1952), p. 13.
5. Trousson, p. 305.
6. See, for example, Lenz as Tantalus, but also Klinger and Maler Müller, who both identified with the Titans.
7. Trousson, p. 311.
8. The influence of Shaftesbury on the *Sturm and Drang* artists was thoroughly analysed by Oskar Walzel, *Das Prometheussymbol Von Shaftesbury zu Goethe*, in *Wortkunst*, VII (Munich: Hueber

1932). George Chapman, in 'The Shadow of the Night' (1594) (*The Poems of George Chapman,* ed, Phyllis Brooks Bartlett (New York: Russell and Russell, 1962)), preceded Shaftesbury in this particular use of the Prometheus myth, since in this work, he named 'Promethean poets' those who knew how to invent and create, as opposed to the artists who limit themselves to repetition and imitation.

9. The original manuscript, given to Charlotte von Stein, was rediscovered in 1878. In 1818, a copy deriving from Lenz's papers was given back to Goethe, who published it in 1830 in tome XXXIII of his works.

10. On the possible sources of the fragment, see Trousson, pp. 312–13.

11. Johann Wolfgang von Goethe, *Prometheus,* in *Early Verse Drama and Prose Plays,* ed. by Cyrus Hamlin and Frank Ryder, trans. by Robert M. Browning, Michael Hamburger, Cyrus Hamlin, and Frank Ryder (New York: Suhrkamp, 1988), p. 240.

12. Ibid., p. 243.

13. Duchemin, p. 122.

14. Ibid., p. 124

15. Goethe, *Prometheus,* trans. by Browning, Hamburger, Hamlin, and Ryder (New York: Suhrkamp, 1988), p. 240.

16. Duchemin, p. 124.

17. Cf. lines 23–24 and 45–47 in Goethe, *Prometheus,* pp. 240–41.

18. Duchemin, p. 125.

19. See above, pp. 14–15.

20. Goethe, *Prometheus,* p. 242.

21. Ibid., pp. 242–43.

22. Trousson, p. 317.

23. Goethe, *Prometheus,* p. 246.

24. Ibid., p. 242.

25. Trousson, p. 326.

26. Ibid., p. 326.

27. Ibid., p. 332.

28. Rousseau's thought, especially on Nature and society, had a major impact in Europe, with the result that most writers felt that they had to express their views on Rousseau's theories in order to define their own positions.

29. Goethe, *Prometheus,* p. 250.

30. Published without Goethe's agreement by Jacobi in 1785, and officially in 1789

31. Trousson, p. 343.

32. See Boyd, *Notes to Goethe's Poems,* I, pp. 73–76.

33. Ibid., pp. 74–75.

34. Trousson, p. 336.

35. Ibid., p. 342.

36. H. Lichtenberger, *Pandore. Goethe.* (Strasbourg: Faculté des Lettres de l'Université de Strasbourg, booklet 57, 1932), p. 370.

37. See above, pp. 18, 16, 25.

38. See H. M. Wolff, *Goethe in der Periode der Wahlverwandschaften (1802–1809)* (Berne: Francke, 1952), pp. 121–22.

39. H. Lichtenberger, *Pandore. Goethe.,* p. 369.

40. See above, pp. 8, 16.

41. Duchemin, p. 124.

42. Despite Goethe's inspiration and talent, his *Pandora* had no great influence on the perception of the mythological character, and, his attempt to give a positive ethos to the first woman did not change the general interpretation of the Pandora myth. His *Pandora* was thus more relevant to a personal myth than to the Pandora myth as such.

43. *Goethe, Selected Poems,* ed. by Christopher Middleton, trans. by Michael Hamburger (Princeton: Princeton University Press, 1983), l. 42–45

44. Trousson, p. 321.

45. Ibid., p. 321.

46. Johann Johann Friedrich Reichardt (1752–1814) set Goethe's ode to music, and later composers such as Jan Willem Frans Brandt-Buys (1868–1933), Julius Röntgen (1855–1932) op. 99, and most notably Hugo Wolf (1860–1903), *Goethe Lieder* n°49, all set *Prometheus* to music.

47. Paul A. Bertagnolli, 'Gesture and Convention in Beethoven's *Ballet d'Action*', in *Prometheus in Music* (Aldershot: Ashgate, 2007), pp. 27–93.

48. Even if, when they eventually met, this admiration proved to be limited to the artistic level. Beethoven found Goethe too bourgeois, and Goethe found Beethoven too wild

49. Trousson, pp. 421–30.

50. Franz Schubert, *Prometheus* (1816) D461, now lost.

51. Franz Schubert, *Prometheus* (1819) D674, in *Gesänge*, Band III (Frankfurt: C. F. Peters), pp. 213–16.

52. For a detailed musical analysis of the lied, with reproductions of the score, see Bertagnolli, 'Episodic Structure of Schubert's *Prometheus*, D. 674', in *Prometheus in Music*, pp. 116–29.

CHAPTER 2

The Romantic Revolution:
Byron and Shelley

Percy Bysshe Shelley, Mary Shelley and Lord Byron were all fascinated by the Prometheus myth, and all three authors, in one way or another, used it in their work. We shall not linger on Mary Shelley's *Frankenstein*, subtitled *The Modern Prometheus*, since the links between her work and the Prometheus myth itself are more tenuous in Byron's and Shelley's treatments of the Greek figure. Although the Prometheus myth and Promethean creation were a source of inspiration, she did not express her interest in the Greek figure along the same lines as those followed by Byron and Shelley. In Mary Shelley's novel, Victor Frankenstein, like Prometheus, makes a man — or rather, fails to make one — and by doing so, he breaks the natural law. This brings us back to Hesiod, and, to a certain extent, to Aeschylus's perspectives. But unlike Prometheus, Victor fails to enlighten and educate his creature. Richard Holmes stressed that *Frankenstein* retells a creation myth, a profane one, and that a confrontation is at stake, as in Shelley's *Prometheus Unbound*. That confrontation, between power and suffering, is embodied by Zeus and Prometheus, as it is by Victor and his creature.[1] But the motives, means, and nature of Victor and Prometheus contrast greatly. Moreover, the main reason why Mary Shelley's character and her friends' interpretations of Prometheus are in a different vein rests on the fact that Victor Frankenstein is not a hero. Whereas a coherence between the work of Byron and Shelley on the Titan is perceptible, Mary Shelley's work is not centred on him as such, and her view on the myth remains on the fringe.

However, the 1816 Genevan summer the three writers spent together was marked by a shared passion for the Titan, and we have to examine the way two great friends and rivals like Shelley and Byron interpreted the same myth. In 1816, Lord Byron wrote a famous three-stanza poem entitled 'Prometheus' and Mary Shelley claimed, retrospectively, that at the same period, Shelley started to work on his *Prometheus Unbound*. It is difficult to determine which of the three writers originated this interest in the figure of Prometheus, and recent critics have challenged the idea that the Prometheus theme emerged simultaneously in their works during the summer of 1816. They were certainly inspired by each other, but when Byron was at Harrow, *Prometheus Bound* was one of the plays he had to read three times a year,[2] and he was therefore familiar with Aeschylus's play from an early age. As Peter Thorslev noted, even if Shelley treated Prometheus as a key figure within his philosophical system, 'the references to Prometheus in Byron's poetry and in his correspondence before the two poets met in 1816 are legion; the references to Prometheus in Shelley's poetry or letters are practically non existent. When he did refer to him in the notes to the youthful *Queen Mab*, it was only as the villain who had by the gift of fire first enticed man away from his vegetarian diet (note to Act VIII)'.[3] Byron, was certainly the first to transmit his passion for Prometheus, and the first, in 1816, to publish a work related to him. There are similarities in Shelley's and Byron's interpretations of the myth, and Byron's ode on the Titan is also close to Goethe's, although there is no reason to think that Byron or Shelley knew his work at that time.[4] Because *Prometheus Unbound* was the result of a long maturation, and because it appeared as the accomplished and complex expression of Shelley's philosophy, we shall start our analysis with the study of Byron's 'Prometheus', which was also the first to be published.

In the context of the Greek War of Independence that was to break out in 1821, and which both poets fervently supported, their predilection for a heroic Greek figure under the yoke of an oppressive power was to resonate strongly with the revolutionary spirit that animates both treatments of the myth.

'Making death a victory'

'Of the Prometheus of Aeschylus I was passionately fond as a boy. [...] The Prometheus — if not exactly in my plan, has always been so much in my head — that I can easily conceive its influence over all or anything that I have written'[5] (Lord Byron)

Byron used Prometheus and the Promethean reference several times in his work, but with various aims in mind. A myth, by definition, relies on symbolic thought, which explains why it is bound to evolve, and why it is constantly open to new interpretations. In this respect, it is not surprising to find different uses of the same myth from the pen of the same writer. This was the case for Byron, who used the figure of Prometheus as a metaphor to express his thoughts, but also as a persona. These two applications take very different forms. Although both rely on the symbolic aspect of the myth, its use as a metaphor plays on an inflexible pattern, whereas the use of Prometheus as character or persona relies on an evolution of the myth.

In *Don Juan*, Canto I, 127, Byron associates Prometheus with the theme of love, around the metaphor of the fire of love:

But sweeter still than this, than these, than all
Is first and passionate love [...]
And life yields nothing further to recall
Worthy of this ambrosial sin, so shown,
No doubt in fable, as the unforgiven
Fire which Prometheus filch'd for us from heaven.[6]

In *Don Juan*[7], Byron also uses the figure of Prometheus to evoke physical pain. In *Childe Harold*, 'the ceaseless vultures' represent moral pain, and in *Manfred*, he bases human dignity on 'the mind, the spirit, the Promethean spark,/ The lightning of my being'.[8] Even though those evocations of Prometheus and the Promethean fire are interesting inasmuch as they show their power over Byron, they remain topoi, and we are therefore more concerned with his treatment of Prometheus as a persona in the perspective of the evolution of the myth.[9] His poem 'Prometheus' makes such use of the mythical material, and reflects the impact of Aeschylus's play on him.

First of all, if Aeschylus influenced Byron, it was through a Romantic reading and interpretation of *Prometheus Bound*. Translations of his plays were still often approximate, and the conception English poets had of Aeschylus during that period was probably not very different from that of Victor Hugo, who saw in him a Greek Shakespeare (bearing in mind that Shakespeare himself was perceived as a Romantic playwright). The second reason why Byron's 'Prometheus' cannot appear as a mere rewriting of *Prometheus Bound* comes from his very personal conception of Prometheus's nature. We have to be mindful of these two characteristics in our reading of 'Prometheus'.

The first strophe of the poem emphasizes the link existing between Aeschylus's Prometheus and his own. The way in which Byron evokes the suffering of the Titan echoes Aeschylus's pathetic depiction of Prometheus bound to his rock. However, the means the two poets use to convey such a feeling diverge. Whereas Aeschylus based this pathos on a 'lamento' produced by Greek rhythms, and, of course, on the visual intensity of drama, Byron renders pathos through a succession of iambic and binary rhythms that create an effect of hypotyposis. This trope has the particularity of giving a pictorial quality to poetry, by creating an impression of coincidence between what is depicted and the means of depiction. Its effect is strengthened by the fact that it follows the inaugural address to Prometheus, which takes the form of a fluent eulogy:

> Titan! To whose immortal eyes[10]
> The sufferings of mortality, seen in their sad reality,
> Were not as things that gods despise;
> What was thy pity's recompense? (lines 1–4)

The hypotyposis that follows therefore contrasts with the previous lines:

> A silent suffering, and intense;
> The rock, the vulture, and the chain,
> All that the proud can feel of pain, The agony they do not show,
> The suffocating sense of woe,
> Which speaks but in its loneliness, And then is jealous lest the sky
> Should have a listener, nor will sigh until its voice is echoless.
>
> (lines 5–10)

The skilled play on rhythms (with an acceleration of rhythm in line 6, followed by a continuous amplification which maintains the 'phrasing' until the end of the strophe) conjures up the pathetic image of Prometheus on his rock, reproducing Prometheus's suffocation under the pain. We can also note in this first strophe that in contrast to Goethe's conception of Prometheus, at the opening of the poem the Titan is represented as superior to man. Although he appears as their benefactor, he is not part of mankind, and in this Byron appears as Aeschylus's heir. To reinforce this idea, the seventh line, in which Prometheus is called 'the proud', introduces the notion of hubris, characteristic of Greek tragedies.

However, from the second strophe, Byron's poem departs from his source of inspiration, inasmuch as the gods are depicted as fundamentally unfair and evil:

> Titan! To thee the strife was given
> Between the suffering and the will,
> Which torture where they cannot kill;
> And the inexorable Heaven,
> And the deaf tyranny of Fate,
> The ruling principle of Hate,
> Which for its pleasure doth create
> The things it may annihilate,
> Refused thee even the boon to die: (lines 11–19)

Such an 'impious' conception of the Olympian gods may rely on the Romantic bias and peculiar reading of Aeschylus mentioned above. However, it is probably at this stage that Byron's original perception of Prometheus clearly intervenes. A first element shows that Byron departs from the Greek in lines 14 to 16 quoted above. Indeed, they make Prometheus's hubris impossible, since injustice is presented as the main attribute of the gods. It implies that Prometheus's transgression obeys a superior order, as opposed to the gods' gratuitous acts. The following lines of the strophe relate the original myth: Prometheus's immortality is stressed, a traditional depiction of Zeus is sketched ('the Thunderer', line 21, in whose 'hand the lightnings tremble', line 27), and in line 24, Byron comes back to the etymology of Prometheus's name ('foresight'), to play on it. Even the theme of the secret regarding the fatal offspring to be born to Thetis and Zeus is present in the second strophe of the poem ('The fate thou didst so well foresee/ But would not to appease him tell;/ And thy silence was his sentence,' lines 24–26). But in spite of the 'traditional' aspect of the mythological material of this part of the second strophe, lines 14, 15, and 16 ensure that Prometheus is glorified as a hero in the third strophe, a characteristic which establishes the originality of Byron's interpretation of the Prometheus myth.

After the use of those narrative elements, the third and last strophe appears as an analysis of Prometheus's acts, following a very clear and logical structure within the poem. In the wake of the denunciation of the gods' injustice, this analysis is filled with particular significance. It takes the features of a retrial of Prometheus's infamy, and entails even more than his discharge:

> Thy Godlike crime was to be kind,
> To render with thy precepts less
> The sum of human wretchedness,
> And strengthen Man with his own mind; (lines 35–38)

We notice first that the theft of fire is absent here. Prometheus's main gift to mankind, as in Goethe's works, is the awakening of conscience. This modification therefore appears as granted at this stage of the myth's history. Secondly, the verdict which is given here is very far from the one returned by Aeschylus in *Prometheus Bound*, and probably still further from the one he gave in his Promethean trilogy. Although Prometheus's intentions towards mankind are good, he is nonetheless guilty of hubris. His means are good, but the end of his acts, which, according to Aeschylus, would eventually be his own good, is a violation of the rules of the gods. World order and harmony combined with justice still rely on them, and to come back to the original balance, Prometheus's crime has to be punished. The focus of Byron's 'Prometheus', from that point of view, diverges greatly from that of Aeschylus. Prometheus no longer appears as a transgressor, which means that he is not a faulty link in the chain the world order represents. In Byron's thought, Prometheus himself embodies another world, with its own values, and whose purpose is to outstrip that of the Olympian gods. In this context, the adjective 'Godlike' is particularly enlightening. If one considers the enumeration of the gods' attributes in the second strophe of the poem, they are degenerate as such. Because Prometheus represents what overthrows this set of values, he appears as a legitimate god, should he make that claim. The rest of the poem is also revealing, given the value the word 'Spirit' takes:

> But baffled as thou wert from high,
> Still in thy patient energy,
> In the endurance and repulse
> Of thine impenetrable Spirit,
> Which Earth and Heaven could not convulse,
> A Mighty lesson we inherit; (lines 39–43)

Byron emphasizes the fact that Prometheus is the representative of a divine principle. The noun 'Spirit', with a capital letter, is used by Byron to conjure up Christian images (especially with the contiguity of the word 'impenetrable', line 35), and more particularly the image of Jesus Christ:

> Thou art a symbol and a sign
> To mortals of their fate and force;
> Like thee, Man is in part divine,
> A troubled stream from a pure source;
> And Man in portions can foresee
> His own funereal destiny;
> His wretchedness, and his resistance,
> And his sad unallied existence: (lines 45–52)

Prometheus is here identified in his nature with Jesus Christ, and especially in lines 39 and 40. With this parallel, Byron adopts one of the major Romantic interpretations of Prometheus. Indeed, Romanticism truly established the link between the Titan and Jesus Christ so dear to the critics' hearts. With Byron, this identification is rooted in the idea that Prometheus, like Jesus Christ, is not deprived of his divine origins, but is also a man. Here, as in Goethe's works, Prometheus's love for men leads him to become part of mankind. Line 37 is particularly important: it appears as a climax in the poem, and defines the value of Prometheus's figure. As 'a symbol and a sign' of their 'fate and force', he represents the essence of mankind.

This identification between Prometheus and mortals is mainly based on the fact that both have a dual nature. We have already shown that Prometheus, in his opposition to gods and their attributes, becomes associated with mankind. Unlike Prometheus, man is mortal, but he is partly divine thanks to his conscience and soul:

> To which his Spirit may oppose
> Itself — an equal to all woes,
> And a firm will, and a deep sense, (lines 53–55)

The spiritual qualities with which Byron endows mankind appear as truly divine. In the final lines, which take the form of an apotheosis, Byron operates a fusion between men and Prometheus.

> Which even in torture can descry
> Its own concentrated recompense,
> Triumphant where it dares defy,
> And making death a Victory. (lines 56–59)

This does not only raise the question of the specificity of men of power facing their destiny. Although they are not named as such, Prometheus's agonies and suffering are conjured up one last time to symbolize the particular fight of mankind, and this fusion within a symbol has a deep effect. Prometheus does not appear as a god or a prefiguration of Jesus Christ, but, because he transmits his force to men, as a hero, to whom the crown of laurels is given in the last line. Besides the deep links existing between Byron's Prometheus and men, his essential function in the poem is to be an example of perseverance and strength for them. We cannot therefore agree with Trousson that Byron's 'Prometheus' is merely a traditional rewriting of the Prometheus myth. The figure of the Titan allows him to personify his conception of the Romantic hero, as a positive figure freed from sin which entirely departs from the tragic hero. In a passage of *The Prophecy of Dante* (canto IV), a poem written five years after 'Prometheus', Byron used the figure of the Titan once again to embody a great genius endowed with all the Romantic traits. Misunderstood, solitude is his fate:

> Many are poets but without the name
> For what is poetry but to create
> From overfeeling good or ill; and aim
> At an eternal life beyond our fate,
> And be the new Prometheus of new men,
> Bestowing fire from heaven, and then, too late,
> Finding the pleasure given repaid with pain,
> And vultures to the heart of the bestower,
> Who, having lavish'd his high gift in vain,
> Lies chain'd to his lone rock by the sea-shore[11] (lines 10–19)

Prometheus's heroism is based on a superb Romantic pride, which is at the opposite pole to the Greek hubris. Whereas in *Prometheus Bound*, the Titan, because of his hubris, is invariably the transgressor of the world order, Byron's Prometheus is great precisely because of his immoderation.

In the Romantic set of values, Prometheus, freed from his sin, and his rebellious side combined with his creative talents, becomes the ideal figure to identify with. According to Peter Thorslev, Prometheus is 'certainly the most sublime of all the Romantic heroes, and at the same time the most refined. Since he is the Romantic Hero apotheosized, he is pure allegory; there is nothing in him of the Gothic, nothing of the dark mystery or taint of sin of the other Romantic heroes.[...]

Although Prometheus lends "Promethean" characteristics to all the rest of these heroes, he borrows nothing from them.'[12] Prometheus is different from the English 'Gothic' Romantic type Thorslev is referring to, as he is presented by Byron as a pure rebel, and, to a certain extent, as a pure spirit, and a pure will. It is in this sense that Byron sees Prometheus as 'pure allegory', which has to be understood as an archetype.

The figure of Prometheus appealed greatly to Romantic poets. Although Goethe strongly denied being a Romantic author, and is considered as a second-generation classicist by German scholars, there was an undeniable community of thought between him and Byron, and other great Romantic artists. Thorslev suggests that the last line of Byron's 'Prometheus' 'curiously enough, echoes the very sentiment of the close of Goethe's fragment, although there could of course be no question of influence.'[13] The influence which was really at stake here was certainly that of the figure of Prometheus himself, who, within the history of the myth, had gradually gained a new significance. Nonetheless, an important distinction needs to be made between Byron's and Goethe's 'Prometheus'; in Goethe's works, Prometheus does not suffer the terrible punishment he has to endure in ancient versions of the myth and in Byron's. This difference left its stamp on German interpretations of the Prometheus myth, and notably in the pictorial field. In Percy Bysshe Shelley's *Prometheus Unbound* as well as in Byron's 'Prometheus', the punishment of the Titan is central to the treatment of the myth. Whereas, in Byron's poem, Prometheus appears as a refined embodiment of the Byronic hero, in *Prometheus Unbound*, he becomes the keystone of Shelley's poetical and philosophical edifice.

Prometheus at the Heart of Shelley's Cosmogony

> 'Genuine creation, or poetry, creates anew the universe, after it has been annihilated in our mind by the recurrence of impressions blunted by reiteration'
> (P. B. Shelley, *The Defence of Poetry*)

In Este, in September 1818, Percy Bysshe Shelley started drafting *Prometheus Unbound*. After a six-month hiatus during which he worked on *The Cenci*, Shelley wrote the fourth Act of *Prometheus Unbound* together with a few 'lyrical insertions' for the first three acts. As Donald H. Reiman and Sharon B. Powers note, 'though he had first sent *Prometheus Unbound* to be published in England in its three-act original version, Shelley's late additions broadened the scope of his most ambitious work from a myth of the renovation of the human psyche to a renewing of the whole cosmos.'[14] *Prometheus Unbound* appears as a dense and elaborate lyrical drama, and also as the perfect example of a total appropriation of the myth through the means of poetry. Mary Shelley herself, in her note on *Prometheus Unbound*, observed that 'the prominent feature of Shelley's theory of the destiny of the human species was, that evil is not inherent in the system of the creation, but an accident that might be expelled [...] That man could be so perfectionized as to be able to expel evil from his own nature, and from the greater part of the creation, was the cardinal point of his system. And the subject he loved best to dwell on, was the image of One warring with the evil principle, oppressed not only by it, but by all, even the good, who were deluded into considering evil a necessary portion of humanity.'[15] Shelley's model as described by his wife is very close to the definition we previously gave of Promethean man, and we shall have to examine what led Shelley to glorify this type. As a Romantic writer living at a time when established beliefs, values, political and social structures were challenged and threatened, Shelley admired Prometheus's character both as hero, revolutionary and freedom fighter, but also, and above all, as a creator. This latter role takes an even more radical significance than in Goethe's works, in which this aspect was already essential.

Shelley's dénouement, in this respect, is meaningful: purified by his suffering, strengthened by a form of heroism that sublimates pain, Shelley's Prometheus does not want his deliverance to be gained through reconciliation. His release is also bound to the inevitable collapse of a cruel god, who is both the principle and symbol of evil. Persevering until the end in his resistance to Zeus, Prometheus does not disclose the secret with which he threatened Zeus in Aeschylus's play, so that the master of the world carries out his lethal plan of becoming Thetis's lover. This is how Demogorgon was born, who, according to the oracle, is destined to be greater than his father and to overthrow him. It is only after Zeus's fall that Prometheus is delivered by Hercules. This liberation marks the beginning of an era of peace and freedom, a proper golden age for mankind, inasmuch as a recreation of the world is implied by the destruction of Zeus's world order. As Maurice Hindle noted, 'Byron had a less idealistic view of the human possibilities suggested by Prometheus than did Shelley.[...] Byron could never have been so idealistic as to believe that evil can be eradicated from the world by willpower and mental determination. But Shelley, with what Mary called his "more abstract and etherealized inspiration", was sustained by a strong idealism and faith in men'.[16] Prometheus Unbound was not, for Shelley, an attempt to restore the lost drama of Aeschylus, despite the title of the play and his deep admiration for the Greek playwright. The poet, in his preface to the play, mentions that it would have been 'an ambition, which, if [his] preference to this mode of treating the subject had incited [him] to cherish, the recollection of a high comparison such an attempt would challenge, might well abate. But in truth [he] was averse from a catastrophe so feeble as that of reconciling the Champion with the oppressor of mankind',[17] a conclusion which had surely been adopted by Aeschylus in his trilogy, given the character of Zeus in his other plays. Indeed, one of the most important aspects of Prometheus Unbound is the fact that Prometheus's struggle implies a new conception of the world order. This was to have a decisive impact on further developments of the Prometheus myth.

Thorslev's theories on Prometheus and the different world orders at stake in Prometheus Bound and Prometheus Unbound bear closer examination in this respect. Thorslev puts forward the idea that the Prometheus myth 'tends in its Romantic development toward a vision of a naturalistic universe coloured by a humanist faith'.[18] Although it is difficult to build theories on Prometheus Bound, knowing that it is part of a larger structure (a lost trilogy), Thorslev distinguishes three levels in Aeschylus's play: 'the Promethean level, a realm of humanist values, since Prometheus is the patron and guide of man, and his gifts are the things man values, [...] the realm in which Zeus reigns: a vindictive and cruel order, irrational and capricious, at least in the terms of the play.[...] Finally, there is the order of Fate to which Prometheus appeals in his soliloquy, and which is obviously conceived as being above both Prometheus and Jove.'[19] It is however problematic to concur fully with Thorslev on the individuation of three levels in a Greek tragedy like *Prometheus Bound*, since the Greek world order is definitely whole. It is ultimately governed by a superior power, Fate or *Moira*, but Zeus is part of this order, in that he ensures its stability. Prometheus, in this context, appears as a transgressor of this world order, which does not necessarily imply that he represents another realm. He destroys the balance of the world order, but as one of its elements. Thorslev goes on to say that 'the order in Shelley's Promethean universe is also on three levels, since as the play opens, we have Prometheus, who stands for humanist values (although admittedly with the significant addition of the quality of mercy which is absent in both Aeschylus and Goethe); Jupiter or Jove, who is capricious and cruel as in the two previous dramas; and finally, "Demogorgon's mighty law" to which all spirits are apparently subject.'[20] It is true that the levels we perceive in *Prometheus Unbound* are different from those in *Prometheus Bound*, and they allow us to take full measure of the turn the Prometheus myth took in the nineteenth century. However, we prefer to distinguish two antagonistic world orders, not three levels, here. It appears in *Prometheus Bound* that Zeus's power, together with the order he represents, is the mental creation of man. Northrop Frye's explanation of the particular trait of the human mind Shelley develops in *Prometheus Unbound* is enlightening: 'Man is a myth-making as well as a tool-using animal, but constant vigilance is needed to make sure that he keeps control of what he makes, for it is with myths as it is with technology: just as man invents the wheel and then talks about a wheel of fate or fortune overriding everything he does, so he creates gods and then announces that the gods have created him. He makes his own creation, in short, a power to stop himself from creating'.[21] Effectively, Shelley assumed that Zeus was nothing but a mental projection, which meant that the human race would avoid improving itself. When the moment of Zeus's fall comes, he becomes identical to his phantasm. When Prometheus addresses the phantasm, in the first act of *Prometheus Bound*, he notes:

> Tremendous Image! As thou art must be
> He whom thou shadowest forth.[22] (I, lines 246–47)

Nonetheless, even if the image of a personal god such as Zeus is the product of man's mind, it is real and oppressive. *Prometheus Unbound* would thus be the account of man's liberation from this burden. To a certain extent, the collapse of Zeus would therefore represent the burial of old myths, whereas Prometheus's freedom would be the expression of the myth-making power of man. As Northrop Frye puts it, 'Prometheus is now the human mind confronting the objective world with its own desire, and Jupiter is the mental block which prevents man from trying to conceive and reshape a world beyond that order.'[23] The real nature of Zeus, that is a mental image created by man, is unveiled when he disappears:

> Let hell unlock
> Its mounded oceans of tempestuous fire,

> And whelm on them into the bottomless void
> The desolated world, and thee, and me
> The conqueror and the conquered, and the wreck
> Of that for which they combated[24] (III, 2, lines 74–79)

Prometheus Unbound appears as the account of a new creation of the world, underlain by the consciousness man gained of his myth-making power. The poem is also the expression of this quest and conquest. As early as the first act of the play, the fourth spirit mentions the force of mythopoetic powers:

> On a Poet's lips I slept
> Dreaming like a love-adept
> In the sound his breathing kept;[...]
> He will watch from dawn to gloom
> The lake-reflected sun illume
> The yellow bees I' the ivy-bloom
> Nor heed nor see, what things they be;
> But from these create he can
> Forms more real than living man,
> Nurslings of immortality! — [25] (I, lines 737–49)

These beautiful lines at the beginning of the play appear as an announcement of the recreation of the world to come. When the ancient world order is eventually overthrown by Prometheus, we witness the accomplishment of these powers through the realization of a new cosmogony in the fourth act:

> VOICE OF UNSEEN SPIRITS
> Bright clouds float in heaven,
> Dew-stars gleam on Earth,
> Waves assemble on Ocean,
> They are gathered and driven
> By the storm of delight, by the panic of glee!
> (IV, lines 40–44)

The entire fourth act is an evocation of this cosmogony, in which music is omnipresent. An interesting aspect of this recreation is that it entails an eternal suspension of time and therefore a rejection of history, while a latent ideal world arises:

> Spectres we
> Of the dead hours be,
> We bear Time to his tomb in eternity.[26]
> (IV, lines 12–15)

The conception of such an ideal world, in which the notion of time does not exist, may be attributed to Shelley's avid reading of Plato, whose conception of a fore-world governed by an Absolute named 'One', also central to Shelley's play, gave the poet the foundations on which to build his own idealism.[27] This absolute principle seems close, once again, to the Greek *Moira*, except that when fully accomplished, the notion of time does not apply to it. The Greek fate on the other hand is inevitably bound to it. It seems also relevant that the king of the new ideal realm Shelley creates is neither Demogorgon or Prometheus, but man:

CHORUS OF SPIRITS
>
> And our singing shall build,
> In the Void's loose field,
> A world for the spirit of Wisdom to wield;
> We will take our plan
> From the new world of man
> And our work shall be called the Promethean.[28]

The attribution of this realm to men raises the problem of religion in *Prometheus Unbound*. In a nineteenth-century context, Prometheus's triumph over Jupiter in Shelley's play would have been read as a victory over a religion associated with an oppressive Christianity. The figure of Jesus Christ is evoked several times in *Prometheus Unbound*, and is clearly affiliated to that of Prometheus himself. However, we have to be cautious and note that Christianity is not entirely rejected, since the Christlike figure emerges in the poem as an emblem of a magnificent hope, but a hope which was deceived. The Church is enabled to put an end to the sufferings of mankind:

> One came forth, of gentle worth,
> Smiling on the sanguine earth;
> His words outlived him, like swift poison
> Withering up truth, peace, and pity.[...]
> Hark that outcry of despair!
> 'Tis his mild and gentle ghost
> Wailing for the faith he kindled.[29] (I, lines 546–55)

We note here that despite Jesus Christ's failure in his mission, similarities exist between him and the Titan. Because of the intensity of his suffering, because of his total devotion to men, and, most importantly, because of biblical references linking Prometheus with Jesus Christ, the mythological character, in *Prometheus Unbound*, appears as a sublime incarnation of man. The allusions to the Passion on Golgotha and to the crucifixion, quoted above, play an important part in the poem. This parallel enabled Shelley to lend weight to the depiction of the Titan as a fighter for freedom and revolutionary character, since it illuminated the human side of Prometheus's persona. If we were to make a synthesis of Prometheus's features in Shelley's play, as opposed to his counterpart in *Prometheus Bound*, he appears as a victim devoid of resentment, and one whose creative power is crucial to elaborate Shelley's ideal world. His main innovation, in terms of the perception of Prometheus, lies in the fact that he combined two aspects of the Titan's persona that were previously separated: his search for freedom, and his love for mankind.

However, even if the Christian model, or anti-model, is apparent in *Prometheus Unbound*, another influence is undeniable: the restoration of many of the elements of pre-Christian Greek culture. In a draft of *The Defence of Poetry*, Shelley says of the century preceding the death of Socrates: 'It is as if the continent of Paradise were overwhelmed and some shattered crag remained covered with asphodel and amaranth which bear golden flowers.' Indeed, for Shelley, Greek culture and religion were less oppressive in imposing belief. According to Northrop Frye, it also 'preserved the intuitive sense of identity with natural forces; its polytheism enabled the scientific and philosophical views of the world to develop independently'.[30] *Prometheus Unbound* would then be an account of the recovery of this 'identity with natural forces', which would explain why the recreation of the world is the only possible conclusion of the play. With Shelley therefore, we reach a paradox within the myth, in that Prometheus, no longer responsible for the loss of the golden age, is on the contrary the hero who conquers it, an element which paves the way for Symbolism. At this stage in the evolution of the myth, the humanization of the Titan seemed to appear as a given fact, and we shall now see that this was true not only of its interpretation in Germany and England. Beyond the irreducible particularities of style, imagery, and thought, there appeared a coherence in the treatment of the Prometheus myth across Europe, and the work of Victor Hugo, Franz Liszt and Honoré de Balzac testify to it.

Notes to Chapter 2

1. Richard Holmes, *Prometheus²: The Two Shelleys and Romantic Science*, lecture given on 27 October 2011 at the School of Advanced Studies, London.
2. Letter to John Murray, Venice, 12 October 1817; see *Byron's Letters and Journals*, ed. Leslie A. Marchand, (London: John Murray, 1976), vol. 5, p. 268.
3. Peter L. Thorslev, Jr., *The Byronic Hero, Types and Prototypes* (Minneapolis: University of Minnesota Press, 1962), pp. 123–24.
4. See J. M. Carré, *Goethe en Angleterre*, 2nd edn (Paris, Etude de Littérature Comparée, 1920), p. 78, note I, and E. M. Butler, *Byron and Goethe, Analysis of a Passion* (London: Bowes and Bowes, 1956), especially pp. 191–93, where it is stated that in spite of their mutual admiration, Goethe and Byron, during the writing of their *Prometheus*, did not know that they were working on the same subject.
5. Letter to John Murray, Venice, 12 October 1817, *Byron's Letters and Journals*, ed. Leslie A. Marchand, 5, p. 268.
6. *Lord Byron, The Major Works*, ed. Jerome J. McGann (Oxford: Oxford University Press, 1986, 2000), p. 409.
7. Ibid., p. 452.
8. Ibid., p. 279.
9. Byron also drew a parallel between the figure of Prometheus and that of Napoleon. See above, p. 79.
10. *Lord Byron, Selected Poetry*, ed. by Jerome McGann (Oxford: Oxford University Press, 1994), p. 64.
11. *Lord Byron, The Complete Poetical Works*, ed. Jerome McGann (Oxford: Clarendon Press, 1986–92), vol. 4, p. 234.
12. Thorslev, *The Byronic Hero*, pp. 112–13.
13. Ibid., p. 122.
14. *Shelley's Poetry and Prose*, ed.Donald H Reiman and Sharon B. Powers (New York, London: Norton and Company, 1977), p. 130.
15. Mary Shelley, *The Poetical Works of Percy Bysshe Shelley* (London: Edward Moxon, 1839), II, pp. 133–34.
16. Maurice Hindle, *Frankenstein* (London: Penguin Critical Studies, 1994), p. 135.
17. *Shelley's Poetry and Prose*, ed. by Donald H Reiman and Sharon B. Powers, p. 133.
18. Peter Thorslev explains that 'by a naturalistic universe [he]mean[s] an amoral universe, one which is morally indifferent but which is nevertheless ordered, but ordered so that what is strong is also successful; in other words, [...] the universe as it is generally presented to us by the evidence of modern science. By a humanist faith, [he] mean[s] the belief that the heart or the soul of man is so constituted that given the conditioning of a moral and reasonable environ-

ment, and given a normal hereditary endowment, he will most of the time choose the good.' (*The Byronic Hero,* p. 117).

19. *A Study of English Romanticism*, p. 88.

20. Thorslev, *The Byronic Hero*, p. 118.

21. Ibid., p. 119.

22. *Shelley's Poetry and Prose*, ed. Donald H. Reinman and Sharon B. Powers, p. 143.

23. *A Study of English Romanticism*, p. 95.

24. *Shelley's Poetry and Prose*, ed. Donald H. Reinman and Sharon B. Powers, p. 182.

25. Ibid., p. 157.

26. Ibid., p. 194.

27. In his preface to *Prometheus Unbound*, Shelley mentions his reference: 'I have, what a Scotch philosopher characteristically terms, "a passion for reforming the world": what passion incited him to write and publish his book, he omits to explain. For my part I had rather be damned with Plato and Lord Bacon, than go to heaven with Paley and Malthus'.

28. *Shelley's Poetry and Prose*, ed. Donald H. Reinman and Sharon B. Powers, p. 198.

29. Ibid., p. 152.

30. *A Study of English Romanticism*, p. 100.

CHAPTER 3

The Mask of the Artist: Victor Hugo, Franz Liszt and Honoré de Balzac

Although the turning point in the interpretation of the myth appears in its most striking form in Germany with Goethe, and in England with Shelley and Byron, some of France's most famous artists of the first half of the nineteenth century found in the Prometheus figure a perfect image to express their ideals and/or fears. They took hold of Prometheus so well that the Titan became — whether intentionally or not — an artistic model to identify with. Different features of Prometheus as a symbol or as a myth appealed to them, and although different, there are probably no better examples of this new 'cult' devoted to Prometheus than his treatment by Hugo and Balzac in literature, and Liszt in music.

Titanic Hugo

Victor Hugo conjured up the figure of Prometheus several times in his poetry, at various periods of his life. However, although we might find here and there possible allusions to the Titan in his poetry, only eight times did Hugo clearly evoke Prometheus: in 'Le Génie'[1] ('The Genius'), in 'La vision des montagnes'[2] ('The Vision of the Mountains'), in ' Le couchant flamboyait à travers les bruines'[3] ('The Setting Sun was Blazing through the Drizzle'), in 'La fin de Satan'[4] ('The End of Satan'), in *Dieu*,[5] in 'Quand Eschyle au vautour dispute Prométhée'[6]('When Aeschylus against the vulture defends Prometheus'), in 'L'Expiation',[7] in which Hugo identifies Napoleon with the Titan, and in his preface to *Les Burgraves (The Commanders)*. Considering Hugo's monumental output, it is interesting to note that, in spite of the relatively few mentions of Prometheus in Hugo's poetry, other poets perceived a close link between him and Victor Hugo. I shall return to that point later. Before examining the reason for this discrepancy, I shall consider the significance of Prometheus in some of these poems.[8] As these have not been translated into English, a literal translation will be provided when necessary.

I shall not analyse the poem from *La Fin de Satan* here, as Trousson has already done so.[9] Moreover, the treatment of the Prometheus figure in this poem is not along the line of Hugo's other interpretations of the Titan, since he represents him as the harbinger of progress and sciences, close to the positivist understanding of Prometheus. Amongst Hugo's poems on the theme of Prometheus, 'Le Génie' is the most valuable for understanding the significance of the Titanic figure for Hugo. 'Le Génie' is dedicated to François-René de Chateaubriand. To the young Hugo — then a royalist, an 'ultra' whose Catholic faith was very strong — he represented the perfect literary model and accomplished artist (the poem was composed in 1820).[10] The poem has as its epigraph a quotation from Lamennais, a contemporary politician who embodied Hugo's values and beliefs:

> Circumstances do not shape men, they reveal them: they unveil, so to speak, the kingship of genius, the last resource of extinct peoples. These kings who do not bear that name, but who truly reign by their strength of character and greatness of thought, are chosen by the events they have to control. Without ancestors or posterity, alone of their race, they disappear once their mission is fulfilled, leaving to the future the orders it will faithfully execute.[11]

This definition of genius was certainly meant to apply to Chateaubriand, although we can also perceive the echo it might have had, after the *Sturm und Drang* movement and the importance the term 'genius' had taken, to designate the power of individual creation and inner forms. If we also consider the importance of Victor Hugo's ethos as a poet, soon to be apparent in 'Le Génie', we can assume that the use of the term 'genius' is also meant to apply to Hugo himself. The second major element of this epigraph is the expression of a very strong and almost religious faith in man, which is an important aspect in relation to the Prometheus myth.

The first strophe of the poem contains the precise evocation of the Titan:

> Malheur à l'enfant de la terre,
> Qui, dans ce monde injuste et vain,
> Porte en son âme solitaire
> Un rayon de l'Esprit divin!
> Malheur à lui ! L'impure envie
> S'acharne sur sa noble vie,
> Semblable au Vautour éternel,
> Et, de son triomphe irritée,
> Punit ce nouveau Prométhée
> D'avoir ravi le feu du ciel.[12]

> [Woe betide the child of earth
> Who, in this unfair and vain world,
> Bears in his solitary soul
> A beam of the divine Spirit!
> Woe betide him! Impure envy
> Dogs his noble life,
> Like the eternal Vulture,
> And, irritated by his triumph,
> Punishes this new Prometheus
> For the theft of Heavenly fire]

We see that the first strophe bears similarities with the third strophe of Byron's ode, in which the double nature of man, both animal and spiritual, is also mentioned. However, whereas in Byron's poem, man transcends the 'troubled stream' of his nature eventually to triumph, in spite of, or rather thanks to, his dual nature, in Victor Hugo's 'Le Génie', man's 'impure envy', that is to say his animal side, is presented as the punishment itself. In the poems we previously examined, the oppressive element within the Prometheus myth was always embodied by divine transcendence. But we are now confronted with the fruitful idea that the Promethean fight is a human internal conflict, between man's spiritual and carnal sides. Here again, 'heavenly fire' is a metaphor for Spirit, that is genius, which is represented as the main attribute of gods, stolen by man, 'the child of earth' and 'new Prometheus'. The Titan is thus indirectly mentioned, used as a symbol: man is punished for his theft, as Prometheus was before him. However, from the second strophe, the nature of the tormentor changes:

> La gloire, fantôme céleste,
> Apparaît de loin à ses yeux;
> Il subit le pouvoir funeste de son rire impérieux!
> Ainsi l'oiseau, faible et timide,
> Veut en vain fuir l'hydre perfide
> Dont l'œil le charme et le poursuit;
> Il voltige de cime en cime,
> Puis il accourt, et meurt victime
> Du doux regard qui l'a séduit.

> [Glory, celestial ghost,
> Appears from afar before his eyes;
> He undergoes the fateful power of his imperious laugh!
> And the bird, weak and shy,
> Wants in vain to escape the perfidious hydra
> Whose eye charms and pursues him;
> He flutters from peak to peak
> Then he rushes up, and dies, victim
> Of the sweet look that seduced him.]

'Impure envy' does not appear as the punishment of the 'new Prometheus' any more. The chimera of glory follows it, and, very unexpectedly, the symbol of the 'new Prometheus' is replaced by the image of a bird. Although the bird in question is an albatross,[13] not the vulture of the Prometheus myth, such a choice, following the first strophe, seems rather confusing. Moreover, in the third strophe, although the metaphor of the bird is long-drawn-out, it is associated with the noun 'the immortal', linked to Prometheus. Both images are surprisingly combined. The bird, more than mankind, seems to represent the figure of the artist: in fact, with his laurel, he is confronted by 'mistake, lofty ignorance/ unpunished offence and hatred', that is to say by other men, not the illusion of glory. The myth of Prometheus is still used in the rest of 'Le Génie', but in a more allusive way. The second part of the poem makes the link between the bird-artist and Chateaubriand, who 'accepts his genius', because he feels 'in his soul/ the celestial flame rising', whereas in the second strophe of the second part of 'Le Génie', Hugo evokes one more time his literary idol, who 'Received from the sky this fateful gift/ which hurts our jealous pride'. Here again Hugo chooses Prometheus as a symbol, but by taking Chateaubriand as a model and by presenting himself in the poem, he uses Prometheus to a wider extent as the figure of the artist, which is fraught with consequences. The third and final part of the poem is mainly devoted to the exile of Chateaubriand during the French Revolution, and to the exaltation of the religious and political thoughts the young Hugo and Chateaubriand had in common. The concluding strophe develops the symbol of the albatross rather than that of Prometheus. Freed from 'envy, the attribute of wicked minds', the bird flies up, and, 'far from the noises of Earth,/ lulled by his solitary flight,/ will fall asleep in heaven'.[14]

Although the Prometheus myth is not the central element of 'Le Génie', used as it is as a symbol and combined with another one, it is nonetheless interesting to notice that the Titan is associated with the figure of the artist of genius.

The myth was used again in a similar way by Hugo in the 1850s, in his poem 'Le couchant flamboyait à travers les bruines'.[15] It is not dated, but the power of the ocean being omnipresent in the poem, we can legitimately assume that it was composed in Jersey, at the beginning of Hugo's exile in the wake of Napoleon III's coup. The contemplation of the ocean by the exiled poet was an important motif in Hugo's poetry during this decisive period of his life. The figure of the outlaw in his poems and drawings is omnipresent, and in the poetical field as well as the pictorial, Hugo almost always depicted this figure on a rock, facing the ocean, which also conjures up our imaginary representation of Prometheus. It is precisely after an inaugural atmospheric description of the ocean that the Titan is evoked in 'Le couchant flamboyait à travers les bruines':

> Lugubre immensité! profondeurs redoutées!
> Tous sont là, les Satans comme les Prométhées,
> Ténébreux océans!
> Cieux, vous êtes l'abîme où tombent les génies,
> Oh! combien l'œil au fond des brumes infinies
> Aperçoit de géants![16] (lines 13–18)

> Dismal infinity! feared depths!
> All are there, Satans as well as Prometheuses,
> Gloomy oceans!
> Heaven, you are the abyss in which geniuses fall,
> Oh! how numerous at the bottom of infinite mists
> The giants the eye catches sight of!

As in 'Le Génie', genius is again associated with the figure of Prometheus. However, the Titan is in this context part of a group of outlaws, which also includes the figure of Satan. Such a partnership is particularly fertile if one considers the fact that the Romantic conception of Satan in England and France largely derives from Milton's *Paradise Lost*, in which Satan is presented less as the dark embodiment of Evil than as a rebel.[17] This is the Romantic image Hugo calls up here with that of Prometheus, to strengthen the depiction of the outlaw the poet represents and in this, there is a coherence in Hugo's representation of Prometheus thirty years or so after the writing of 'Le Génie'. A development of the Prometheus figure is even perceptible: whereas in 'Le Génie', he appeared as a symbol of human genius, a symbol which was linked to Chateaubriand and thus to the artist, in 'Le couchant flamboyait à travers les bruines', the figure of the poet is totally projected on those of 'Prometheuses' and 'Satans'. Hugo adds:

> J'habite l'absolu, patrie obscure et sombre,
> Pas plus intimidé dans tous ces gouffres d'ombre
> Que l'oiseau dans les bois[18]

> [I live in the country of the Absolute, dark and obscure,
> No more intimidated in this abyss of shadow
> Than the bird in the wood]

A subtle identification between the outlaw poet contemplating the ocean and Prometheus is now seen in the use of the Titanic figure by Hugo, and it hinges on his conception of genius.

Hugo adds an important feature in 1856, with 'La Vision des montagnes' ('The Vision of Mountains'), a poem dated 2 July. Although it was composed later than 'Le couchant flamboyait à travers les bruines', it is the opening poem of *Toute la Lyre*, and of its first section, untitled 'L'Humanité' ('Mankind'). The general meaning of 'La Vision des montagnes'[19] is problematic, as the poem is composed of different mythological and biblical pictures whose linking remains partly enigmatic. However, the first scene of the poem is that of Prometheus bound on Mount Caucasus. It is perceived by the poet, from above 'black rolling clouds':

> Ce faîte monstrueux sortait de l'ombre obscure;
> Ses pentes se perdaient dans le gouffre inconnu;
> Sur ce plateau gisait, fauve, terrible, nu,
> Un géant, dont le corps se tordait sur la pierre;
> Il en coulait du sang avec de la lumière;
> Sa face regardait le ciel sombre, et ses pieds,
> Ses coudes, ses genoux, ses poings, étaient liés
> D'une chaîne d'airain vivante, impitoyable;
> Et je voyais décroître et renaître effroyable
> Son ventre qu'un vautour rongeait, oiseau bandit.
> Le patient était colossal; on eût dit
> Deux montagnes, dont l'une agonisait sur l'autre.
> — Quel est, dis-je, le sang qui coule ainsi? — Le vôtre,
> Dit le vautour. Ce mont dont tu vois les sommets,
> C'est le Caucase. — Et quand t'en iras-tu? — Jamais.
> Et le supplicié me cria: Je suis l'Homme.

> [This monstrous summit emerged from the dark shadow,
> Its slopes vanishing in the unknown abyss;
> On this plateau was lying a giant,
> Wild, terrible, naked, his body convulsing on the stone;
> Blood and light were flowing out of it;
> His face was looking at the dark sky, and his feet,
> His elbows, knees, and wrists, were bound
> With a chain of living bronze, pitiless;
> And I saw his entrails awfully diminish and regrow,
> Eaten away by a vulture, a criminal bird.
> The patient was colossal; it was like
> Two mountains, one of which was dying on the other
> — Whose, I said, is this flowing blood? — Yours,

Said the vulture. This mount, of which you can see the summits
Is Caucasus. — And when will you leave? — Never.
And the martyr told me screaming: I am Mankind.]

The scene which follows this depiction of Prometheus is that of the Flood and
Noah's Ark, which leads the poet to ask:

— Quoi! dis-je, est-on créé pour être anéanti?
O terre! Est-ce ta faute? O ciel! est-ce ton crime? (lines 32–33)

[— What! I said, were we created to be annihilated?
O earth! Is it your fault ? O heaven! Is it your crime?]

We can see here that the issue of the relationship between a creator and his
creatures is raised. The third scene represents Olympus, the place where 'reigned
the horrible joy' (line 38), and in which mankind is the target of the gods' arrows.
The fourth depicts Moses on Mount Sinai,

Un homme face à face avec Dieu dans un rêve,
Un prophète effrayant qui recevait un glaive,
Et qui redescendit plein d'un céleste ennui
Vers la terre, emportant de la foudre avec lui...
Et l'infini cria: Sinaï!

A man face to face with God in a dream,
A frightening prophet who was given a sword,
And who climbed down again full of celestial boredom
Towards the earth, taking lightning with him...
And the infinite shouted: Sinai!

And, the fifth and last scene is an evocation of Calvary:

Un homme expirait là, cloué sur un gibet,
Entre deux vagues croix où pendaient deux fantômes;
[...]
Et le supplicié me cria: Je suis Dieu.

A man was dying there, nailed to a gibbet,
Between two vague crosses where two ghosts hung
[...]
And the martyr told me screaming: I am God.

Although it is not clear how to interpret the biblical episode of Moses on Mount
Sinai given the changing aspect of Hugo's beliefs towards religion and rites, it
nonetheless appears that the unifying theme of the poem is the persecution of
man by God(s), the climax of the poem being when a god himself, because he is
also human, becomes a martyr. The use of the Prometheus myth in this context is
therefore a fruitful one. More than a simple myth character, the Titan appears as
a powerful symbol of mankind. Parallel to the use of this symbolic material, the
poem develops the themes the myth itself contains: the injustice of the gods, and
the incomprehensible punishment which derives from it. Even if Hugo does not
use the Titanic figure to represent the poet himself in 'La Vision des montagnes',
Prometheus, here again, is associated with Jesus Christ. Whereas on the one hand
the godlike Titan claims he is mankind, on the other, the one who appears as a

man claims that he is a god. The choice Hugo made to represent Jesus Christ on his cross is surely deliberate, since this episode of the Bible coincides with the moment when Jesus Christ feels he is abandoned by God, and cries out 'My God, why have you forsaken me?'.[20]

This passage from the Bible particularly appealed to French Romantics,[21] as it perfectly illustrated man's anguish and the impossibility of understanding the designs of God, should He exist. A link appears with the Prometheus myth, in that this interest in a 'Romantic Christ' coincides with the same concern shown by what Václav Černý[22] calls 'Titanism', a moral attitude rejecting the moral of punishment that suppresses the freedom of man. According to this theory, 'Ancient Titans once rebelled against Heaven. Modern Titans are doing the same. However, they do not wish to replace the Gods. They only want to be men, but they want to be fully men. They try to perfectly accomplish the idea of man, and want to do so by creating free individualities, driven by autonomous moral laws. Such is their individualism. They believe their aspirations are justified by Reason and human moral sense. In the name of those, they protest and rebel against the regime *de facto*, established on earth by a divinity, a regime which to human eyes is neither rational nor moral and which even tries to cover up its moral anomalies by pretending it is unintelligible to human reason, that is to say by simply slandering the spirit of man.'[23] Their rebellion would thus be against what is beyond human understanding and generates an unjustified guilt. If we consider this theory, the association of Prometheus with Jesus Christ by Hugo in the inaugural poem of 'L'Humanité' makes perfect sense, and also casts light on the title of this section. In fact, both figures, although coming from different sources, reflect the anguish of man facing the Absolute, whatever form it might take. In a poem dealing with the ill-founded persecution of man, the striking scene of the Titan's martyrdom combined with that of Jesus Christ on the cross offers the perfect illustration of Titanism. It might be because Hugo's poetry and use of Prometheus reflects the Romantic concerns that he himself was associated with the Titan's figure, even if he is not omnipresent in his poetry.

It is noteworthy that other poets contributed to developing a link between Hugo and Prometheus, in different ways. Charles Baudelaire, in his *Fusées*, comments: 'Hugo often thinks of Prometheus. He applies an imaginary vulture to his breast, which is seared only by the moxas of vanity'.[24] Although Baudelaire takes the opportunity to make fun of Hugo's huge ego, it is interesting to see that in his sarcastic way he nevertheless reveals a process of identification between Hugo and the Titan. It might well have been verbally expressed by Hugo himself, but, with no such evidence, we must conclude that the very use of Prometheus as a symbol, in the forms we previously examined, led Baudelaire to identify Hugo with him. Given the connection made between the figure of the poet and that of Prometheus in Hugo's poems, and given also the fact that the Titanic figure carries Romantic concerns with his martyrdom, this identification was probably meant to be an appropriate one.

Hugo's association with Prometheus could also have been partly rooted in the remnants of a romantic tradition that established a parallel between Napoleon

Fig. 11.3.1 Charles-Gilbert Martin, *L'Olympe* (1876, detail).
Hugo is represented with his arms crossed.

and the Titan. Hugo's personality was larger than life, but could not rival that of the emperor and his extraordinary destiny. Hugo himself, in 'L'Expiation', made of Napoleon a new Prometheus, but in an allegorical manner, Prometheus's rock becoming St Helena, and the vulture being England. Vicenzo Monti was the first to identify Prometheus with Bonaparte in 1797, at a time when some still saw in him the champion of mankind and believed that he would fight for freedom in Europe, spreading the ideals of the revolution.[25] But as Trousson has noted,[26] 'it was neither the victorious General [..] nor the all-powerful Emperor that gave rise to the comparison, but rather [...] the prisoner of Saint Helena, the redoubtable outcast chained to his desert island, watched by the whole of Europe',[27] an aspect that was bound to appeal to Hugo. Byron himself, in his ambivalent *Ode to Napoleon Buonaparte* (1814), which oscillates between a feeling of admiration for the emperor and condemnation of his tyranny, made that parallel in the sixteenth stanza of the ode, which conjures up Aeschylus's Prometheus and sees greater dignity in his destiny:

> Foredoomed by God — by man accurst,
> And that last act, though not thy worst,
> The very Fiend's arch mock;
> He in his fall preserved his pride,
> And, if a mortal, had as proudly died![28]

The association between Napoleon and Prometheus as two outcasts did exist, but remained marginal in the history of the myth.

Whichever part it played in Hugo's own association with Prometheus, its grandeur fed the imagination of the nineteenth-century cartoonist Gilbert-Martin (Fig. II.3.I).[29] However, the main reason for the parallel between Hugo and Prometheus probably lies in the striking visual representation of the outlaw on his rock, facing the sea, which Hugo himself depicted in his drawings, and which he also embodied in pictures for which he posed.[30]

It might also explain why Swinburne 'identified Prometheus punished for his benefits with Hugo the exile, "fate-stricken, and rejected of his own".'[31] Because Hugo wanted to represent the noblest figure, that is, according to him, that of the outlaw, of man fighting for his beliefs, and because he depicted it using the traditional representation of the Promethean martyrdom, he gradually annexed this symbol of human suffering to his personal imagery.

Another French literary Titan was to be associated with the Prometheus myth, but on different grounds. Although Honoré de Balzac, like Hugo, did not often mention Prometheus in his work, each time he did was in a context we cannot ignore, that of an *ars poetica*, in two of the most famous pages of the *Comédie humaine*.

'Prometheus, or the Life of Balzac'

> Tous ses livres ne forment qu'un livre, livre vivant, lumineux, profond, où l'on voit aller et venir et marcher et se mouvoir, avec je ne sais quoi d'effaré et de terrible mêlé au réel, toute notre civilisation contemporaine.[32] (Victor Hugo)

If Honoré de Balzac is often identified with Prometheus, it is mostly because of the biography by André Maurois, entitled *Prometheus, or the Life of Balzac*.[33] Interestingly enough, the title is only justified by one epigraph, a quotation from Balzac on the flyleaf saying: 'Of Faust and Prometheus, I prefer Prometheus'. In the rest of the biography, no mention is made of the Titan, although, in the twentieth century, Maurois's title was enough to establish a link between Prometheus and Balzac. However, it is reasonable to assume that the title was explained by Balzac's unique and gigantic project. In the *Comédie humaine* Balzac set out to create a perfect fictional society which would reflect the real one. This ambition itself — to create an infinite number of characters who would reappear within the cycle and interact together — is of Titanic design, not only because of its gigantic proportions, but also because of its very nature. Balzac was aware that his project of giving literary shape to his countless human creatures was Promethean. As creator, he put himself in the position of a Prometheus *plasticator*. The coherence and achievement of his project depended on his ability to take on this role.

He first took Prometheus as a model in a work which he himself named his 'aesthetic catechism', his *Chef-d'œuvre inconnu* (*The Unknown Masterpiece*), first published in 1831 as part of a trilogy.[34] *Massimilla Doni* and *Gambara* were written at the same time, and in a letter to Mme Hanska,[35] Balzac established the link that connects his three works. In his system,[36] the three short stories were meant to deal with the annihilation of the work of art (and also, in the case of *Massimilla Doni* and *Gambara*, of its musical interpretation) which occurs when the creative principle is excessive. As Pierre-Georges Castex put it, the three short stories 'elaborate on the fundamental postulate of the destructive power of thought, when applied to the field of Arts'.[37] The theme of the 'failure' of the work of art is represented, in *The Unknown Masterpiece*, by that of the imaginary painter Frenhofer. It is at the heart of the questioning of this problem, as part of Balzac's *ars poetica*, that the figure of Prometheus is conjured up. The work of art which does not succeed as such is precisely described as lacking Prometheus's fire. Indeed, Frenhofer, criticizing Porbus's painting, says: 'You had power only to breathe a portion of your soul into your beloved work. The fire of Prometheus dies away again and again in your hands; many a spot in your picture has not been touched by the divine flame'.[38] Further on, he evokes the difficulty 'to fuse [...] two manners in the fire of your own genius'.[39] In these thoughts on aesthetics, we find two elements we have previously encountered in the use of the Prometheus myth: first, the Prometheus figure understood as a creative power, a power which gives life to objects; second, its association with the figure of the artist, and, more specifically, of genius. This emphasis on the Titan as Prometheus *plasticator*, and the fact that his power is circumscribed to the aesthetic and artistic fields, conjures up another myth, in which the figure of the artist is also at stake: that of Pygmalion. Balzac himself throws a bridge between them, and even seems to take one for the other. In *The Unknown Masterpiece*, the great master, Frenhofer, initially corrects Porbus's painting of a woman before the fascinated eyes of young Nicolas Poussin, who, as a novice, is willing to develop his skills. Although Frenhofer pretends he just improved Porbus's painting to make it livelier, the two other painters believe that they are facing perfection. Under the charm, Porbus begs Frenhofer to let Poussin and himself see the painting he has been working on for ten years. His refusal is categorical: the painter, in love with his painting of Catherine Lescault, cannot possibly exhibit his lover, whom he jealously hides from other people. He then explains to Poussin, 'I have been at work upon it for ten years, young man; but what are ten short years in a struggle with Nature? Do we know how long Sir Pygmalion wrought at the only statue that came to life?'.[40] Frenhofer also details at length the nature of his love, or, should we say, blind passion, for his painting. In this respect, his feelings are close to those of Pygmalion, who also fell in love with his work of art: 'Would you have me cease at once to be a father, a lover, and creator? She is not a creature, but a creation',[41] Frenhofer adds. Here, Balzac seems to mix the myth with that of Pygmalion, inasmuch as the novelist, within the Prometheus myth, underlines the power of the Titan to give life, like a god, to his beloved creatures.[42] However, whereas Pygmalion idolizes a statue which is already formed and accomplished, and which he loves as such, Frenhofer tirelessly keeps working on his painting. According to Balzac, it is this very process which dooms him. When, at the end of the short story, he eventually agrees to show Catherine Lescault to Porbus and Nicolas Poussin, the two painters can see nothing but a chaos of paint. Because Frenhofer endlessly strives towards perfection, examines and questions his creation, by doing so, he eventually destroys it.

The fact that he wants to equal God in the process of creation might entail both his failure and the parting between the Pygmalion and Prometheus myths, leading to the predominance of Prometheus. Indeed, in Balzac's thought, as exposed in his 'aesthetic catechism', it appears there is no room for the artist to equal nature and God, and the rivalry with gods traditionally appears as a feature characteristic of the Prometheus myth. Interestingly, Frenhofer himself warns his colleague against the temptation of copying nature (which would be, were it possible, to rival it), although, ironically, he is its first victim: 'The aim of art is not to copy nature, but to express it!'.[43] In fact, if he annihilates his own creation, it is essentially by trying to create the perfect woman, and not the most beautiful painting. However, Frenhofer's words appear as the first rule of Balzac's *ars poetica*. As Félix Davin puts it, in his introduction to *Etudes de mœurs au XIXème siècle*, according to Balzac, 'nature, to be grasped in its deepest truth, had to be analysed, i.e. broken up into its component parts, and then rebuilt, its life given back by a new animation',[44] and not copied. Balzac certainly succeeded in his ambition, if we consider the eagerness of contemporary readers and critics to recognize existing people in Balzac's characters, whereas he wanted to create types, since they gather the particular features of all of those who look like these types, and are therefore paradoxically 'more real'.

In *Cousin Betty*, Balzac refines this thought when one of his characters, commenting on art, suggests that 'Sculpture — like dramatic art — is at once the most difficult and easiest of all of the arts. You have but to copy a model, and the work is done; but to give it a soul, to make it typical by creating a man or a woman — this is the sin of Prometheus.'[45] Apart from defining his own ambition as an artist through his character, the novelist here depicts Prometheus's gift of life as a sin, which would support the idea that Frenhofer is punished for attempting to rival God, as Prometheus was before him. Indeed, even if the way Balzac understands 'sin' does not necessarily rely on the original treatment of the Prometheus myth, like that of Hesiod (and possibly that of Aeschylus's trilogy), in which he was blamed for the loss of the golden age and punished for his hubris, and even if Prometheus's flame allows the creation of the perfect work of art, a reference is nonetheless made to the will to equal God/nature, and to breaking the divine law.

The way in which Balzac interprets the figure of Prometheus, in the light of the Pygmalion myth and with the assumption that the Promethean flame, stolen from the gods, is a gift with almost Faustian implications, presents an original conception of the artist. The Promethean power appears as a magical one, over which it is difficult, not to say impossible, to gain control.

Balzac understands the Prometheus myth as a parable of artistic creation, a conception which derives from one of Prometheus's original features as *plasticator*. Franz Liszt also saw in Prometheus the mask of the artist. Interestingly, he moved in the same social circles in Paris as Hugo and Balzac, and the three men had a strong admiration for one another. Liszt's personal interpretation of the Titan in many ways prefigures the Symbolist one.

Prometheus, the Artist-Apostle

When Franz Liszt started composing his *Prometheus*,[46] he had chosen a new path, as *Kappelmeister* in Weimar (1848–1861). During those years, Liszt was particularly prolific in his output, and such productivity was undoubtedly linked to the fact that he felt it was his duty, through his art, to reveal God to others. According to Mara Lacché, his 'intense activity in Weimar is the result of the influence that the stimulating Parisian intellectual environment and his meeting with Countess d'Agoult had on his musical, aesthetic and literary education',[47] and it is not surprising that such a development took place in what Liszt himself called 'the fatherland of the Ideal'.[48] It was under the influence of Weimar that *Prometheus* was written. It was originally composed by Liszt in 1850 for the commemoration of Johann Gottfried von Herder's birth. On that occasion, a statue of the German poet and thinker was unveiled and Liszt composed an overture and choruses for Herder's *Der entfesselte Prometheus*,[49] entitled *Chöre zu Herders 'Entfesseltem Prometheus'*.[50] Even though Herder was the revered master of Goethe in his youth, his interpretation of Prometheus was very different. Herder used the Promethean figure to illustrate an Idealist conception of history, with Prometheus as the symbol of the perpetual progress of the divine Spirit, which gradually unveils all the extent of the powers of mankind. In the same spirit, Liszt soon developed his overture and choruses to create a symphonic poem and chose to emphasize four characteristics of Herder's Prometheus as a compositional principle.

Audacity, suffering, endurance and salvation were Prometheus's four main attributes and the four themes along which Liszt developed his own philosophy. 'Audacity', the first energetic theme (bars 4 to 6), is formed of eight notes, with the dominance of the fourth, which contributes to the conquering aspect of the theme. However, from bar 28, this 'audacity' is soon followed by the 'suffering' theme. From bar 160, the 'endurance' theme can be heard, the idea of time being ingenuously transposed by contrapuntal writing, which emphasizes linearity. This third compositional part reaches a climax when the first three themes are given simultaneously thanks to the horizontal writing adopted by Liszt, who thus manages to express the main characteristics of Prometheus's persona at once. The last theme, 'salvation', is given from bar 129, and, as Lacché notes, 'answers' the previous theme.[51] Even though there are four themes in Liszt's symphonic poem, the general structure remains a sonata form, based on two principal themes: endurance and salvation.

Liszt was deeply influenced by the ideas of Félicité de Lamennais[52] and the notion of 'people's Christianity'. Lamennais communicated to Liszt the idea that God was revealed through art, and that artists were 'apostles', 'priests of an ineffable mysterious, eternal religion, which germinates and ceaselessly grows in all the hearts'.[53] The word 'apostle' is particularly interesting and proved to be influential, since, in Liszt's foreword to the score of *Prometheus*, the composer explains that he chose to set to music *Der entfesselte Prometheus* because it was 'one of the works of that kind in which the purest and the most generous feelings of the one who was called the apostle of mankind was expressed the best'.[54] These words by Liszt are essential to understanding the value that he attributed to the treatment of Prometheus. He did not perceive the pagan origin of the myth, and did not see the myth itself within Prometheus. Like Herder, he probably saw in him the human accomplishment of godlike designs, but, by association, because the revelations of those designs were also in the hands of artists, Prometheus, according to Liszt, was a typification of the artist. In the foreword to the score, Liszt underlines the 'creative activity'[55] which characterizes the Titan. Even though Prometheus, for Liszt, was part of a divine revelation (modelled by an idealist conception of History), the Titan was for him the archetype of the artist, as was the case with Hugo and Balzac. This interpretation would soon be echoed by Symbolism, but Liszt also had intriguing words concerning the Prometheus myth, anticipating its Symbolist perception: 'it [the Prometheus myth] has always spoken to one's imagination, troubled with the secret correspondences of that symbolic account with our most obstinate instincts, with our sourest griefs, with our sweetest sense of foreboding'.[56]

By examining the specificity of the interpretations of Prometheus during the first half of the nineteenth century, we have seen that the figure of Prometheus was increasingly used to represent the artist, which explains, in Balzac's case, a shift towards the Pygmalion myth. The focus adopted on the Prometheus myth became more and more specific, and strove, in one way or another, towards an identification between the Titan and the artist. When Romanticism started in Europe and England, the Prometheus myth as such started to disappear in the works of artists, in favour of the symbol Prometheus represented. The Titan being now perceived as a man or a pure human form, the set of questions and values contained in the myth changed. Because it took on a metaphysical value, men projected themselves onto the image of Prometheus, who became a typification of man, and, increasingly, of the artist. This pattern was to be of great interest to Symbolist artists.

Notes to Chapter 3

1. Victor Hugo, *Odes et Ballades*, ed. by Pierre Albouy (Paris: Gallimard, 1964), IV, 6, pp. 220–24.
2. Victor Hugo, *Toute la lyre* (Paris: Nelson, 1916), I, pp. 19–21.
3. Victor Hugo, 'Le Moi', *Toute la lyre*, (Paris: Nelson, 1916), IX, pp. 29–30.
4. Victor Hugo, *La Fin de Satan. Dieu*, IV, 'Le Vautour', *Œuvres poétiques complètes*, ed. by Francis Bouvet (Paris: Pauvert, 1961), pp. 1228–29.
5. Victor Hugo, *Dieu (L'Océan d'en haut)* (Paris: Nizet, 1960), p. 51.
6. Victor Hugo, *Les Quatre Vents de l'esprit, Œuvres complètes de Victor Hugo — Poésie III* (Paris: Robert Laffont, 1985).
7. *Selected Poems of Victor Hugo: A Bilingual Edition*, trans. by E. H. and A. M. Blackmore (Chicago: University of Chicago Press, 2001).
8. I shall leave out the preface of *Burgraves*, as 'La Vision des montagnes', thirteen years later (the preface is dated 25 March 1843 and the poem 2 July 1856), uses almost word for word the passage concerning Prometheus: '[Le Voyageur] n'apercevait pas à l'horizon l'immense Prométhée couché comme une montagne sur une montagne...' / '[The traveller] could not see on the horizon the great Prometheus, lying down as a mountain on top of another one'.
9. Trousson, pp. 456–57.
10. For a biography of Victor Hugo, see Graham Robb, *Victor Hugo* (New York: W. W. Norton, 1997).
11. Hugo, *Odes et Ballades*, IV, 6, p. 220.
12. My translation.
13. There is a poetical tradition in France which uses the albatross as a symbol of the poet, the most famous example being Baudelaire's *L'Albatros*.
14. In his notes to the 1820 edition, Victor Hugo mentions that the albatross sleeps on the wing.
15. Hugo, *Toute la lyre*, pp. 29–33.
16. My translation.
17. See Theodore Ziolkowski, *The Sin of Knowledge, Ancient Themes and Modern Variations* (Princeton: Princeton University Press, 2000). Shelley also associated Prometheus with Satan: in his preface to *Prometheus Unbound* (*Shelley's Poetry and Prose*, ed. Donald H. Reinman and Sharon B Powers (London, New York: Norton & Co., 1977), p. 133), Shelley suggests that 'The only imaginary being resembling in any degree Prometheus, is Satan; and Prometheus is, in my judgement, a more poetical character than Satan because, in addition to courage and majesty and firm and patient opposition to omnipotent force, he is susceptible of being described as exempt from the taints of ambition, envy, revenge, and a desire for personal aggrandisement, which in the Hero of *Paradise Lost*, interfere with the interest. The character of Satan engenders in the mind a pernicious casuistry which leads us to weigh his faults with his wrongs and to excuse the former because the latter exceed all measure. In the minds of those who consider that magnificent fiction with a religious feeling, it engenders something worse. But Prometheus is, as it were, the type of the highest perfection of moral and intellectual nature, impelled by the purest and the truest motives to the best and noblest ends'.
18. Victor Hugo, 'Le «Moi»' (IX) in *Toute la lyre*, 2 vols (Paris: Nelson, 1916), II, p. 30.
19. Victor Hugo, 'La Vision des Montagnes' (I) in *Toute la lyre*, 2 vols (Paris: Nelson, 1916), I, pp. 19–21.
20. Matthew, 27:46.
21. This interest derived less from a biblical tradition than from a poetical one which started in the 18th century with Jean-Paul Richter, who imagined a dreamlike episode in which the apparition of Jesus Christ announces the death of God. Vigny, Stendhal, and Baudelaire were Jean-Paul's heirs in this respect, although they transferred the dreamlike scene on Golgotha or the Garden of Gethsemane, in which the human side of Jesus Christ was the strongest. Because he expressed doubt, anguish, and suffering during those episodes, he became an emblem for the Romantics.

22. Václav Černý, *Essai sur le titanisme dans la poésie romantique occidentale entre 1815 et 1850* (Prague, 1935).

23. Trousson, p. 394.

24. Charles Baudelaire, *Intimate Journals*, translated by Christopher Isherwood (Mineola, NY: Dover, 2006), pp. 54–55.

25. Vicenzo Monti, *Poemetti Mitologici* (Turin: Unione Tipografico-Editrice Torinese, undated)

26. Trousson, pp. 421–29.

27. Ibid., p. 455.

28. Byron, *Ode to Napoleon Buonaparte* (London: John Murray, 1814), p. 17.

29. Charles-Gilbert Martin, *L'Olympe*, in *Le Don Quichotte*, 22 July 1876.

30. *Hugo à Jersey sur le rocher dit "des proscrits"*(c.1852), photograph, BNF, MS NAF 13353. This also recalls Euripides on the island of Salamis.

31. Trousson, p. 484.

32. 'All his books are but one, a living, enlightening, and profound book, in which we see contemporary civilization come and go, walk, and move, with this awesome and terrible *je ne sais quoi* mingled with reality.' Honoré de Balzac, *La Comédie humaine* (Paris: Gallimard, Bibliothèque de la Pléiade, 1979), volume I, p. xix.

33. André Maurois, *Prométhée, ou la vie de Balzac* (Paris: Hachette, 1965).

34. Balzac, *The Unknown Masterpiece*, trans. by Ellen Marriage (London: Dent, 1896).

35. Balzac, *La Comédie humaine* (Paris: Gallimard, Bibliothèque de la Pléiade 1979), vol. X, p. 393.

36. Balzac wanted to create a social system analogous to that of nature, inspired by Buffon's theory, that as well as zoological species, social species existed. In this respect, he aimed to include in his system 'studies of manners' (they represented the major part of his work, divided into scenes of the provincial, Parisian, country, political, military life...), 'philosophical studies', to examine the causes of these manners, and, eventually, 'analytical studies', concerning their principles.

37. Balzac, *La Comédie humaine*, vol. X, p. 393.

38. Balzac, *The Unknown Masterpiece*, p. 6.

39. Ibid., p. 7.

40. Balzac, *The Unknown Masterpiece*, p. 16.

41. Ibid., p. 24.

42. Balzac expressed the same idea, and mixed the two myths together in the newspaper *La Silhouette*, in 1830: 'One evening, in the middle of the street, one morning, when getting up, or amongst a jolly orgy, live charcoal, sometimes, touches this head, these hands, this tongue; suddenly a word awakes ideas; they are born, they grow, they are in a ferment. A tragedy, a painting, a statue, a comedy show their daggers, their colours, their outlines, their gibes [...] it is a group worthy of Pygmalion, a woman whose possession would kill even Satan's heart'. The combination of the theme of fire, characteristic of the Prometheus myth, with the myth of Pygmalion, shows once more their link in Balzac's mind.

43. Balzac, *The Unknown Masterpiece*, p. 7.

44. Ibid., p. 418.

45. Balzac, *Cousin Betty*, trans. by James Waring (London: J. M. Dent, 1897), pp. 233–34.

46. Franz Liszt, *Prometheus* (1855), Symphonic Poem n° 5.

47. Mara Lacché, 'L'humanisme de J. G. Herder dans la pensée esthético-musicale de F. Liszt', *Ostinato Rigore* 18 (2001), p. 44.

48. Quoted by Mara Lacché, *ibid.*, p. 44.

49. Johann Gottfried von Herder, *Der entfesselte Prometheus*, in *Sämtliche Werke* (Hildesheim: Olms-Weidmann, 1994).

50. Franz Liszt, *Chöre zu Herders 'Entfesseltem Prometheus'*, R.539, 1850.

51. Mara Lacché, 'L'humanisme de J. G. Herder dans la pensée esthético-musicale de F. Liszt', p. 52.

52. Ibid., p. 45

53. Quoted by Lacché, p. 45.

54. Franz Liszt, *Prometheus* (Leipzig: Eulenburg, 1850)

55. Ibid.

56. Ibid.

PART III

Prometheus and the Crisis of Faith

One is forced to ponder the fact that in almost every epoch of history where the arts flourish and taste reigns we find humanity in decline and can give no single example where in a people a high degree and a general breadth of aesthetic culture go together with political freedom and civic virtue, where beautiful customs go together with good customs and cultivated manners go together with truth.[1]

FRIEDRICH SCHILLER

In order to measure the importance of the Prometheus figure in the artistic field during the second half of the nineteenth century, and especially during the *fin de siècle*, it is necessary to examine Symbolism. To appreciate what Prometheus meant to the artists of this period, and the nature of their relationship with this figure, we must consider the specificity of Symbolism, and its link with the crisis of faith with which Prometheus is associated. I will examine the nature of this so-called movement and what it revealed of an entire generation, and try to clarify as far as possible its relation to Decadence and Aestheticism. A reason for this confusion is that these 'movements' are often associated with different countries, which tends to create a geographical seg-mentation of Symbolism, Aestheticism, and sometimes Decadence. As Symbolism is inseparable from a crisis of faith and values, will take religious borders into consideration, thus identifying the variations that Symbolism took on. One of the crucial aspects we shall envisage during our examination of Symbolism is its very particular conception of 'myth', and its impact in relation to Prometheus.

CHAPTER 1

Symbolism and Myth

United in Spirit: Symbolism, Aestheticism and Decadence

Symbolism was officially born on 18 September 1886, when Jean Moréas published
the Manifesto of Symbolism in *Le Figaro*. Does this mean that Moréas was the
father of Symbolism, its creator and leader, rather than Mallarmé and, to a certain
extent, Verlaine? And was Symbolism originally literary and French? The task
of defining and delimiting the lineaments of Symbolism is not easy, even if this
'event' in September 1886 gives an illusion of clarity and 'classification'. Moréas, for
that matter, was fond of manifestos and definitions: in 1891, he also launched the
'Romanic School', which indicates the need for caution concerning the origin of
Symbolism. Another difficulty with Symbolism is that its best representatives, such
as Mallarmé, often refused to be labelled as Symbolists. They felt they did not truly
belong to any movement, which certainly indicates the main clue for understanding
Symbolism: if it is so difficult to apprehend and discern its coherence as a 'school',
that might be because it was not a movement, but a spirit, a state of mind.
Symbolism embraced artists of many different fields and styles. The most famous
theorist of Symbolism, Paul Valéry, in his attempts to explain the phenomenon,
came up with more than fifty definitions of Symbolism, which highlights the
impossibility of the task. In his *Etudes littéraires*, Valéry explained his failure to give
a final definition of Symbolism: 'The unity that we can name Symbolism does not
rely on aesthetic conformity; Symbolism is not a school. It admits, on the contrary,
a lot of schools, and very different ones, and as I told you: Aesthetics divided them;
Ethics united them.'[2] Symbolism would be a matter of moral or spiritual attitude,
and not a question of movement, leaders, or aesthetic rules. Certain theorists of
Aestheticism and Decadence deplored the absence of manifestos or precise dates of
birth to mark out these 'movements', which they contrasted with Symbolism. The
outlines of those aesthetic trends are nebulous, but certainly no less so than the
contours of Symbolism, despite an alleged date of birth. Worse, the three trends
sometimes seemed to contaminate each other and to be superimposed one upon
the other. Even geographical partitions did not properly constrain the respective
characteristics of each 'school'. For more clarity and consistency, attention will
be paid to the distinctions, or, to be more precise, to the similarities between
Symbolism, Decadence, and Aestheticism.

The birth of Aestheticism is often said to coincide with the publication of
Théophile Gautier's *Mademoiselle de Maupin* in 1835. According to William Gaunt,

in this novel, 'all ecstasies and all excesses were justified in the search for sensation and the delight in beauty which, the author implied, was a law unto itself'.[3] If young 'bohemians', the future Aesthetes, identified with the ideas expressed in the novel, it is surely because it put their own feelings into words: they despised the bourgeois spirit which had developed and expanded with the industrial revolution, and defended values which were at the opposite pole to this new culture. As William Gaunt puts it, 'Bohemians had one law, one morality, one devotion, and that was — Art. It had to be so, for it was their sole justification. They were responsible for it, as, in the previous century, noble patrons had been. They must, now that so few others were interested, preserve it like a sacred mystery'.[4] Hence their motto, 'l'art pour l'art', 'art for art's sake', initially used by Victor Cousin during a lecture at the Sorbonne, which was later adopted by Théophile Gautier. France was not the best land for that doctrine to develop. England, however, appeared to be so, and, from the 1860s, thanks to figures like Walter Pater and Algernon Swinburne, it became Aestheticism. It must be borne in mind that on the continent, nations had to deal with consecutive revolutions, the final trauma being, for France and Belgium, that of 1870. Europe also had to cope with the difficulties entailed by the industrial revolution, whereas England had gone through that process fifty years earlier. What England had to face in the second half of the nineteenth century was 'the spirit of competition and excessive conformity', which 'weighed too heavily on social life'.[5] In this special context, a certain number of artists and individuals tried to escape this 'dead-end' by turning towards the idea of Beauty conceived as the Absolute, and towards the expression of this supreme value. Aestheticism appeared as a true philosophy of life, and was therefore more than the principle of art for art's sake on which it was based. As Bertrand Marchal puts it, 'during the Symbolist period, Aestheticism borders on the religion of Art'.[6] In this element of definition, it must also be stressed that an association is made between Symbolism and Aestheticism.

As for Decadence, the distinction between it and Symbolism is again very difficult to define. All the important names in the Symbolist tradition, such as Stéphane Mallarmé, Oscar Wilde, Charles Baudelaire, or Joséphin Péladan, were classified either as Symbolists or as Decadents. Jean Moréas's manifesto of Symbolism originally put forward the idea that the term 'Symbolists' was a more suitable definition for those who were called 'Decadents'. To make things even more confusing, Count Robert de Montesquiou-Fézensac (the inspiration for Des Esseintes in Huysmans's *A Rebours*,[7] the so-called Bible of Decadence), was considered as the embodiment of the Decadent, when not presented as the Aesthete par excellence. Philippe Jullian makes the following point: 'While England was aesthetic, France was Decadent',[8] implying that the problems of definition and classification we are encountering are in fact a question of geography and cultural identity. However, Jullian immediately qualifies his assertion: 'There were few Decadents in England, apart from certain disciples of Wilde, and few Aesthetes in France, although she can lay claim to the most exquisite of them all, Robert de Montesquiou'.[9] Jullian's position concerning the 'quarrel' about Montesquiou is that he was an Aesthete, not a Decadent. But the exceptions he makes to his original assertion are considerable. Wilde was certainly one of the most important characters in the English artistic milieu at that time (not to say of the European artistic milieu), and such an exception, rather than proving the rule, tends to prove that it is wrong. Another question which divides theorists is whether Oscar Wilde was a Decadent, an Aesthete, or a Symbolist.

It is traditionally said that Decadence is the dark and mystical side of Symbolism, which includes this trend. The individuals who claimed to be Decadents had specific points of reference that were on the fringe of Symbolism. As Bertrand Marchal puts it,[10] the critics used the term 'Decadent' in a pejorative way to define postclassical Latin writers, and Baudelaire and his followers appropriated the word to define their new sensitivity, as opposed to the illusions of progress. Thus they willingly brought back to life, to define the art of that time, the myth of Byzantium and 'byzantinism'. However, the byzantinism in question was another way of expressing the Symbolist quest for the rare and the exotic. Moreover, it is interesting to see that Baudelaire, who considered himself a dandy and an Aesthete, is here linked to Decadence. According to the French poet Edouard Dujardin, who was at the heart of the Symbolist experience, 'two steps have to be distinguished within the grammatical evolution of Symbolism: firstly the "Decadent act of speech"[...] which was an explosion, and which from the beginning resorted to the worst audacities; then what one could call the "Symbolist act of speech", which is its continuation, but a considerably wiser continuation, involving the same patterns, but devoid of the previous excesses'.[11] If it is so difficult to make a distinction between Aestheticism, Symbolism, and Decadence, it is certainly because they are part of the same nebula. Indeed, it is impossible to define those movements when considered as such. However, another way of clarifying what they are would be to examine what Decadents, Symbolists, and Aesthetes reacted against.

All of them were united in their rejection of materialism,[12] with all it involved. The industrial revolution, on the continent and in England, had produced radical changes in society: in its composition, and, on a different scale, in social and religious practices. Cities largely developed into what the Symbolist Paul Verhaeren termed 'sprawling towns', to the point that they were often described as monsters absorbing people. This metamorphosis, which occurred within a relatively short lapse of time, was a real upheaval on all levels: it created wealth, but also considerable poverty. One reaction was that adopted by Symbolists, Decadents, and Aesthetes: idealism, or the antithesis of this predominant materialism. However, their anti-materialism was not just a literary or aesthetic quarrel. It appeared as the result of a deep crisis.

This leads us to the second element of coherence between what are distinctively called Symbolism, Aestheticism, and Decadence. They all derived from the *mal du siècle*, which means that all of them were engendered by Romanticism. As Edward Lucie-Smith put it, 'Symbolism, in the narrow, historical sense of the term, must be approached only as part of a larger whole: the Romantic Movement. Romanticism represents a crisis, a convulsion in the European spirit [...]'.[13] At the end of the century, with a climax in the 1880s, the *mal du siècle* reached its maximum intensity. To take the representative example of France, Henri Scepi, with Paul Bourget's influential *Essais de psychologie contemporaine* as a reference, reminds us of the fact that all the disenchanted generations of the nineteenth century, 'that of 1801, that of 1830', and 'that of 1855', 'all of them knew, according to different fashions and in a variety of contexts, what the temptation of nihilism [...] [and] the neutralising crisis of will were'.[14] The crisis in question appeared as the prolongation of the upheaval Romanticism had originated, by focusing on the examination of the human heart. As Guy Michaud noted, 'All Romanticism gained through the development of positivist rationalism was a critical judgment it was indeed lacking, but which, by giving it the taste of analysis, made this neurosis even more acute'.[15] We shall see later that the Romantic legacy to Symbolism, notably in the interpretation of the Prometheus myth, is extremely valuable. However, according to Scepi,[16] because of the political and social crisis of the second half of the century, a radical doubt spread amongst the generation in question and affected the study of their heart (inherited from Romanticism), which became an exercise in dissection, and resulted in a deep discouragement. One of the answers to this crisis, or, at least, modes of expression of it, was Symbolism.

It cannot be entirely denied that Aestheticism and Decadence had their own particularities. Aestheticism was essentially directed towards the idea and expression of beauty, and therefore less drawn to what was morbid or macabre. Decadence, on the other hand, was particularly provocative, and attracted to artificial paradises, and generally speaking, to exoticism. Moreover, Aesthetes and Decadents were not necessarily artists. Both of those trends were above all philosophies of life (even if, for some individuals, this philosophy was only temporary: the conversion of Decadents into fervent practising Catholics was not uncommon). However, in spite of those differences, both were part of a wider spirit, which can be called Symbolism, since both were included in that Aesthetic expression of the vast nineteenth-century crisis that reached its climax during the *fin de siècle*. It remains for us to examine the detail that characterized this crisis, in order to understand what fed the particular state of mind known as Symbolism.

If the shape of society, together with traditional practices, had totally changed with the industrial revolution, the structure and value on which society and the traditional world relied had slowly disintegrated. What people had to face was a world which had lost its meaning, its coherence, and what used to govern it: the Church, and, more importantly, its symbolic order. As Michael Gibson wrote, 'At the end of the nineteenth century, whilst science and positivism triumphantly announced a brave new world founded on reason and technology, some people were primarily aware of the loss of an indefinable quality which they had found in the former cultural system, in the values and meanings signified by what we might call its "emblematic order".'[17] Thomas Carlyle, in *Sartor Resartus*,[18] which had a noticeable impact on Symbolists, expressed the idea that the Church, the State, language, and Art were symbols, visible forms of spiritual objects, and that men were guided by those symbols, whether recognized as such or not. Carlyle also feared that with the metamorphosis society underwent so quickly, men would be led to lose their faith. Even though this did not happen in England, Carlyle's fear materialized on the continent. In this context, the fact that artists resorted to the use of symbols essentially appeared as an attempt to reach the Absolute people had lost touch with, a symbol referring to an absent reality: in this case, a superior, idealistic order. As Rodolphe Rapetti noted, the Symbolists' 'idealism refuted the validity of material appearances, thereby placing itself outside the prevailing fascination with concrete reality'.[19]

Although Symbolism is usually described as a retreat into an ivory tower, this vision is erroneous. The adepts of unrestrained progress accused the Symbolists of being a small isolated group of incurable conservatives, whereas, as Michael Gibson notes, 'It is thus the nature of Symbolist art to attempt to record a process which had till then been massive, involuntary, and very largely unconscious. Symbols had once been the "cement of the community"'.[20] The Symbolists were perceived as a group of eccentrics, whereas, in their own way — perhaps unconsciously — they wanted to preserve the 'emblematic order' which gave meaning and consistency to the world they lived in. They were certainly a minority turned towards the past, but more profoundly, through this political and aesthetic quarrel, two opposite visions of the world can be perceived: the world of progress, science, commerce, and industry which only discerned one level, nature, as opposed to the world recognized by Symbolists, comprising the level of nature related to that of a transcendency, God or His substitute. In this context, Symbolism was nothing less than a reaction to a deep cultural crisis. Fed on a profound sense of disorientation and loss, it was a spirit, a state of mind striving towards the only thing that made sense to Symbolists, the Absolute. As mentioned earlier, the Symbolist spirit was not limited to France, nor to continental Europe. It ignored geographical boundaries. However, because Symbolism derived from a crisis of faith, it took different forms, depending on where it originated.

A Symbolist Map of Europe

In most cases, geographical boundaries were not directly linked to the shape Symbolism took in Europe: beyond these contours, traditional religions seemed to determine the variations it took. Because Symbolism derived from a crisis of faith, it was logical for it to take different forms depending both on the nature of the faith that was prevalent in the countries touched by that spirit, and on the intensity of the religious crisis. The fact that Symbolism hinges on an acute feeling of a loss, which is that of faith, spirituality, and an ancient set of values providing a meaning for existence, shows that the question of religion is crucial. It determines the various facets of Symbolism, which were particularly striking in the pictorial field: even if traditional religions were rejected or faded during the period we are interested in, the Protestant or Catholic legacies left their traces through Symbolist art. Indeed, the common idea that Symbolism was limited to the Catholic part of the continent will have to be challenged. As we shall examine, Symbolism may have developed to a larger extent there, but it does not necessarily imply that Protestant areas were not significantly affected by it. If the features of Symbolism varied according to religious legacies, there was no specific prevalent model. Moreover, another difficult case will have to be considered, that of Germany, which went through an identity crisis of a cultural rather than religious nature. Its history will also be taken into account to understand the specificity of Symbolism in the new Reich, Austria and Switzerland, and to draw a map of Symbolist Europe.

Symbolism, Catholicism and Protestantism: Belgium and France vs England

> The concept of what is diabolical emerges where that of modernity meets
> Catholicism. (Walter Benjamin)

We have seen that Jean Moréas's manifesto cannot be considered to mark the birth of
Symbolism, but what of the idea that Symbolism was born in a Catholic, continental
and industrial country? Even if the reaction against industrialism is a *sine qua non*
for Symbolism to develop, the consideration of religion to define Symbolism is to
be handled with great care. We might also consider the Pre-Raphaelites, especially
Dante Gabriel Rossetti, as forerunners of this spirit,[21] even before Gustave Moreau.
This is even more true of the work of Edward Burne-Jones, a painter who belonged
to the 'second generation' of Pre-Raphaelites, as we shall see in a later chapter.
On the other hand, the assertion that the intensity and propagation of Symbolism
was stronger in Catholic countries is also true, in the sense that the spiritual crisis
associated with this religion was greater.

The loss of faith was more acutely felt in those countries, because of the fundamental importance of the rituals and emblematic aspect of Catholicism. The social
upheaval industrialization entailed was no greater in Belgium or France: as Michael
Gibson has pointed out,[22] Dr Barnardo's institutions in England took in no less than
50,000 abandoned children from the streets of London. England had been through
the industrial revolution fifty years before continental Europe, which means that
England had possibly already dealt with the acceptance of the radical changes
that had occurred in society. However, the clue to understanding this different
perception of reality probably lies in the fact that poverty was viewed differently.
As Gibson also noted, 'Perhaps, too, the Reformation, whose demands were those
of the pragmatic, new financial and merchant classes, had better prepared Protestant
minds for this event [the industrial revolution]'.[23] Indeed, with the emphasis on
the seven sacraments, the rites, the figure of the Virgin Mary, and, perhaps even
more importantly, on religious imagery and arts, 'magical thinking' was essential
to Catholicism. Catholic culture was steeped in a symbolic system, and, to a large
extent, society relied on the emblematic order which resulted from it. We have to
take the full measure of what it implied. As Bertrand Marchal remarked, taking the
example of France, Symbolism was 'an indication of a wider process of disintegration
of the old orders and the emergence of the individual in a nineteenth-century
society which goes on digesting the Revolution for ever, and learns, willy-nilly, the
relativity of values.[...] As for economy, the absolute guarantee of gold is replaced
by the development of fiduciary currencies. And the entire old order, political,
economical, religious, or literary, found its keystone in God, a God whose king,
gold, or, in His image, the patriarchal figure of Victor Hugo were, in their own
fields, only representatives or substitutes.'[24] French society had gradually neglected
the Church for almost a century, and the values on which it relied had already
crumbled away, but what put the seal on the break-up with the Catholic Church
was the rural exodus which accompanied the industrial revolution. Until then, the
traditional practices which structured society had remained. But now, society had

lost its very roots, and individuals had to face what they often perceived as a sort of disquieting chaos.

Belgium was even more affected by the religious crisis because of its political situation. It became an independent state in 1830, but had been joined to Holland for fifteen years. In reaction against this Calvinist Dutch-speaking country, the Catholic religion had gained even more importance, especially in the upper classes of Belgian society, in which Symbolist art was to develop at the end of the century. Moreover, as Michael Gibson noted, 'between 1860 and 1914, the country enjoyed unprecedented industrial and economic development [...]. This influx of wealth helps to explain the sudden development of the arts in Belgium.'[25] As we can see, all the elements previously identified in the emergence of Symbolism were therefore gathered in Belgium. The righteous atmosphere that reigned in this prosperous country resulted in a strengthening of the moroseness felt by Symbolist artists. The deep spiritual crisis Belgium went through is essential to understand why, for Belgian artists such as Félicien Rops, Jean Delville, Fernand Khnopff, and James Ensor, the Decadent and macabre aspect of Symbolism was extremely strong. In order to clarify this point, it is worth comparing the works of Khnopff with those of Edward Burne-Jones.[26] The aesthetic similarities between them are strong: the eerie androgynous characters, the idealized faces that return again and again in their respective works, the motionless figures, and the mellow light. However, whereas the work of Burne-Jones has a mysterious and magical quality, Fernand Khnopff's characters are often seen in a deleterious atmosphere. Individual irreducible features aside, this difference could partly be explained by the dissimilarity of the spiritual crisis which was at the origin of their art.

In Catholic countries like France and Belgium, Symbolist art almost always evoked the sacred, which artists felt so powerfully deprived of. This is true despite this reference often taking the intense form of a violation of the sacred, which explains why Decadence was generally perceived as a profane attitude and why Belgian and French Symbolist artists frequently used traditional Catholic imagery or cult objects to express their uneasiness.[27] But, as Don Juan had challenged God before, those artists, in their own way, were searching for a form of the sacred with which they had lost touch. It could be said that in this Catholic part of Europe, where the emblematic order had been so fundamental, the need to find a substitute for this form of spirituality had been stronger than in England. Indeed, in the United Kingdom, the development of Symbolism resulted more from a lassitude linked to the lack of depth of a materialistic and pragmatic philosophy of life than from a true religious crisis. Catholicism, during the industrial revolution, had shown itself inadequate to 'support' its flock, whereas Protestantism had prepared believers for it, and this essential difference between the two cults had an effect on the way artists depicted their subjects. After this brief explanation of the major variations entailed by Protestantism (more precisely Anglicanism) and Catholicism, we must consider Germany, Austria and Switzerland during this period, in order to understand the context in which painters like Böcklin and Klinger, who both depicted Prometheus, were working.

A Special Case: Germany and Switzerland

The question of religious borders in Germany in the 1870s is a delicate one, since the most important problem during that period appeared to be that of the preservation or rather dispersion of a shared culture. In the context of the foundation of the Reich, the religious question was only part of a larger cultural crisis. In William Vaughan's words, Germany 'was known to most as the land of thinkers and poets, unworldly people with relatively little political power or economic strength. This image was to change dramatically during the nineteenth century, being replaced after the establishment of the German Reich in 1870 with the image of a powerful, organised and technologically advanced country which has remained more or less in place ever since.'[28] The unification of Germany into the Reich had been a dream as far back as the time of the Holy Roman Empire, but it did not satisfy all expectations.[29] Indeed, the Reich failed to give a tangible cultural existence to Germany, which resulted in an identity crisis that was magnified amongst artists. As Walter Pape noted, 'after 1871 many thoughtful Germans were gripped by a mood of mingled pride and disenchantment; pride in the power and the unity of the Reich, disenchantment with the culture of the Empire, with the fact that beneath the crust of prosperous politics the old Germany was disintegrating, pulled apart by modernity — by liberalism, secularism, and industrialism. Common were the lamentations about the decline of the German spirit, the defeat of idealism by the forces of realism in politics and materialism in business.'[30] These descriptions of the effects of modernity on the German soul, as we can see, are very close to those which triggered the Symbolist crisis in England, France, and Belgium. Moreover, because of the redefinition of its borders, the new Germany excluded what had been absolutely essential to its cultural identity. William Vaughan pointed out that 'Swiss Germans and Austrians, who would have thought of themselves as an integral part of "Germany" in the early nineteenth century, now found themselves outsiders. This in itself contributed to a growing tension between the cultural and political concept of what was "German".'[31] The concept of a 'Kulturnation' German intellectuals had dreamt of proved to be illusory, and instead of coherence, what emerged was a feeling of cultural estrangement.

Only now that this cultural and political background has been sketched can we tackle the problem of religion in Germany, since the cultural issue, in the development of 'German' Symbolism, was more at stake than the religious problem, which only strengthened the identity crisis. When the Reich was founded, North Germany was traditionally Lutheran, whereas the south was Catholic. However, there is little clear difference in the inspiration and style of the Symbolist works made in the northern and southern parts of what was Germany. Symbolist artists like Max Klinger and Arnold Böcklin, who both used the Prometheus figure, found their pictorial expression in a vitalist imagery which spread in the new Reich, and which also appeared as the result of that identity crisis. As if to remedy it, they drew their inspiration from an idealized golden age, coming either from Greek and Roman or from old Nordic mythology, possibly because the foundation of the Reich brought to their mind the dream of a renaissance as well as of a unity around a mutual past, through ancient myths. However, although German Symbolism reflects this dream, the Reich being unable to protect, build, and develop a German culture, German Symbolist art also shows the artists' focus on nightmarish visions. If we take the example of the work of the Swiss German Arnold Böcklin,[32] we see that it is peopled with demons and malevolent creatures, who confer a Decadent atmosphere. However, it lacks the evanescent and dreamy aspect that imbues most Decadent paintings, such as Fernand Khnopff's, for example. That difference of atmosphere relies on Böcklin's bright palette, which endows his paintings with vitalist qualities.

Interestingly, German-speaking Symbolist artists seemed to make up for the political unification and cultural disintegration of the Reich by reacting against the arts establishment. In Belgium, France, and England, the reaction against religion and politics had taken shape through an aesthetic style, but in Germany, artists went further and organized themselves to defend this characteristic style through the foundation of the Secession: first in Munich in 1892, then in Vienna in 1897, and eventually in Berlin in 1899. 'There was thus a constant ferment of ideas, to which new currents were added from throughout the German-speaking world [...]. Artists influenced by Symbolism appeared in both Catholic Bavaria and Protestant Prussia.'[33] That underlines the specificity of Switzerland, Austria, and Germany in the Symbolist map of Europe. Gibson adds 'There was not, in Germany, this clear religious split which opposed, for example, Belgium and Holland. There was not either the fight between the Church power and that of the lay Republic which touched France so deeply at the end of that century.'[34] A wider questioning about the identity of the countries affected by the foundation of the Reich had indeed surpassed this.

We have considered through this Symbolist map of Europe that the forms Symbolism took were often based on the traditional religious imagery of the cult that was prevalent before the crisis of faith, and that despite a variety of modes of expression, there was also a consistency in Symbolism across Europe. In all cases, it emerged as the result of an upheaval of society when industrialization developed. The rapid changes in the social, religious, and political structures at the end of the nineteenth century entailed a crisis of faith, and, more generally, a crisis of identity and values. Symbolism appeared as a form of idealism whose (sometimes unconscious) aim was to compensate for the feeling of loss. Having tried to show the origins and nature of Symbolism, we now have to study the value myths held for Symbolist artists in this age of upheaval.

The Symbolist Perception of Myth

> Recent poets have considered myths and legends in a different way. They looked for their permanent significance and ideal meaning; where some saw tales and fables, others saw symbols [...]. A myth is the resounding conch of an idea.[35] (Henri de Régnier)

A crisis of belief, values, and representation: in the context that has been sketched in the previous paragraphs, it is not surprising that the Symbolists took a deep interest in myths. The Greek word *mythos* originally meant 'anything delivered by word of mouth, word, speech'.[36] In Sophocles and Euripides, *mythos* means both a saying, a proverb, and the talk of men, rumour. Traditionally opposed to the word *logos*, which also refers to the word, or that by which the inward thought is expressed, *mythos*, being 'delivered [...] by mouth', has a physiological quality. Those elements of definition are not fortuitous, as they all underline the idea that myth is by essence the protean creation of man.

This is why a myth implies a particular relation to time, which also has tremendous consequences for the Symbolist perception of myth. Since myths are adopted and recreated by each generation, and since it is in the nature of myth to appear as a palimpsest on which the 'fabula' (the material of the story, in its chronological development) would be perpetually rewritten, the origins of myths are impossible to define from a precise historical point of view. As Mircea Eliade put it, 'a myth is an account of events which took place *in principio*, that is, "in the beginning", in a primordial and non-temporal instant, a moment of *sacred time*.'[37] Such a characteristic is fraught with consequences for the artistic choice to make use of a myth, since 'in narrating a myth, one reactualises, in some sort, the sacred time in which the events narrated took place.[...] The myth is supposed to happen — if one may say so — in a non-temporal time, in an instant without duration, as certain mystics and philosophers conceived of eternity.'[38] We can easily see why the sacred aspect of myths particularly appealed to Symbolist artists: since their idealism led them to look for new forms of spirituality, different from that of the Church, myths gave them the possibility to express their longing for the sacred. What they rejected by despising materialism was also, by and large, a rejection of the form history took. And, Eliade goes on, 'the myth takes man out of his own time — his individual, chronological, "historic" time — and projects him, symbolically at least, into the Great Time, into a paradoxical instant which cannot be measured because it does not consist of duration. This is as much as to say that the myth implies a break-away from Time and the surrounding world: it opens up a way into the sacred Great Time.'[39] In other words, myths gave Symbolists the ability to escape from history and materialism. They gave them the means to retreat into an ideal world thanks to a particular apprehension of temporality. We could even go further, and suggest that myths also projected Symbolist artists into a new perception of space. Indeed, as is generally accepted today, myths (and not only cosmological myths) often represent natural elements and forces, like the sun, the earth, the moon, which is to say that the narration of a myth also implies the understanding of the universal cycle, and through its physiological characteristic ('delivered... by mouth'), its appropriation. The myth appears as a unique mode of expression of a world which no longer exists as such: on a temporal and spatial level, the myth allowed Symbolists to reconnect with the 'spiritual' world they thought they had lost.

Such contact was not made through the diachrony of history, but through the synchronic structure and understanding of myth. What particularly appealed to Symbolist artists was the fact that myth appeared as a way of reaching totality in a world that, in their eyes, was collapsing and crumbling. According to Françoise Grauby, '[Symbolist] uses of the myth merge in the same call: that of the past'.[40]

Through the aspect of totality linked to the myth, Symbolist artists were surely looking for the roots of their culture and spirituality. In this, 'the myth [was] a means to communicate with the past, but, most of all, with the beyond'.[41] This is indeed a specificity of Symbolism to associate culture and faith, because the loss of those two was felt by the artists who underwent the *fin de siècle* crisis. As Grauby notes, 'the myth is the scene of reconciliation and syncretism [...] [The Symbolist] philosophy does not linger on any ideal of perfection, but on that of totality, which would be a fusion of knowledge and faith'.[42] This partly explains why many scholars involved in the Symbolist trend made extensive researches into myths. People like Edouard Schuré in France, and George William Cox in England, highlighted correspondences between myths, peoples, and religions, which leads Grauby to define their research as 'anthropological'.[43] It is also on this perception of the myth that Richard Wagner, one of the most important figures for Symbolist artists, based his art. What Wagner wanted to achieve through his musical dramas was, in Bertrand Marchal's words, 'a collective unconscious'.[44] As George Lehmann notes, '[Wagner's music-drama] was total by its virtue of being both mythical and musical: its pure humanity and its extreme generalization in the hero-legend was intended to give it the widest possible audience — to bring together all humanity, eventually, without regard for race or state.'[45] This attempt relied on the power of myths, since, for Wagner and his acolytes, they were 'the natural support of an art based on symbol', and the best way to 'make a religious celebration of his dramas'.[46] In other words, Wagner wanted to use the totality inherent in myths to achieve his *Gesamtkunstwerk*.

This leads us to an important point. We have to take the whole measure of what the crisis of values Symbolist artists went through really meant. By challenging the entire structure society relied on, Symbolists underlined the fact that their disbelief had reached the level of a crisis of representation. From the moment the structure of society, with God at its top, starts collapsing, 'all religious, but also political, economic, and social systems, are nothing but representations solely articulated by language. Society, Democracy, the Republic are not realities as much as effects of speech'.[47] And, the material of myths being language, we come naturally to this somewhat paradoxical conclusion: '[Society, Democracy, the Republic] are contemporary mythologies which, like Ancient myths, are nothing but words taking advantage of the obviously perpetuated citizens' credulousness'.[48] One of the most important figures of French Symbolism, Stéphane Mallarmé, shared this view. According to him, myths were deepest illusion, and mythology was nothing but organized speech having forgotten its own original meaning and the significance of words. Mallarmé went so far as to say that 'any divinity is never anything more than a word that has lost its word's memory, its etymology'.[49] According to Mallarmé, there was nothing beyond words, which explains his syntactic and neological experiments: poetical creation could only be based on the sole tangible material he was in possession of, i.e. words. As Bertrand Marchal rightly states, 'Mallarmé's criticism of myths, which dissolves gods into language, joins thus the criticism of a poetry that perpetuates outdated myths, together with the illusion of a meaning beyond words'.[50] It is somewhat unsettling to consider that one of the most important Symbolists had such views on myths, given that at the same time, myths gave Symbolists the means to express their most vivid concerns. However, the paradox we are encountering here is not as impenetrable as it seems.

Although Mallarmé is particularly virulent about myths, one of the works he valued most in his own oeuvre was *Hérodiade*. Mallarmé's poem is not exactly faithful to the myth, since, in the first place, the creature he so names is in fact Salome.[51] More importantly, what appealed to him in the myth was the name 'Hérodiade', and the dream this 'dark word, and red, like an open pomegranate',[52] entailed. Thus Mallarmé's creative process obeys his conception of language and his famous 'il faut céder l'initiative aux mots'.[53] Nonetheless, it is worth noticing that of all ancient myths, Mallarmé chose by far the most popular among Symbolists, a choice which is surely not accidental. Indeed, in spite of Mallarmé's view of myths, their undeniable evocative power also appealed to him, which is to say that he too recognized their spiritual power. What he seemed to reject, more than mythology, was the scholarly and somewhat ossified approach to myths, revering them as sacred texts, not as the ever-changing, lively material intrinsic to *mythos*. The poetry of the Parnasse, the main trend before the appearance of Symbolism, made extensive and erudite use of mythology, by drawing on its allegories. Yet despite a common interest in myths, Symbolists and Parnassians treated them in a totally opposite way. Symbolism was an attempt to create or conjure up what we might call a supra-natural world, a fore-world, through the power of evocation, whereas Parnassians, by using traditional allegories, wanted to produce a learned poetry. The Parnasse school did not use Prometheus in its poetry, although it used most of the main Greek mythological figures. The Symbolist theorist Mockel provides a clue to this surprising omission.

In *Propos de littérature*,[54] Mockel attempted to compare allegory and symbol, to show the power of the latter, and established the following points: 'The allegory would be the explicit or analytical representation, through an image, of a PRECONCEIVED abstract idea; it would also be *conventional* — and in that explicit — of that idea, as we can see with the attributes of heroes, gods, goddesses, who in a way are the labels of that convention. On the contrary the symbol implies the intuitive search for various ideal elements scattered in forms'.[55] Mockel distinguishes between the two tropes as follows: 'Ceres, Vulcan, are allegorical characters; the attributes explaining them are true emblems since, without their conventional meaning, Ceres and Vulcan would not be more than an ordinary blacksmith and a woman crowned with spikes. But a poet or a sculptor translating the Prometheus myth, would easily make a symbolic work of it; since Prometheus stealing the fire, Prometheus bound, can entirely express himself through his only attitude'.[56] Although Mockel did not explain precisely why Prometheus appeared to him as 'symbolic material', rather than simply a thief, or a torch bearer, or even a tortured man, the comparison he drew between allegorical mythological figures and the Titan is sufficient to give an insight as to why Parnassians did not choose to develop the Prometheus figure. By that time, the Titan had inspired so many giants of European literature that he had already reached the status of a symbol, whose artistic interpretation was constantly changing. Moreover, he was epitomising mankind at that stage of the myth's evolution, and therefore could not find his place in the Greek pantheon, so dear to the Parnassians' hearts. Prometheus's status is ambiguous, and the interest Symbolist artists took in him is surely linked to the ambivalence they felt. Even if Prometheus represents mankind, its suffering, and also its glory, and even if his becoming man appears as a conquest in the evolution of the myth, the Titan's origins cannot be totally erased. And Prometheus's double nature, in this context, is of great interest.

The Symbolist choice of myths is certainly not a matter of chance. In order to understand why, we have to come back briefly to a point mentioned earlier in this chapter, which is that Symbolists had pushed the examination of their sensitivity and moods even further than the Romantics. The *fin de siècle* crisis had affected the Symbolist psyche, and instead of finding certainties, unity, and a solid rational ground through the examination of their own sensitivity, they only discovered further reasons for doubting. As Bertrand Marchal noted, 'the omnipresence of the soul in Symbolist poetry refers less to a spiritual or sentimental principle [which might have been the case with Romanticism] than to a strange and sometimes disquieting reality perceived at the depth of oneself'.[57] The fragmentation they saw everywhere around them was also present in themselves,[58] and 'a certain Symbolism thus discovers the inside space, explores this new reality the *fin de siècle* psychology now named the Unconscious, and which [...] can only be phrased in the language of the image, in poetry'.[59] Such an observation is important in the perspective of the Symbolist apprehension of myths (and especially in that of the Prometheus myth, as we shall see), since it appears that the great Symbolist myths show a sort of fascination for 'otherness' (which is also another way of defining the unconscious). It seems that Symbolists were drawn to myths involving creatures which were neither entirely human, nor absolutely transcendent. This may prove an important key to understanding Symbolist interest in the Prometheus myth.

The most famous characters of Symbolist mythology have in common an intrinsic mysterious quality, which mainly relies on the fact that something uncanny makes them both human and inhuman. As Françoise Grauby put it, with 'Salome, the androgyne, the sphinx, three different lights are shed on the woman, the disquieting creature, the monster and the animal in us. Those beings, who are only loosely linked to mankind, show that the centre of interest shifted'.[60] This shift can easily be explained by the disturbing discovery of the unconscious, and, therefore, by the very presence of the otherness in oneself. Grauby argues that the main difference between the Romantic and Symbolist mythologies lies in the fact that the Romantic mythology was that of man, whereas the Symbolist one '(was) not interested in the individual perceived as a productive being any more'.[61] However, if we examine the main Symbolist figures named above, it is interesting to see that, although they are not human beings as such, they all have human qualities: those myths 'have kept a few human behaviours while staying out of mankind. The myths do not exalt superhuman heroes, and do not condemn monsters either. They are just one of the possible aspects of mankind...'.[62] In other words, Symbolist artists favoured myths which reflected the ambiguity and mystery of the human psyche, and their disquieting feeling facing the discovery of this 'unknown territory'. Interestingly,

Symbolist artists focused their attention on characters taken in a tragic conflict, and the human side of these creatures essentially relied on this tragic quality. Narcissus, the main Symbolist mask of the androgyne, has to face the impossible fulfilment of his love; the femme fatale, with the features of Salome or Medea, has to kill to satisfy her passion; and the Sphinx was treated by Symbolists as a chimera, who, as a mermaid, was in fact another femme fatale. Thus, we can see that the main Symbolist characters are linked to mankind because of the nature of their passions, even if they are too great to be human. And this is because those passions lead them to an unsolvable conflict that they are quintessentially tragic characters.

If we apply all the Symbolist characteristics detailed above to Prometheus, we can understand why he inspired Symbolist artists. He, more than any other character, had the tragic quality which appealed so much to Symbolists. This was certainly inherited from Aeschylus and Shelley, but the very nature of the Prometheus myth already contained all the elements of a tragedy. The myth is essentially, and originally, the supreme conflict between Prometheus and the Olympian gods. However, with the evolution of the myth, the essence of the *agon* was not hubris any more, but the injustice of the gods. The Titan was not the black sheep among gods: the conflict was now between mankind and gods, that is between two sets of values and two different conceptions of the world. The myth had evolved so much that by taking the side of men, it looked as if Prometheus's choice also implied that of his 'identity', human or godlike. This leads us to an important point. Prometheus may be the Symbolist myth par excellence, precisely because of his double nature. He epitomizes mankind, but his godlike origins remain, since they give the Titan's acts all their value and significance. He represents mankind, or, to be more precise, its greatness, and for this reason, he is above human nature. He is a symbol and an archetype. The fascination of otherness could not have been greater than in the character of Prometheus, who is so close to man, whose tragic suffering is greatest, and yet who is so far above mankind. The infinite ambiguity of Prometheus triggered the Symbolist interest in otherness.

In conclusion, it seems that his duality defined the two different existing attitudes towards Prometheus in the context of this crisis of faith. The first consisted in exalting his human, the second, his sacred side. The perception of Prometheus during the *fin de siècle* period appears as a reflection of the general religious questioning. During this period the history of the Prometheus myth met history itself, and the reality of the religious crisis. The Prometheus symbol was fed by the richness and significance acquired by the myth throughout its history.

Notes to Chapter 1

1. Friedrich Schiller, 'Über die ästhetische Erziehung des Menschen in einer Reihe von Briefen' 10. Brief, in *Werke* (Nationalausgabe) vol. 20 (Weimar, 1949–1993), p. 339. Walter Pape's translation.
2. Paul Valéry, *Variétés, Etudes Littéraires,* in *Œuvres,* ed. by J. Hytier, vol. I (Paris: Gallimard, Bibliothèque de la Pléiade, 1968), p. 694.
3. William Gaunt, *The Aesthetic Adventure* (London: Jonathan Cape, 1945), p. 8.
4. Ibid., p. 10.
5. Philippe Jullian, *Dreamers of Decadence: Symbolist Painters of the 1890s* (London: Pall Mall Press, 1971), pp. 25–26.
6. Bertrand Marchal, *Lire le Symbolisme* (Paris: Dunod, 1993), p. 174.
7. And also for Baron de Charlus in *A la recherche du temps perdu*
8. Jullian, *Dreamers of Decadence,* p. 28.
9. Ibid., p. 28.
10. Bertrand Marchal, *Lire le Symbolisme,* p. 173.
11. Quoted by A. G. Lehmann, *The Symbolist Aesthetic in France 1885–1895* (Oxford: Blackwell, 1950, 1968), p. 17. My translation
12. The Symbolist rejection of Naturalism, a movement best represented by Emile Zola, was another way of rejecting materialism. In actual fact, the naturalist school had chosen to depict nature and the consequences of materialism as realistically as possible. Naturalism and Symbolism embodied two opposite attitudes regarding materialism. Whereas Symbolism turned its back on materialism for a realm governed by idealism, Naturalism, on the other hand, tackled the immediate consequences of materialism through an aesthetic which examined them with great scrutiny.
13. Edward Lucie-Smith, *Symbolist Art* (London: Thames and Hudson, 1972, 1977), p. 23.
14. Henri Scepi, *Les Complaintes de Jules Laforgue* (Paris: Gallimard, 2000), p. 33.
15. Guy Michaud, *Le Symbolisme tel qu'en lui-même* (Paris: Nizet, 1961), p. 27.
16. Ibid., p. 34.
17. Michael Gibson, *Symbolism* (London: Taschen, 1995), p. 17.
18. Thomas Carlyle, *Sartor Resartus,* ed. by Kerry McSweeney and Peter Sabor (Oxford: Oxford Paperbacks, 2000)
19. Rodolphe Rapetti, *Symbolism* (Paris: Flammarion, 2005), p. 7.
20. Gibson, *Symbolism,* p. 24.
21. The work of Millais was sometimes criticized for showing an interest in the traditional Catholic depiction of religious subjects, and for his choice of those subjects, but the Pre-Raphaelites were nevertheless part of a Protestant culture.
22. Gibson, *Symbolism,* p. 13.
23. Ibid., p. 12.
24. Marchal, *Lire le Symbolisme,* p. 22.
25. Gibson, *Symbolism,* p. 87.
26. The respect and admiration they had for each other is well known: Khnopff's *Study of a Woman* (1896, private collection, Turin, 23 × 15 cm), which he gave to Burne-Jones, is a testimony to this mutual interest.
27. To give an example among many, *La Tentation de St Antoine,* by Felicien Rops, 1878 (73.8 × 54.3 cm, Cabinet des Estampes, Bibliothèque Royale Albert Ier, Brussels), which depicts a sensual naked woman replacing Jesus Christ on the cross, appears to reveal the deep spiritual crisis experienced by artists of Catholic culture.
28. William Vaughan, 'Spiritual Landscapes', in *Kingdom of the Soul: Symbolist Art in Germany 1870–1920,* ed. by Ingrid Ehrhardt, and Simon Reynolds (Munich: Prestel, 2000), p. 79.
29. Vaughan, (p. 79) specifies that the new Germany, 'at once industrialized and authoritarian, [...] was neither the reconstituted feudal Holy Roman Empire dreamed of by right-wing romantics, nor the utopian democracy that those on the left had sought to engineer'.
30. *1870/71–1989/90 German Unifications and the Change of Literary Discourse,* ed. by Walter Pape (Berlin, New York: Walter de Gruyter, 1993), p. 5.

31. Vaughan, p. 79.
32. The work of Arnold Böcklin (1827–1901) probably shows better than any other the identity crisis which characterized Symbolism in Germany. Even though, from a cultural point of view, he belonged to Germany, after the foundation of the Reich he left for Italy. As William Vaughan puts it, 'This was a self-imposed exile. He resisted attempts to lure him to Germany with official positions. In a sense, however, the creation of the Reich also imposed an exile on him. For he was, after all, Swiss and the Swiss-German community could no longer be considered a part of Germany after 1870' (p. 82).
33. Gibson, *Symbolism*, pp. 102 and 125.
34. Ibid., p. 125.
35. Henri de Régnier, *Figures et Caractères* (Paris: Mercure de France, 1901), p. 336.
36. Definitions from Liddell and Scott's *Greek-English Lexicon*.
37. Mircea Eliade, *Images and Symbols*, trans. by Philip Mairet (London: Harvill Press, 1952, 1961), p. 57.
38. Ibid., p. 57.
39. Ibid., p. 57.
40. Françoise Grauby, *La Création mythique à l'époque du symbolisme: Histoire, analyse et interprétation des mythes fondamentaux du symbolisme* (Paris: Nizet, 1994), p. 71.
41. Ibid., p. 71.
42. Ibid., p. 71.
43. Ibid., p. 71.
44. Marchal, *Lire le Symbolisme*, p. 98.
45. Lehmann, *The Symbolist Aesthetic in France 1885–1895*, p. 229.
46. Marchal, *Lire le Symbolisme*, p. 98.
47. Ibid., p. 23.
48. Ibid., p. 23.
49. Bertrand Marchal *Lecture de Mallarmé*, (Paris: Corti, 1985), p. 173.
50. Ibid., p. 173.
51. Hérodiade, Herod's wife, is Salome's mother. Mallarmé, in calling Salome by a different name, wanted to avoid the conjuring up of the dense imagery attached to her, namely the sensuality of her famous dance, and the archetype of the femme fatale.
52. In a letter to his friend Lefébure, dated February 1865, he rejects all the historical and literary documentation his friend had sent him, saying that he owes his only inspiration to the name 'Hérodiade'. He adds 'I want to make of her a purely dreamt being, absolutely independent from history'.
53. 'The initiative must be left to words'.
54. A. Mockel, *Propos de littérature*, 1894, republished in *Esthétique du Symbolisme* (Brussels: Palais des Académies, 1962)
55. Ibid., p. 85.
56. Ibid., p. 87.
57. Marchal, *Lire le symbolisme*, p. 17.
58. It is probably in this light that we have to understand Arthur Rimbaud's famous 'Je est un autre', 'I is another'.
59. Marchal, *Lire le symbolisme*, p. 17.
60. Grauby, *La Création mythique à l'époque du symbolisme*, p. 21.
61. Ibid., p. 21.
62. Ibid., p. 21.

CHAPTER 2

'The Twilight of the Gods'

In order to understand why the history of the myth entered into conjunction with history itself at the end of the nineteenth century, it is necessary to return briefly to Goethe, who was largely responsible for the Prometheus myth reaching a crucial point: the Titan became a man, and, perhaps even more importantly, the mythological character became a symbol of mankind, its suffering, and its nobility. However, the impact that Goethe's works on Prometheus had on the myth and the perception of the Titan had even deeper consequences. Prometheus claimed that he equalled the gods with his creative power, denounced their injustice, implied that men themselves created their gods, and, most of all, put wisdom and reason (in the person of Athena) on the side of mankind. Man was therefore 'freed from God', since, to a certain extent, He was the creation of man. Although Goethe himself did not go as far as announcing the death of God, this is nonetheless what his two *Prometheus* lead to, and it is not surprising to notice the great influence they had on philosophers, the most important being Karl Marx and Friedrich Nietzsche. We shall first examine Friedrich Nietzsche's interpretation of the Prometheus myth, because the importance of Prometheus was greater in his work than in that of Marx, and because Nietzsche can be regarded as a Symbolist philosopher, and certainly as a remarkable analyst of the turmoil of the *fin de siècle*.

The Era of Mankind

> If I speak of Plato, Pascal, Spinoza, and Goethe, I know that their blood runs in mine.[1] (Friedrich Nietzsche)

Friedrich Nietzsche

Nietzsche's interpretation of Prometheus sheds light on the way the Titan might have been perceived during the later years of the nineteenth century, especially in Germany. His interest in Prometheus was more than admiration for Goethe or Aeschylus. Although Prometheus is rarely a major figure in Nietzsche's work, he nonetheless makes recurrent appearances in key passages. From an early age, Nietzsche had shown a particular interest in the Titan: when he was fifteen years old, he wrote a play entitled *Prometheus*. Even if *The Birth of Tragedy* (1872) was his first published philosophical work, Prometheus had already inspired Nietzsche's pen, in a piece of work that was probably the first to be completed. Even more revealing is the fact that, when *The Birth of Tragedy* was about to be published, Nietzsche proved to be particularly enthusiastic about the vignette that he decided to put on the cover of his work. The vignette in question was not a representation of Dionysos, as might have been expected, nor of Apollo. In late November 1871, Nietzsche sent his publisher E.W. Fritzsch an illustration of Prometheus by his friend Leopold Rau. Nietzsche considered it a masterpiece, and the dedication he wrote in the copy of *The Birth of Tragedy* that he presented to Richard Wagner demonstrates the pride he took in his book, in the vignette affixed on it, and in the fact that *The Birth of Tragedy* was written under the Titan's sway: 'I am picturing to myself, my esteemed friend, the moment when you received my book. I can see you returning from some walk in the snow, on a winter evening, contemplating the *Prometheus Unbound* of the vignette, reading my name, and you being already persuaded that, whatever the content of this work, the author has deep and impressive things to say...'.[2] This calls for an examination of Prometheus's role in *The Birth of Tragedy*, as well as for interpretation of its recurrence in later works, inasmuch as Nietzsche's interest in Prometheus was to be long-lasting.

In *The Birth of Tragedy*, Nietzsche perceives in a very clear way what is at stake in the evolution of the Prometheus myth, before dealing with Prometheus's persona as such. By taking into account the versions of the myth by Aeschylus and Goethe, Nietzsche extracts from his observation the revolution introduced by Goethe in his interpretation of the myth:

> What the thinker Aeschylus had to say to us here, but what as a poet he only allows us to sense in his symbolic image, the youthful Goethe was able to reveal to us in the audacious words of his Prometheus:
>
> > 'Here I sit, forming men
> > In my own image,
> > A race to be like me,
> > To suffer, to weep,
> > To delight and to rejoice,
> > And to defy you,
> > As I do.'
>
> Man, rising to Titanic stature, gains culture by his own efforts and forces the gods to enter into an alliance with him because, in his very own wisdom, he holds their existence and their limitations in his hands.[3]

What Nietzsche implies is that the myth, as treated by Aeschylus, already potentially contained Prometheus's embodiment of mankind, although Goethe was the first to reveal it fully. In other words, Goethe allowed the birth of Promethean man. Because Nietzsche perceived the value of Prometheus's persona in the context of the myth's history, he saw Prometheus's manhood as a conquest, and therefore as a victory over God. This special focus on Prometheus surely conditioned the deep interest he took in the Titan, who soon became a model for Nietzsche, on different grounds.

One of the main characteristics of Prometheus in Nietzsche's works is that he appears as the model of what the philosopher calls active sin, as opposed to the Judeo-Christian passivity which he abhorred. This element of Prometheus's persona is already present in *The Birth of Tragedy*: 'The Prometheus story is an original possession of the entire Aryan[4] community of people and evidences their gift for the profoundly tragic. Indeed, it does not seem improbable that this myth has the same characteristic significance for the Aryan character which the myth of the fall has for the Semitic character, and that these are related to each other like brother and sister'.[5] Nietzsche puts forward the idea that primitive men, because of the power of fire and what it involved, felt guilty for disposing freely of fire. The fire, if not 'a present from heaven, either as a lightning bolt or as the warming rays of the sun', was surely the fruit of 'a robbery of divine nature'.[6] The Prometheus myth being an explanation of the end of the golden age, it appears as the equivalent of the biblical myth of the Fall. However, because of the notion of 'active sin' as described above by Nietzsche, the myth, for Goethe, became that of a liberation and a rebirth, rather than a loss. This allows us to understand why, in Nietzsche's perspective of freeing man from his chimeras, the figure of Prometheus appeared as a fundamental model for mankind.[7]

There is a second important point concerning Prometheus in *The Birth of Tragedy*: the fact that he is not, so to speak, an isolated figure. Prometheus is presented as a 'mask of Dionysos', who was so important in the philosopher's thought, and who also appeared, as we shall see, in other guises. Nietzsche establishes a link between the two Greek characters: 'The Titanic impulse to become, as it were, the Atlas for all individuals, carrying them on a broad back, higher and higher, farther and farther, is what the Promethean and the Dionysian have in common. In this respect, the Prometheus of Aeschylus is a Dionysian mask'.[8] Many commentators have emphasized the fact that, in Nietzsche's writings and letters (included those preceding his lapse into total insanity) the philosopher associated and even superimposed Dionysos onto Zarathustra, which allows us to suggest that Prometheus was part of the same lineage in Nietzsche's thought, and also confirms that the Titan was a constant model and inspiration.

Prometheus reappeared in Nietzsche's work in a more definite and decisive way, as a prototype of the superman. In *The Will to Power*, the philosopher explained that society had reached a point at which the 'tools' (men) it needed for it to function in an optimal way was a new model of man: 'The increasing dwarfing of man is precisely the driving force that brings to mind the breeding of a stronger race — a race that would be excessive precisely where the dwarfed species was weak and growing weaker (in will, responsibility, self-assurance, ability to posit goals for oneself)'.[9] In the two following fragments, Nietzsche describes the qualities of the new model of man, as opposed to the characteristics of the current majority: 'Our psychologists, whose glance lingers involuntarily on symptoms of Decadence alone, again and again induce us to mistrust the spirit. One always sees only those effects of the spirit that make men weak, delicate, and morbid; but now they are coming: new barbarians (cynics; experimenters; conquerors) union of spiritual superiority with well-being and an excess of strength'.[10] We recognize here the attributes of the man Nietzsche will later name 'superman'. He goes on to make a link between those attributes and Prometheus himself: 'I point to something new: certainly for such a democratic type there exists the danger of the barbarian, but one has looked for it only in the depths. There exists also another type of barbarian, who comes from the heights: a species of conquering and ruling natures in search of material to mould. Prometheus was this kind of barbarian'.[11] In this respect, we can see that although the figure of Prometheus never appears as central to any of Nietzsche's works, it is nonetheless omnipresent, and essential in what it represents. As truly as Goethe gave birth to Promethean man, Nietzsche uses the Titan as a model for mankind to follow. He wants to make of a symbol and an emblem a model *in praxis*. Men had to get rid of their chimeras (God and 'morality' being the two most important, according to Nietzsche), and have faith only in themselves and their creative power in order to inaugurate a new era in which man would be his own dignified master.

This brief examination is essential if we consider Nietzsche's enormous impact on German Symbolist artists. Nearly all the most important German sculptors and painters devoted one of their works to Nietzsche — Max Klinger,[12] Curt Stoeving, and Karl Donnorf[13] all made busts of him — or of a particular aspect of his works, as we shall see in a later chapter. Another influential German philosopher, Karl Marx, used Prometheus to embody one of his most important ideas, an interpretation which was not without consequences for the evolution of the myth.

Karl Marx

Although Nietzsche and Marx developed different philosophies, and the ways in which they structured their thought had little in common, both took a great interest in the Prometheus myth, and their perception of the Titan shared many similarities, amongst which was the fact that both took him as a model for mankind. Marx's first reference to Prometheus may be found in his first philosophical work, his doctoral dissertation. Written between 1840 and March 1841, and completed when he was only twenty-three years old, it was entitled 'Difference between the Democritean and Epicurean Philosophy of Nature'.

One of the aims of Marx's dissertation was to rehabilitate Epicurus, whose philosophy until then had been considered as similar, but inferior, to that of Democritus. Such a defence of Epicurus was largely justified by the fact that Marx was in sympathy with the thought of the ancient philosopher. On the question of Nature and its laws, Marx tried to prove that, as H.P. Adams put it, 'Epicurus, and indeed, earlier thinkers, had shown that the planets were not gods but merely collections of atoms'.[14] That idea had fundamental consequences, and explains Marx's interest in Epicurus's philosophy. Adams continues, 'But how shake off the inexorable laws, which are the first, the "naïve" form in which reason embodies itself in phenomena? Here we reach the ultimate crisis of the dialectical progress, and here Epicurus-Marx recurs to the fundamental doctrine of "abstract possibility", which is nothing short of the dogmatic assertion that whatever is could be otherwise'.[15] This brings us to one of the central points, if not the central point, of Marx's philosophy: 'The human mind, armed with this medusa-shield of its own self-consciousness in which Nature's independence is reflected and overcome, thus vindicates its own absolute freedom and security. The victory makes us equal to the gods'.[16] Although the dissertation was his first work, Marx's essential idea of the supremacy of human consciousness, which later led him to analyse and denounce man's alienation, was already evident, and already crucial. So crucial, in fact, that Marx's foreword to the thesis focuses the attention of his readers on this question, through his evocation of Prometheus, who appears as an illustration of the rejection of Plutarch's famous dictum: '[bringing] philosophy before the forum of religion'. After this, Marx introduces a quotation by Hume, and, eventually, Prometheus's lines from Aeschylus's play.

The first important point to make about Marx's perception of Prometheus, as opposed to that of Nietzsche, is that, even though he too recognized Prometheus as a very important figure, Marx quoted Aeschylus, not Goethe, in order to develop his thoughts. However, if we examine the texts in question, Marx seems to have read Aeschylus after Goethe, and, without any doubt, it was Goethe's *Prometheus* rather than *Prometheus Bound* which had the greater influence on his thought, even if he did not admit it. According to the young Marx, Goethe was too conservative to be a point of reference. As we have already seen, Goethe's opinions, especially his conception of God and the Absolute, evolved and changed during his long life. That explains the abundant literature and frequent disagreements about this burning question. However, Goethe's works on Prometheus clearly claimed predominance for 'Genius' over the Olympian gods, which gave full impetus to the perception of Prometheus as man, rather than God. Marx had a deep knowledge of Goethe's writings, and he quoted from him on several occasions,[17] but because of his mixed feelings of admiration and disagreement, it seems Marx decided to quote Aeschylus rather than Goethe to evoke the Titan.

Marx puts Prometheus's words into the mouth of a personified, if not deified, Philosophy. After violent criticism of Plutarch, Marx continues: 'Philosophy, as long as a drop of blood shall pulse in its world-subduing and absolutely free heart, will never grow tired of answering its adversaries with the cry of Epicurus: 'Not the man who denies the gods worshipped by the multitude, but he who affirms of the gods what the multitude believes about them, is truly impious'.[18] Philosophy makes no secret of it.'[19] It is at that point that Marx, or rather Philosophy, makes use of Prometheus's credo: 'In one word, I feel hatred for all the gods',[20] which is a compression of lines 974 and 975[21] of Aeschylus's *Prometheus Bound*, to which Marx added, '[This] confession of Prometheus is its own confession, its own aphorism against all heavenly and earthly gods who do not acknowledge human self-consciousness as the highest divinity. It will have none other beside'.[22] We note that Marx's use and analysis of this quotation enables him to introduce an explanation of why he chose to compare the philosophies of Democritus and Epicurus, i.e. to declare the idea that human self-consciousness is above everything, including God (or the gods). Marx's personified Philosophy appears as representative of the free man, free because he makes use of his freedom and self-consciousness to think.

Marx then quotes Aeschylus again, with Prometheus's answer to Hermes:

> I would not change my painful plight
> On any terms, for your servile humility.
> Being bondslave to this rock is preferable, no doubt,
> To being the trusted messenger of Zeus, your father. (lines 965–68)

Fig. iii.2.i Anonymous, *Karl Marx as Prometheus* (1842)

These last two lines are in fact sarcastic in the mouth of Hermes[23] in the original text, and not another provocation from Prometheus. The 'discreet' condensation (in the first quotation) and reinterpretation (in the above quotation) of Aeschylus's play emphasize the revolutionary aspect of Prometheus, and could very well disguise an attempt to give a Goethean coloration to his references. Goethe's *Prometheus* fragment in particular would have given the same weight to Marx's words and interpretation of the Titan's opposition to the Olympian gods.

The novel aspect of Marx's interpretation of Prometheus is that the Titan's claim that he despises the gods, and therefore belongs to mankind, relies on the fact that self-consciousness, understood as the most precious possible attribute, is properly human. Prometheus's manhood stems from his embodiment, in Marx's foreword, of the power of human self-consciousness. Thus, for Marx, Prometheus's attitude appears as an invitation for man to make full use of his attribute. In that, he is presented by the German philosopher as a symbol and model for mankind. A print of Marx as Prometheus (Fig.III.2.1), published in 1842[24] to criticize the censorship of his articles for the *Rheinische Zeitung*, tends to prove how influential his interpretation of the Titan was, and it is telling that John Goodwyn Barmby, who coined the word 'communism', did so in a work untitled *The Promethean: or Communist Apostle* (1842).

Marx concludes his foreword with the provocative remark 'Prometheus is the most eminent saint and martyr in the philosophical calendar',[25] since, as opposed to Plutarch, philosophy and mankind must not be evaluated in comparison to religion or gods. Later in the twentieth century, the figure of Prometheus took on an important significance in communist imagery, especially in Russia, where he became some sort of variation on Stakhanov, the archetype of the worker.[26] During the period we are interested in, the transposition of Marx's theories into the political world had not yet occurred, and his ideas did not have the deep impact that they later had. Moreover, Marx's doctoral dissertation was far from being his most influential text. However, it is important to mention the value Marx gave to the figure of Prometheus since, together with that of Nietzsche, it appears as symptomatic of German thought during the second half of the nineteenth century. In order to understand the value of Prometheus's representations in the German world, especially in the pictorial field, we now have to synthesise and examine in a larger context what is revealed by Marx's and Nietzsche's perceptions of Prometheus.

German Thought and the Birth of Vitalist Prometheus

Prometheus, as seen by Marx and Nietzsche, represented more than a symbol for mankind. Following Goethe, they did not make Prometheus a symbol for human suffering, but, like him, they chose to highlight the nobility of mankind in Prometheus by emphasising the rebellious aspect of his persona. However, whereas Prometheus's harangue against the Olympian gods in Aeschylus's play had a tone both desperate and resolute, both philosophers made of Prometheus the model of a conqueror who overcame his own chimeras. In Goethe's fragment and in the *Prometheus* ode, the Titan, thanks to his genius and creative powers, can equal the gods, and does equal them by choosing his human side. But this implies that the gods still rule. Marx's and Nietzsche's interpretations of Prometheus derive from Goethe, but the common ground of their thoughts on the value and meaning of Prometheus's act, implied by Marx and claimed by Nietzsche, is that gods are products of the human mind, and that the awakening of self-consciousness is the real issue in the myth. The theme of transgression is replaced by that of man's realization and awareness of his own powers, which makes of Prometheus an entirely positive character.

It is noteworthy that Nietzsche used Prometheus to illustrate the idea of 'active sin', inasmuch as this concept suppresses the guilt accompanying the biblical original sin or the loss of the golden age. Given this change of perspective, Prometheus is finally freed from the responsibility for the origin of human misery and for Pandora's mischief. This is even more true of Marx's perception of the Titan, as he does not evoke any aspect of the Fall. For Marx, the acceptance of Prometheus as a model of self-consciousness coincides with the original acceptance of man for what he really is, that is a potentially free being. For Marx and Nietzsche, Prometheus's opposition to the gods appears as a symbolic scene of the moment at which man realizes that, through his conscience, he is an autonomous and free being, with his own ability to create. Prometheus seems to be presented as the model of a new man, born without the weight of original sin, and with an infinite number of possibilities offered to his creative and mental powers. This new German interpretation of Prometheus was that of a rebirth for man, on this new basis.

We can understand why this perception of the Prometheus myth developed in the German context of the newly created Reich, relying on the dream of a strong and united Germany. The rebirth of man through the example of Prometheus was equalled by the (hoped-for) rebirth of Germany, which had never before had a real geographical and political consistency. Although the expectations of Germans were later disappointed, their hope in a rejuvenated Germany found a direct expression in pictorial art, which created an imagery of Arcadia and a fantasy of a new eternal golden age. Nature, athletic bodies, often nudes, and scenes from classical mythology were exalted for their vitalism. The works of Hans von Marées, Max Beckmann, and Ludwig von Hoffmann are the most representative of this idealization of the golden age. The paintings of Arnold Böcklin, peopled with fauns and representations of Pan, also reflect the vitalism which spread in German art during the second half of the nineteenth century. His interpretation of Prometheus will be the subject of a later chapter.

Through an examination of Nietzsche's and Marx's interpretations of Prometheus, we have been led to consider the fact that the crisis of faith which spread in Europe during the second half of the nineteenth century took a special form in Germany, and that the perception of Prometheus was affected by it. In the particular cultural and political context of the Reich, it seems that hope, rather than being directed towards religion, turned towards man and his potential, which explains why, in Prometheus's dual nature, mortal and divine, his belonging to mankind was emphasized, and why he was presented as a model for man. However, in most of the rest of Europe, his godlike nature was also to play an important part.

As an answer to the crisis of faith, it could be said that the Symbolist tendency, in German-speaking countries, was to proclaim that religion had only been a step within the evolution of mankind, who was now freed from chimeras and from the burden of original sin, and ready to enter the era of its full achievement. In this respect, they did not entirely deplore the destruction of the ancient order, since they considered that what was felt as a new historical period was in fact stemming from the end of that structure. The only difference was that their faith was placed in man, not in God. However, another Symbolist attitude was indirectly to return to what they had lost, that is to say God or the Absolute. Such an approach implied an attempt to rebuild a form of religion, based on what they had previously known. It could be said that, whereas, in German-speaking countries, most Symbolist artists turned towards an idealized golden age to emulate the great powers of man, in the rest of Europe, Symbolists generally attempted to recreate a meaningful world, in which a supernatural principle, not man, was central. Applied to the myth of Prometheus, it is therefore not surprising to consider that this other Symbolist reaction to the crisis of faith coincided with an emphasis on Prometheus's divine origins.

Notes to Chapter 2

1. A.H.J. Knight, *Some Aspects of the Life and Work of Nietzsche, and particularly of His Connection with Greek Literature and Thought* (New York: Russell and Russell, 1933, 1967), p. 8.
2. Quoted in Dominique Lecourt, *Prométhée, Faust, Frankenstein, Fondements imaginaires de l'éthique* (Paris: Livre de poche, 1996), p. 152. My translation.
3. Friedrich Nietzsche, *The Birth of Tragedy*, trans. with commentary by Walter Kaufmann (New York: Vintage Books, 1967), p. 69.
4. It must be remembered that the appropriation of this terminology by the Nazis should not affect our reading of Nietzsche, who always loathed anti-Semitism.
5. Nietzsche, *The Birth of Tragedy*, p. 70; this idea is recurrent in Nietzsche's work. See, for example, *The Will to Power*, ed. by Walter Kaufmann (New York: Vintage Books, 1968), p. 445: 'The idealization of the man of *great sacrilege* (a sense of his greatness) is Greek; depreciation, slandering, contempt for the sinner is Judeo-Christian.'
6. Ibid., p. 70.
7. At the end of the first edition of *The Gay Science*, 14 years after *The Birth of Tragedy*, Nietzsche wrote: 'This book marks the conclusion of a series of writings by Friedrich Nietzsche, whose common goal is to erect *a new image and ideal of the free spirit*'.
8. *The Birth of Tragedy*, p. 72.
9. *The Will to Power*, edited by Walter Kaufmann, translated by Walter Kaufmann and R. J. Hollingdale (New York: Vintage Books, 1968), fragment 898, pp. 477–78.
10. Ibid., fragment 899, p. 478.
11. Ibid., Fragment 900, pp. 478–79.
12. Max Klinger, *Friedrich Nietzsche*, 1902–1903, bronze, Museum der bildenden Künste, Leipzig.
13. Karl Donndorf, *Bust of Nietzsche*, 1901–1902, plaster of Paris, Weimar, Stiftung Weimarer Klassik, Nietzsche-Archiv.
14. H. P. Adams, *Karl Marx in his Earlier Writings* (London: Allen and Unwin, 1940), p. 37.
15. Ibid., p. 37.
16. Ibid. p. 37.
17. See, for example, *Debates on the law on Thefts of Wood*, in *Collected Works*, by Karl Marx and Frederick Engels, vol. I (London: Lawrence and Wishart, 1975), p. 246, and, in the same volume, *Debates on the Freedom of the Press*, p. 137. However, a sign of his (secret?) admiration for Goethe is also is mixed attitude towards him: see the satirical poem he wrote about him, 'False Wandering Years', pp. 578–80.

18. In Greek in Marx's doctoral dissertation. *Collected Works,* I, p. 30.

19. *Collected Works* I, p. 30.

20. In Greek in Marx's doctoral dissertation. *Collected Works,* I, p. 30. For consistency, I am using Philip Vellacott's translation of *Prometheus Bound.*

21. 'In one word, I detest all gods who could repay/ My benefits with such outrageous infamy', Aeschylus, *Prometheus Bound,* trans. with an introduction by Philip Vellacott (London: Penguin Books, 1961), p. 49.

22. Karl Marx and Frederick Engels, *Collected Works,* I, p. 30.

23. In Philip Vellacott's translation, line 967 reads: 'To being the trusted messenger of Father Zeus', p. 49.

24. *Prometheus Bound* (1842), anonymous.

25. Karl Marx and Frederick Engels, *Collected Works,* I, p. 31.

26. For the development of this aspect of Prometheus, see Theodore Ziolkowski's *The Sin of Knowledge, Ancient Themes and Modern Variations* (Princeton: Princeton University Press, 2000).

Prometheus at the
Heart of Symbolist Syncretism

Re-Establishing a World Order

Although there were different Symbolist reactions to the *fin de siècle* crisis, this did not imply that they were mutually exclusive or antagonistic. As well as the specific German answer to the crisis of faith, one of the Symbolist attitudes to spiritual turmoil was to point out the state of dereliction of the world, often in a cynical way, which was therefore commonly called 'Decadent'. However, another Symbolist reaction, truly idealistic, was the conception and creation of a new world order to replace the structure of values and beliefs that had disappeared. Where German Symbolism had tried to move forward by claiming that the new era was that of mankind, this other trend of Symbolism tried to re-establish a world order, consciously or unconsciously based on the Judeo-Christian one.

The essence of this new world was the notion of the Absolute, which they felt so deprived of. Most Symbolist artists had retained some Christian sensitivity, which re-emerged in their works of art. However, at first it was inconceivable for them[1] to base a new world and aesthetic on the religion whose very collapse brought with it the meaning of society. They rejected the dogma of religion, but not its poetical aspect. They rejected the Church, but not spirituality. The element they retained from religion was its transcendency, together with the unequalled beauty and evocative power of its symbols. They sought the Absolute, which explains why Symbolism raised art to the level of religion. This is what one of the main references for Symbolists, Richard Wagner, noted when he said: 'One might say that when religion becomes artificial, it is reserved for art to save the spirit of religion by recognising the figurative value of the mythic symbols which the former would have us believe in their literal sense and revealing their deep and hidden truth through an ideal representation'.[2] Symbolist artists saved the spirit of religion, by creating a new form of art based on their own syncretism, made of myths and symbols of very different origin.

To appreciate the coherence of this syncretism, we have to remember that the basis of Symbolism was the religious nature of art. These artists based their art on symbols, because, for them, this was the only form of expression which could designate the hidden truth and meaning of the world behind its immediate perception. We mentioned earlier that language appeared as a part, and as a reflection, of the general structure of society. But with the disappearance of the values which sustained and justified this very same structure, language itself appeared as a delusion. The symbol, suggestive in essence, therefore appeared as a privileged means to reach the truth and Absolute behind the apparent reality. As Mockel put it, 'the symbol implies the intuitive search for the various scattered ideal elements in forms',[3] which is to say that the symbol relies on an active participation of the reader, who, as an initiate, has to discover the ideal world suggested by symbols.

The role of the artist was to reveal the superior kingdom Symbolism was aspiring to. In Dorothy Kosinski's words, 'The artist is capable of deciphering the hieroglyphs of this world, of penetrating the mysterious truth of the ideal realm, and of communicating the hidden correspondences between the two realities in a universal language of symbols'.[4] This leads her to name the Symbolist artist 'the artist-priest'.[5] An almost supernatural function is ascribed to him, for he gives expression to the Absolute. Taking the example of Mallarmé, Kosinski highlights the fact that he 'departs from the Romantic tradition of the poet who expresses personal emotions which he sees reverberate in nature. Instead, the Poet is the mouthpiece or medium for the divine truth which finds expression in the chastened purity of the work'.[6] All these elements tend to show Symbolism almost as a religion, the poets playing the part of priests by revealing the ideal behind reality, and the notion of the Absolute, traditionally represented by God, being replaced by that of Beauty. In spite of a shift from established religions and dogma, the sacred was at the very heart of Symbolism, and, to a large extent, founded it. Furthermore, this form of spirituality gave coherence to the Symbolist syncretism, whose composition we now have to examine.

The basis of Symbolist syncretism, its credo, so to speak, is the affirmation of a belief in Beauty perceived as the Absolute, as the truth to strive towards. However, facing the discrepancy between the cultural, sociological, and historical period they were living in and this ideal precept, Symbolism had to rely on the idea of a 'fore-world', of a hidden ideal realm. Without this primary assumption, Symbolists would have belonged to the category of Utopians (they were often considered as such in any case) and not to that of idealists, in the literal sense of the term. With regard to the conception of a fore-world, Symbolists were the heirs of Romanticism, while the Romantics themselves had been part of an idealist tradition that could be traced as far back as Ancient Greece. Shelley, and, to a certain extent, Goethe, had been inspired largely by Plato, and, as Richard Jenkyns puts it, by 'the Platonist doctrine that all transient things are merely appearances'.[7] Before the enthusiasm of Shelley and his friends, this interest was 'not shared by scholars. Plato began exciting interest at Cambridge in the 1820's. He did not appear on the syllabus at Oxford until 1847; twenty years later he dominated it.'[8] Plato's best advocates were Walter Pater and Oscar Wilde. Since then, his thought, notably his dialectics, has been extensively examined, discussed, and studied, in the light of new translations, but, during the period we are interested in, Plato's conception of the world was very much perceived as dual, divided between a 'real world', that of appearances — as described in Plato's famous allegory of the cave — and an 'ideal world', that of truth and beauty, an interpretation which largely sustained the idealism of a Shelley. Plato, as interpreted in the nineteenth century, had a strong influence on the thought of the most important figures of Romanticism, and, as far as the Prometheus myth is concerned, on the same Romantic figures who showed a deep interest in the Titan. The Symbolist artists who inherited this interest also inherited the idea of a fore-world from this generation. In this regard, Symbolist syncretism was indebted to Romanticism.

However, with regard to what made the specificity of the Symbolist fore-world, we also have to look at its inheritance from the previous Romantic generation, in particular that of Charles Baudelaire. Baudelaire might be considered as the father of Symbolism, as he gave striking expression to what, to a large extent, defined and gave coherence to the Symbolist ideal realm we have just mentioned. Although the theory of synaesthesia and correspondences is not Baudelaire's invention, his poems gave substance to it.[9] As Bertrand Marchal puts it, the theory of correspondences is a 'philosophico-mystic notion linked to the conception of a universe governed by the principle of analogy, which became famous with the sonnet by Baudelaire that was named after it. But above all, Baudelaire gave all the poetical impetus to this notion by using it as the privileged instrument for transcending reality'.[10] This definition allows us to understand why correspondences were a central notion for Symbolist artists. The establishment of an analogy between the reality they loathed and the fore-world they were aspiring to justified their creation and the foundation of their syncretism. The notion of synaesthesia is part of that of correspondences, since this word is applied to what Marchal terms 'horizontal correspondences',[11] that is to say the level of sensation, that of the five senses, which, according to this principle, communicate. In this respect, the first step to access the Symbolist fore-world is this horizontal level of synaesthesia, on which the communication and unification of sensible perceptions create correspondences. From this basis are derived essential Symbolist features and values. As Dorothy Kosinski puts it, 'Synaesthesia and the *total work of art* are ideas which represent the Symbolists' attempt to surpass the limited, descriptive vocabulary of the ordinary work of art, and to embrace this universal language of symbols. Music [...] is adopted as the ideal art form because of its non-mimetic, immaterial quality'.[12] We might even suggest that the Symbolist perception of the world in its totality is similar to that of a musical piece, in which the harmonics (the non-descriptive symbols) eventually create a figured harmony and understanding of the entire work. The Symbolist view of the world would therefore rely on its ultimate model: the musical one. The theory of correspondences and synaesthesia, and, by extension, the musical ideal, appear as the pillars of the Symbolist syncretism. But we now have to examine the different threads intermingled in this syncretism, and what constituted its own 'Bible' to understand Prometheus's importance within it.

Symbolism rejected Judeo-Christianity, but its syncretism being based on the Judeo-Christian model, it is interesting to see that Symbolist artists looked into other forms of spirituality, and that they took a particular interest in Eastern spirituality and art. Such an interest was not entirely new in France, since the poet Leconte de Lisle, in his *Poèmes antiques* (1852), along with the evocation of 'traditional antiquity', had introduced his readers to Indian antiquity. However, the

Symbolist enthusiasm for the eastern world represented a debt to another author, more precisely, a philosopher. The Symbolists discovered Buddha thanks to Arthur Schopenhauer, who was himself dubbed the 'contemporary Buddha'. However, this fact itself shows that the Symbolist 'Orientalism' was in fact very European, and was itself known through what was already an appropriation. Schopenhauer's philosophy proved to be particularly influential on French Symbolism.[13] The first French translations appeared in France in 1877, and 1880 saw the publication of *Thoughts, Maxims and Fragments,*[14] a book which to a certain extent gave shape to the pessimism of Decadence,[15] even though it was a compilation of extracts from various of the author's works.

One of Schopenhauer's most important philosophical ideas is that the world's vital force is the Will, and that the Self, being also ruled by this inner force, is a phenomenal illusion. According to Schopenhauer, life is pure, endless suffering, which implies that the only two acceptable ways to escape the damnation of the Will are, firstly, Art and Science, inasmuch as they make man strive towards the contemplation of the essence of things, and, secondly, a moral attitude consisting in self-denial, that is to say in a form of asceticism, the model for which was Buddhism.[16] Schopenhauer, although overtly atheist, had sympathy for Catholicism because of its ascetic dimension. In such a context, one can understand why he appealed to Symbolists, because of both the exotic foundations of his philosophy and the development of his pessimism. The acknowledgement of human suffering was the principle of his philosophy, which, as a result, did not give false hope to man. His theories perfectly matched the despair of the *fin de siècle* generation, as the asceticism he preached matched their resignation in facing life. Buddhism, as represented by Schopenhauer, had a direct influence on French Symbolist poets such as Gustave Kahn and Jules Laforgue, but the Symbolist interest in Eastern spirituality is more apparent in the pictorial field.[17] However, India and Buddhism were not the only elements of Eastern spirituality which appealed to Symbolist artists. Their interest in Chinese and Japanese culture, together with their European perception of the Arabic world, also left its mark on Symbolist paintings, whether in the depiction of exotic objects in the background, or in the subject matter itself.[18]

Some of the fundamental legends of Symbolist syncretism, the most famous being that of Salome, are Biblical stories. In the perspective of the Symbolist rejection of Judeo-Christianity, it might appear paradoxical to consider such material as part of Symbolist syncretism. However, if we examine the case of Salome (mentioned in the Gospels of Matthew [14, 1–12] and Mark [6, 14–29]), it is worth noting that, whereas in the Bible she is only presented as being responsible for John the Baptist's death,[19] the focus shifted with the Symbolists, for whom she became the archetype of the femme fatale, a sort of fascinating anti-model of the Victorian woman. In this respect, the Symbolists made a myth out of the Biblical story by highlighting the exoticism of the account, together with its pagan aspect and the poisonous timeless beauty of Salome[20].

Another way of evoking the Bible indirectly was to replace its parables and stories by what we might term parallel accounts and myths. Greek mythology, in particular, provided Symbolism with many accounts which had the evocative and symbolic power of Biblical texts, albeit bereft of their dogmatic aspect. It is for this reason that Nietzsche praised the Prometheus myth as a variation on the myth of the Fall, since it developed the notion of 'active sin', and ignored that of original sin. Symbolists were probably sensitive to this characteristic in their interest in Prometheus, but this element of the myth was not the one they were going to emphasize in the elaboration of their syncretism. We have noted in the first chapter of this work that Prometheus, especially during the phase of evangelization, was identified with Jesus Christ, mainly because both endured intense suffering. However, a similar association emerged anew in the nineteenth century, even if, at that time, the figure of Prometheus was used to reflect that of Christ, and not the other way round. We now have to examine to what extent Prometheus appeared as a substitute for God within Symbolist syncretism.

Prometheus as Substitute for God

As we saw in Chapter One, the extensive use by scholars of the misleading quotations from Tertullian, 'Hic est verus Prometheus, Deus omnipotens blasphemiis lancinatus',[21] and 'Crucibus Causarum', made a large contribution to shaping an identification between Jesus Christ and Prometheus. In the nineteenth century, Tertullian's quotations were still being similarly used, by Edgar Quinet among others. As Jacqueline Duchemin noted,[22] he seems to have confused a few quotations by Tertullian to make his point, probably without knowing that the original text from which he drew them was not as clear as he thought. In 1838, Quinet published his *Prométhée*,[23] a work which largely illustrates the way in which he interpreted Tertullian's words, and which also follows the lines of the Romantic vision of Prometheus. Although Quinet was not a Symbolist, an examination of his work may allow us to understand better the position of Symbolists in relation to the comparison that was established in the nineteenth century between Jesus Christ and Prometheus.[24]

Edgar Quinet's dramatic poem *Prométhée* borrows from Aeschylus's trilogy the titles of its three parts: 'Prométhée inventeur du feu', 'Prométhée enchaîné', and 'Prométhée délivré'.[25] However, although the general frame of Quinet's work seems close to that of Aeschylus, its orientation is very different, each section of the poem being punctuated by quotations from Tertullian or Lactantius, and, as Duchemin put it, by 'Christian premonitions'.[26] In 'Prométhée inventeur du feu', Prometheus creates Hesione, the mother of mankind, thanks to a spark stolen from the volcano of the Cyclops, but as soon as men are created, they ask for gods. The chorus of Cyclops fears human thought, which challenges pagan gods:

> Il part, vaisseau bercé sur le roulis des âges
> Pour aborder chez d'autres dieux.[27]

> ['She leaves, the ship rocked by the rolling of ages,
> To reach the land of other gods'.]

In the second part, 'Prométhée enchaîné', Prometheus is crucified on his rock on Mount Caucasus, where he is visited by Ocean, the father of the Oceanids, who reports to Prometheus the ungratefulness of men: they are devoted to his enemies, the gods. After the death of Hesione, Prometheus, prophet-like, foretells the death of the Olympian gods, after which he adds:

> Le croirez-vous? Mes yeux voient un autre Caucase...
> Quel est, sur la sainte colline,
> Cet autre Prométhée à la face divine?...
> Est-ce un Titan esclave? Un Dieu crucifié?
> O Prodige! Il bénit l'univers qui l'opprime.
> Les cieux obéissants s'inclinent sous ses pieds...[28]

> [Will you believe it? I can see another Caucasus
> Who is, on the holy hill,
> This other Prometheus with a divine face?
> Is he an enslaved Titan? A crucified God?
> O miracle! He blesses the Universe that oppresses him.
> The obeying Heavens bow under his feet...]

In the third and final part of Quinet's poem, the fusion between mythology and Christianity proves even more daring, when the archangels Michael and Raphael, coming down from Heaven, glimpse Prometheus on his rock, and stop in order to listen to his story,[29] after which they free him. Then Michael himself pierces the vulture with one of his arrows. When Prometheus asks the archangels whom he has to thank for his deliverance, Michael answers:

> Celui qui nous envoie et qui sait tes misères.
> Ton père est Jéhovah, et nous sommes tes frères.
> Des liens du sépulcre archange racheté,
> Il est temps de rentrer dans la sainte cité.[30]

> [The one who sends us and knows your misery.
> Your father is Jehovah, and we are your brothers.
> From the Tomb's bonds, redeemed archangel,
> It is time to return to the Holy city.]

Quinet is very daring, since he makes an archangel of the pagan hero and puts his martyrdom on the same level as the crucifixion of Jesus Christ. As Jacqueline Duchemin puts it, 'The author himself does not know how to situate his hero in regard to the new faith, and fails to integrate him clearly into the development of Genesis'.[31] But Quinet's originality here is precisely his attempt to combine myth and religion, and to glorify the latter by doing so. Quinet's approach to a comparison between Jesus Christ and Prometheus is not to throw light on religion by examining myths, as much as to make a synthesis of them in order to enrich the Christian dogma. But even if such a parallel was not in itself new, such a synthesis was. Indeed, before Quinet and Tertullian, and at the beginning of evangelization, religious scholars were careful not to draw a parallel between Prometheus and Jesus Christ, despite their common traits.

This might seem surprising when such scholars were not usually reluctant to use the theory of pagan forebodings, and make use of mythological characters to explain the Bible. The main reason for their unwillingness to emphasize the similarity between these two characters lies in the fact that the pagan one embodied the idea of transgression. The passages of the Bible that mainly justify the parallel between Jesus Christ and Prometheus are the story of the Agony in the Garden, and the Crucifixion itself. However, even if Jesus Christ expresses his misunderstanding of God's silence on Calvary, the next step is not taken, since 'the ways of God are unfathomable'.[32] Christ's 'My God, why have you forsaken me?' is a question, not a cry of revolt. In this respect, it is easy to perceive why religious scholars were unwilling to make use of Prometheus's figure to highlight the Bible.

However, in the nineteenth century, the main shift in the perception of the Prometheus myth had already occurred, and the aspect of transgression was now seen as secondary to the dual nature and human side of Prometheus. The fact that Quinet could compose a poem linking Prometheus and Jesus Christ reveals the evolution of the perception of Prometheus. If there were a parallel between the Prometheus myth and the Bible, it was now based on the personae of Prometheus and Jesus, not on the sin of Prometheus. At the end of the nineteenth century, the perception of Prometheus and the main trait of his persona made of him the benefactor of mankind, and the great sacrificial victim, hence the identification with Jesus Christ. However, even if for the previous generations of Romanticism, Christ had to a certain extent become a literary character, the situation changed in the context of the crisis of faith. In the light of the new syncretism, many Symbolist artists avoided referring to him. Although some Symbolists, like Jules Laforgue, were not afraid of using him in their poems — usually simply depicted as a man — most Symbolist artists attempted to build their syncretism entirely away from the Judeo-Christian system. But as the latter remained their point of reference, even if a negative one, the consequence of this characteristic of the Prometheus myth was that the Titan, for artists whose spirituality remained strong in spite of the disorientation of their faith, became the double of Jesus Christ.

Percy Bysshe Shelley, in *Prometheus Unbound*, had already compared one to the other, but Symbolist artists superimposed them. It is particularly striking in the pictorial field, where the traditional way in which Jesus Christ was represented was then applied to the Titan. In our final chapter, we shall make a detailed study of Gustave Moreau's depictions of Prometheus, which clearly refer to Christ, and are probably the most revealing examples of the use of Prometheus as a substitute for Him. However, a less famous painting, Briton Rivière's *Prometheus*,[33] depicts the Titan crucified on a sheer cliff, which has the same verticality as Christ's cross.

The eagle in the top centre of the canvas highlights the three-quarter viewpoint, and prolongs the bent elbow of Prometheus, thus producing the visual effect of a cross. The positioning of Prometheus's body — notably his feet — together with his bearing and the inclination of his head, are in line with the traditional Christian depiction of Jesus, and this assimilation was not restricted to the pictorial field.[34]

By the end of the nineteenth century, Symbolist artists were not alone in finding Prometheus appealing as a substitute for God. Paradoxically, although positivism was all that the Symbolists despised, it found in Prometheus the image of a sort of invincible conqueror. The Titan embodied mankind, with unlimited — godlike — powers, gained through the mastery of sciences. Although positivism does not necessarily imply a rejection of religion, its values were nonetheless not easily compatible with the idea of God. In this respect, Prometheus appeared as the perfect emblem of the belief that man had replaced God. However, such a use of the Promethean figure relied on the original myth itself, with the symbol of fire and the idea of transgression, and not on the persona Prometheus had eventually gained through history. However, it is worth noting here, since Prometheus as perceived through positivist eyes had a long life, and determined the interpretation of the Titan in the twentieth century, and even the twenty-first. It was with this interpretation of Prometheus in mind that the French state organized a competition at the time of the 1867 Exposition Universelle to commission a cantata to be performed in the newly built Palais de l'Industrie. Camille Saint-Saëns, who won the competition, used the Prometheus theme to extol France's industrialism, even though his cantata was not in the end performed.[35]

Prometheus was not the only mythological character to be used by Symbolist artists as a substitute for God. Orpheus also appeared as a key figure within Symbolist syncretism, and, intriguingly, artists who used the subject of Prometheus very often drawn to Orpheus as well.

Prometheus's Association with Orpheus

The figure of Orpheus within Symbolism had an essential and complex role, which was the subject of the exhaustive study by Dorothy Kosinski, *Orpheus in Nineteenth-Century Symbolism*,[36] to which frequent reference will be made. A contextualization of both myths is again required for the understanding of their affiliation, since the nature of their association lies fundamentally in the Symbolist appropriation of their symbolic value. Symbolist artists who took Prometheus as their subject also often count among their works a treatment of Orpheus. Franz Liszt, Gustave Moreau, G. F. Watts and Jean Delville all made use of both subjects, and occasionally drew noticeable stylistic parallels between Orpheus and Prometheus through the way in which they depicted them. We are therefore entitled to wonder what kind of link might have existed for Symbolist artists between the two Greek mythological characters.

Orpheus, both as myth and as persona, had evolved throughout history. In the Symbolist context, the Orpheus myth, like the Prometheus myth, took on a very particular meaning. Orpheus appears as a favourite Symbolist subject, but artists from that period mainly concentrated on his death rather than on other elements of the myth.

Orpheus the Thracian, son of the muse Calliope, had the power to enchant men, trees, stones, animals, streams, and even gods when striking the golden lyre that Apollo had given to him. He won the heart of Eurydice, but, while they were dancing during their wedding feast, a snake bit her heel and she died that same day. Inconsolable, Orpheus eventually went to the gates of Hades, to seek his beloved where no mortal could go. Orpheus succeeded in his attempt, since his music enchanted Charon, Cerberus, and Pluto himself, who decided to let Eurydice go back to the world of the living. However, Pluto warned Orpheus not to look behind to check if Eurydice was really following him until reaching the upper air. This is how Orpheus, too eager to see his wife, lost her for the second time. Faithful to Eurydice, the bereaved Orpheus did not smile back at any of the women who would have liked to console him. One day, Orpheus did not heed the outcry of the Maenads, a troop of women frenzied by Dionysian rites, who invited him to join their revels. Furious, they tore him to pieces. Thus scattered in Nature, his head nonetheless carried on singing to the miraculous sound of his lyre.

From this short account of the Orpheus myth we note that one of Orpheus's essential characteristics is that he appears as an enchanter. The second important element of the myth is not inherent to his persona, but an account within the myth: the love story between Orpheus and Eurydice. The mysterious death of Orpheus and its symbolic import forms another coherent aspect. Kosinski notes that 'the Symbolists demonstrate relatively minimal interest in the role of Eurydice, the Romantic tale of Orpheus' undying love, the gothic horror of his quest in Hades. [...] It is especially Orpheus' death which most fascinated the Symbolists. In contrast to images from earlier periods, the Symbolists eschew the sexually aggressive image of the onslaught of the crazed Maenads, in favour of the aftermath of the Bacchic destruction'.[37] From this we can see that the Symbolists focused and shaped their interpretation of the Orpheus myth on the third main element of the myth.

It is not surprising that Symbolist artists turned towards the most mysterious part of the myth, those linked to Orphism and to the symbolic disintegration of Orpheus in nature.[38] Symbolism being an attempt to regain a lost harmony, its understanding of the Orpheus myth was to perceive it as the symbol of a symbiotic connection with nature, and furthermore, the symbol of the synaesthetic ideal. It implies that the death of Orpheus, to Symbolist artists, appeared as the expression of their fulfilled ideal. Such an interpretation had an immediate consequence on the Symbolist pictorial treatment of the Orpheus myth. In such treatments of the subject, the landscape takes on a special significance. The Theosophist Edouard Schuré described these as 'psychological landscapes, playing a role analogous to that of the Wagnerian orchestra. Through nuances and harmonies it modulates emotions of the interior drama, prolonging those feelings in time and space. The Symbolists develop an anti-naturalist concept of the landscape, exploring the popular concepts of synaesthesiae and correspondences, to create landscapes which express an interior reality'.[39] In the case of Orpheus's death, what was expressed, more than an 'interior reality', was a communication, or even a communion, between the world of our perception and the Symbolist ideal fore-world.

This constitutes the first parallel with the Symbolist Promethean figure. If we view the two myths as pure literary accounts, it is pointless to look for a parallel between Orpheus and Prometheus. However, on a symbolic level, what they represent is striving towards the same end. Symbolists chose both Prometheus and Orpheus as symbols of a new realm, even if the means to reach that end differ in the two myths. In both cases, the new world order, characterised by the symbiosis with Nature, comes as the result of transgression. As we have already seen, in the Prometheus myth the new order arises from a glorification of action. In the case of Orpheus, however, the death of the mythological character, which marks the same cosmic accomplishment, symbolically takes the form of a harmonious fusion. In the Prometheus myth there is conquest; in the Orpheus myth, symbolic rebirth. This is why William Pencak expressed the idea that 'Orpheus is a gentler counterpart of Prometheus, giving humanity a taste of the bliss, rather than the power, enjoyed by the gods. Both are prophets of freedom, and thus rebels and outlaws who defy an old order of heaven and earth that would confine people and deprive them of the joy and sensitivity they need to be more than cogs in earthly or supernatural machinery'.[40] The 'active sin' of Prometheus, as Nietzsche calls it, is the obvious reason for his punishment, but Orpheus's 'sin' can be perceived on different levels. He goes where no living man had been before, which is in itself a clear demonstration of hubris. However, if we follow Dorothy Kosinski in focusing on Orpheus's death, his sin also relies on his 'revelation of secrets or mysteries to mankind'.[41] Orpheus would thus be close to Prometheus, who reveals self-awareness to mankind. However, both myths ultimately refer to a cosmogony, which probably explains why they are so important within Symbolist syncretism, and, most importantly, why an association was formed between both characters. Kosinski has examined closely the parallel between Orpheus and Jesus Christ[42] in Gustave Moreau's work, and we shall study in our next chapter the figure of Prometheus in Moreau's work. We shall now attempt to illustrate the nature of that association with the works of Jean Delville and George Frederic Watts.

With the exception of Briton Rivière and William Blake Richmond, Watts is the only British Symbolist artist known to have depicted Prometheus during the period we are interested in, and his picture of Prometheus is one of the most striking within Symbolism because of the dreamlike though energetic atmosphere that it conjures up. In *Prometheus* (Fig. III.3.1),[43] Watts chose to depict the powerful Titan on a rock, to which no chains bind him. Surrounded by comparatively small female figures, most probably the Oceanids, he gazes into the distance, sitting up, legs crossed and raised on his elbow, in a relaxed and meditative attitude. In the background of the painting, a textural semi-circle can be clearly perceived above Prometheus's head. This has a strong compositional effect, since the female figures at Prometheus's feet mirror that shape, with Prometheus thus represented in the middle of a circle. The upper semi-circle was originally intended as a flaming sun, emphasizing Prometheus's element, but Watts eventually decided to keep its outline only (Fig. III.3.2).

It is noteworthy that this painting is linked to *Chaos*, of which one version was entitled *The Titans*.[44] Watts had the habit of modifying and reworking his paintings, so that even though he started *Prometheus* on his return from Asia Minor in 1857, he was still at work on it in 1904, the year of his death. He was working on it while painting *Chaos*, which he had considering entitling *Cosmos*, or, even more interestingly, *Chaos passing to Cosmos*.[45] *Chaos* and *Prometheus* were part of the same vision. The landscape and the setting in which the Titans are represented, the female figures and the mysterious dawn are the same in the two paintings. Watts himself said that 'Silent and Mighty Repose should be stamped upon the character and disposition of the giants; and revolving centuries and cycles should glide personified by female figures of great beauty, beneath the crags upon which the mighty forms should lie'.[46] Since the Oceanids, here, are the symbolic representation of time,

FIG. III.3.1. Picture taken before Watts decided to cover up the flaming semi-circle

Fig. iii.3.2. George Frederic Watts, *Prometheus*, 1857–1904, Watts Gallery.
© Watts Gallery

Prometheus has to be interpreted accordingly. The figure of the Titan is part of this powerful atmospheric and symbolic landscape, and part of this cosmos at stake. The fact that Prometheus is encircled by the female representations of Time and by the globe-like outline he is gazing at takes on a new significance: the round pattern appears as a symbol for cosmic regeneration, and Prometheus is turning towards the dawn of a new world. Watts's focus on Prometheus here is the same as the Symbolists' focus on Orpheus: Prometheus is depicted endowed with cosmogonic powers, not with the mask of the rebel or the great martyr. Like the image of Orpheus, that of Prometheus is used by Watts to represent the symbolic ideal, and indeed Symbolist harmony with Nature.

The parallel between the two mythological figures is even clearer in Jean Delville's paintings entitled *Orphée aux enfers*[47] and *Prométhée*.[48]

The similarities are so great that, even though the latter was painted more than ten years after *Orphée aux enfers*, the two paintings seem almost to form a diptych. The narrow frames focus on the full-length figures in motion of the two mythological characters, Prometheus being presented in profile — emphasising the musculature of his body — whereas Orpheus' twisted torso, at a three-quarter angle, creates an impression of swirling motion that makes of his lyre a prolongation of his body. Their poses are almost identical, but treated from different viewpoints. The two landscapes in the background of the paintings are particularly striking. The compositions appear as full-length portraits, in which the landscape represents a mere part in terms of surface. However, it is much more than a simple setting. In the case of *Orphée aux enfers,* the landscape has two different functions: a narrative one, since Pluto, Persephone and Eurydice can be seen in the distance, and, more importantly, it also highlights the power of Orpheus. Indeed, his lyre seems to create a turmoil of the elements, a swirl in the Underworld, an effect which underlines Orpheus's cosmogonic powers. In this respect, even if Delville's painting refers to the love story of Orpheus and Eurydice, and not to the death of the mythological character, the magic power of Orpheus the enchanter is at the heart of his composition. In spite of the subject treated here, Eurydice herself is almost imperceptible in the background. It is paradoxical to note that *Orphée*,[49] Delville's most famous painting, depicts the favourite Symbolist topic within the myth — his severed head on his lyre floating on the water — but that the emphasis on Orpheus's power over nature is not as clear as in *Orphée aux enfers.*

If we now examine *Prométhée*, its background, composed of a similar chaotic landscape, seems to indicate that a cosmogony is at stake. Prometheus sheds light all around him. His titanic feet are surrounded by men, which emphasizes both the fact that his creatures are made to his own image, and are symbolically enlightened by him. His head, amongst planets, glows with fire. Symbolic dark clouds disintegrate around him. As Orpheus brandished his lyre above his head, so Prometheus carries the instrument of his cosmogonic powers above him: a radiant star encircled in a globe, which may symbolize self-awareness and the creative power of mankind. This depiction of Prometheus, with his luminous globe, recalls the illustrations of William Blake's myth-making work *The Urizen Books*, which also represent essential primitive forces and depict with great strength symbols of a cosmogony.[50]

An important detail shared by *Prométhée* and *Orphée aux enfers* comes from the depiction of the heads of the two mythological characters, surmounted by a sort of halo probably partly meant to represent the crown of martyrdom. In *Prométhée*, the star plays that role, as well as emphasizing the idea that the Titan's love for mankind is also the reason for his martyrdom. In the case of *Prométhée*, which was painted when Delville was deeply influenced by theosophy, the halo also symbolized the elemental force of fire. However, an examination of the preliminary sketches for the painting would tend to suggest the haloes were an essential aspect of the composition of Delville's paintings, since they reveal one of the main links between Orpheus and Prometheus. Indeed, their association might stem from the fact that both mythological characters were used by Symbolists as a substitute for Jesus Christ. It is particularly interesting that the composition of another of Delville's paintings, which is representative of his treatment of Christian subjects, *L'Homme-Dieu (The God-Man)*,[51] is very similar to that of his *Prométhée*.

Most troubling is the title, which could also apply to the Titan. In *L'Homme-Dieu*, a luminous Christ rises above a pyramid of men, smaller in scale, a procedure which will later be emphasized in *Prométhée*, whose composition was surely influenced by Delville's depiction of Christ. Indeed, in one of the first sketches of *Prométhée*,[52] in 1892, Delville had planned to represent Prometheus on his rock, freshly unbound and weakened, near the dead eagle that had tormented him. In a later sketch[53] dated 1904, Delville represented Prometheus rising on his rock again, but only to bring the 'traditionally' haloed muscular conqueror closer to the sky.

The bust of the Titan in that sketch is very similar to its depiction in the final version, in which Delville added the features shared by *Prométhée* and *L'Homme Dieu*, the presence of men on a small scale, and the dramatic sky. Such an evolution of the conception of *Prométhée* tends to prove that Delville's treatment of Jesus Christ influenced his perception and depiction of the Titan. Even more troubling is his last depiction of Prometheus, for the score of Scriabin's symphonic poem *Prometheus, the Poem of Fire* (Op. 60), in 1911.[54]

The influence of freemasonry and Theosophy on Delville dominates that drawing, which is a complex intermingling of symbols, amongst which are fire (the flame of Wisdom), and a lyre, the traditional emblem of Orpheus. The lotus, which represents the spirituality of Asia, earth, and Lucifer's five-branch star are also shown in this complex drawing. Radiating from the central design are stars, constellations, and systems seemingly in the making. Delville's interest in theosophy probably encouraged him to represent the other arch-rebel and bringer of light. We shall examine Scriabin's work and its significance in the perspective of the *Gesamtkunstwerk*, dear to the Symbolists' hearts, in the final chapter, in which we shall also consider the relationship between Theosophy and the last generation of Symbolists. However, we can see that Delville's drawing, with its combination of the Prometheus and Orpheus figures, is also representative of their close association within Symbolist syncretism. The identification of Orpheus with Christ by Symbolist artists was as considerable as that of Prometheus with the Biblical figure, and its roots were probably as deep. Dorothy Kosinski explains that 'the basis for this association of Orpheus and Christ is, of course, the similarity between the image of

Orpheus surrounded by animals tranquillised by his music and Christ as the Good Shepherd [...] This identification of Orpheus and Christ may depend, moreover, on other important similarities as well.[...] Christ's passion and resurrection echo the central episode of the Orphic theogony — Zagreus Dionysus' death and rebirth'.[55] It is interesting to note that Orpheus and Prometheus were associated with Christ for different qualities. Although both figures were used as substitutes for Christ, neither can be perceived as substitutes for each other. Both are identified with Christ because of their 'martyrdom', which recalls Christ's Passion, but if we only take that episode into account, we might put forward the idea that in respect of what they embody within the Symbolist syncretism, Prometheus and Orpheus are complementary characters.

Whereas the identification of Prometheus with Christ hinges on a shared love for mankind, which leads both of them to sacrifice, that of Orpheus with Christ seems to be based on death, and what ensues. The resurrection that follows Christ's Passion and Orpheus's mysterious song after his death present similarities. It is true that the deaths of most martyrs, as described in the Bible, are also of a supernatural nature, but the symbolic link existing between Jesus Christ and Orpheus is based on more than this characteristic of martyrdom. The manifestations of Christ and Orpheus after their deaths mark in both cases the beginning of a new understanding of the world. The miraculous resurrection of Christ marks the origin of Christianity as a cult, while the song of Orpheus's severed head symbolizes the source of a symbiotic relationship with nature. In this respect, Orpheus's mysterious death would be to the Symbolist syncretism what the resurrection of Christ is to Christianity, that is to say the symbolic origin of a religion established as such. Of course, Christianity derives from the belief in a God, and in a dogma, whereas Symbolism is not a cult as such: Symbolist syncretism stems from the belief in an Absolute, Art, and relies on a few essential principles, amongst which is the theory of synaesthesia and correspondences. Orpheus appears as the symbol par excellence of those notions appropriated by Symbolism, while Prometheus embodies the very freedom of mind (which also engenders the creative power) that paves the way for the Symbolist fore-world. In contrast to Christ, who is an object of adoration and who is perceived by Christians as a guide and tangible historical figure towards which Christianity converges, Orpheus and Prometheus are only two elements within the body of symbols that constitutes Symbolism.

This specificity of Symbolism explains their association as substitutes for Jesus Christ. Although most Symbolist artists rejected Christianity, their references were nonetheless Judeo-Christian, and the image of Christ, in the pictorial, literary, and artistic field at large, had left its mark on those artists, who tried to find a set of symbols to conjure up the evocative power that His image conveyed. The Prometheus and Orpheus myths, which present many similarities with the story of Jesus Christ, were ideal symbols to conjure up such power, despite the fact that each myth only partially evoked Christ's story. The nature of their association appears complementary, bearing in mind that the elements from those myths that communicate with the Bible are the same episodes that appealed to the Romantics, before they transmitted this interest to the Symbolists.

Now that we have put into perspective why Prometheus played such an important role within the Symbolist syncretism and what significance his figure could take in the context of the crisis of faith, notably through his association with Jesus Christ and Orpheus, it is now time to examine how the sets of symbols that he embodied during the Symbolist period took shape in artistic works of the time. We shall see that Prometheus retained his protean quality at the end of the nineteenth century, and that the treatment of his myth highlighted all the richness of the use of symbols at that time. In the Symbolist context, homogenised by the common goal of reaching a fore-world, whatever form it took, the Promethean figure appeared as a protean but coherent image. Prometheus's image varied according to different criteria, but the multi-faceted aspect that the Titan took at the end of the nineteenth and the beginning of the twentieth century was not the symptom of a fragmentation of the symbol that he became. It did not mark the death of the Prometheus myth as such, after its transformation into a symbol. We should rather perceive the Prometheus symbol as a prism, whose facets condensed the various beams of representation of the Titan. It is in order to see the coherence of the Prometheus figure behind his multiple masks that I shall opt for a typology in the final chapter of this study.

Notes to Chapter 3

1. Some Symbolists, such as Joris-Karl Huysmans, eventually returned to their original faith.
2. Richard Wagner, *Religion and Art*, in *Prose Works*, vol. VI, trans. by Ashton Ellis (London, 1897).
3. A. Mockel, *Propos de littérature* (1894) in *Esthétique du Symbolisme* (Brussels: Palais des académies, 1962), p. 85.
4. Dorothy M. Kosinski, *Orpheus in Nineteenth Century Symbolism* (London: U.M.I Research Press, 1989), p. 67.
5. Ibid., p. 69.
6. Ibid., p. 64.
7. Richard Jenkyns, *The Victorians and Ancient Greece* (Oxford: Blackwell, 1980), p. 228. Writing of Goethe and the influence of Plato on his works, Jenkyns states that 'Goethe bends Plato in a less abstract direction: it is not dialectic that leads us on but the Eternal feminine'.
8. Ibid., p. 228.
9. Swedenborg, in *The New Jerusalem*, had already put forward the idea of correspondences, but it was Baudelaire's poems, in particular 'Correspondances' and 'La Vie antérieure' which made the theory popular.
10. Marchal, *Lire le Symbolisme*, p. 173.
11. Ibid., p. 176.
12. Kosinski, *Orpheus in Nineteenth Century Symbolism*, p. 67.
13. The work of Jules Laforgue, for example, can be seen as a poetical version of Schopenhauer's philosophical texts. However, the writings of Thomas Mann also reflect a strong interest in Schopenhauer.
14. In 1874, Ribot had published *La Philosophie de Schopenhauer*.
15. In Joris-Karl Huysmans's novel *A Rebours*, Des Esseintes devotes a whole page to an apologia for the German philosopher.
16. Schopenhauer was the first Western philosopher to have access to translations of Indian Vedic and Buddhist texts.
17. Odilon Redon, *Le Bouddha*, c. 1905, pastel on paper, 98 × 73 cm, Musée d'Orsay, Paris, is the best example of this interest.
18. Symbolist artists, following the model of Des Esseintes, themselves often collected exotic objects, most of the time Chinese. However, Lord Leighton and the French writer Pierre Loti,

who both had an entire room made in the style of an Arabian mosque, could not match the extravagance of the fictitional character.

19. Listening to the advice of her mother Herodias, Salome agrees to dance for Herod providing that he grants her John's head.

20. On the theme of Salome, see Robert Ross, 'A Note on 'Salomé', in *Salomé*, by Oscar Wilde (London: Faber, 1989), pp. xv–xvii, and Tomoko Sato, 'Salomé, the Legacy of Oscar Wilde', in *The Wilde Years*, ed. by Tomoko Sato and Lionel Lambourne (London: Barbican Centre, 2000), pp. 60–73.

21. 'Here is the real Prometheus, the omnipotent God, pierced by blasphemy'.

22. Duchemin, p. 112.

23. Edgar Quinet, *Prométhée* (Paris, 1838).

24. For a detailed study of Edgar Quinet's *Prométhée*, see Duchemin, pp. 112–15.

25. Which would be the equivalent of *Prometheus porphyros*, whose significance, however, would be 'Fire carrier' more than 'inventor', and, naturally, 'Prometheus Bound' and 'Prometheus Unbound'.

26. Duchemin, p. 112.

27. Quinet, *Prométhée*, I, iv, p. 53.

28. Quinet, *Prométhée*, II, v, pp. 75–79.

29. As Duchemin sees it, p. 116, Quinet tries to link Prometheus's account to that of Genesis.

30. Quinet, *Prométhée*, III, iii, p. 121.

31. Duchemin, p. 117.

32. Romans 11.33.

33. Briton Rivière, *Prometheus,* 1889, oil on canvas, 89.5 x 58.7 cm, Ashmolean Museum, Oxford.

34. In 1900, Jean Lorrain and Ferdinand Hérold wrote a lyrical tragedy set to music by Gabriel Fauré, a tragedy characterized by a return to God. Paul Bertagnolli has studied this work, noting that it was 'designed for a giant amphitheatre in Béziers, [and] articulates Languedoc's regional identity and honors populist theatrical traditions' (Paul Bertagnolli, *Prometheus in Music: Representations of the Myth in the Romantic Era* (Aldershot: Ashgate, 2005), p. 189).

35. Ibid., p. 204. George Bizet, Jules Massenet, and Peter Benoit also entered the competition, but Bizet's and Massenet's cantatas are now lost.

36. Kosinski, *Orpheus in Nineteenth-Century Symbolism* (London: U.M.I. Research Press, 1989).

37. Ibid., p. xiv.

38. Orphic cults did not appear before the sixth century B.C. and their leader, Orpheus, is not the same as Hesiod's. However, Kosinki notes that their personae are 'inextricably intermingled' (ibid., p. 2). Although Orphic cults were devoted to Zagreus-Dionysus, Kosinski notes that 'Orpheus' own fate — his descent into Hades and death by dismemberment — parallels the story of the Orphic deity himself' (ibid.). Therefore, the intermingling of both Orpheuses is particularly clear in the Symbolist interpretation of the myth, since it emphasizes, through the focus of Orpheus' death, the symbolic reunification and communion with nature.

39. Kosinski, *Orpheus in Nineteenth-Century Symbolism*, p. xiv.

40. William Pencak, 'Lyres against the Law', *Legal Studies Forum*, 23.3 (1999), 293–314 (p. 294).

41. Kosinski, *Orpheus in Nineteenth-Century Symbolism*, p. 189.

42. Ibid., pp. 69–73; 151–55; 192–98.

43. George Frederic Watts, *Prometheus*, 1857–1904, oil on canvas, 53.3 × 66 cm, Watts Gallery, Compton, Surrey.

44. *Chaos* was part of a scheme for a fresco in a great hall. The first version, a study in blue and gold, was *Chaos, or The Titans*, 1873–75, oil on canvas, 71.1 × 111.8 cm, Watts Gallery, Compton, Surrey; the other versions are *Chaos*, 1882, oil on canvas, 302 × 104 cm, Tate Britain, London, and *Chaos*, 1882, oil on canvas, 317.5 × 104 cm, Watts Gallery, Compton, Surrey.

45. Cf. Mary Watts's catalogue at the Watts Gallery, Compton, Surrey, p. 24.

46. Ibid., p. 24.

47. Jean Delville, *Orphée aux enfers*, 1896, oil on canvas, dimensions unknown; private collection, reproduced on the website www.jeandelville.org.

48. Jean Delville, *Prométhée*, 1907, oil on canvas, 500 × 250 cm, Free University, Brussels, reproduced on the website www.jeandelville.org.

49. Jean Delville, *Orphée*, 1893, private collection.
50. Delville greatly admired the work of Blake, which he may have discovered through his Pre-Raphaelite friends.
51. Jean Delville, *L'Homme Dieu*, 1901–03, oil on canvas, 550 × 500 cm, Groeningemuseum, Bruges.
52. Jean Delville, Study for *Prométhée*, 1892, ink and watercolour on paper, 34 × 22 cm, private collection, reproduced on www.jeandelville.org.
53. Jean Delville, Study for *Prométhée*, 1904, ink on paper, 16 × 12 cm, private collection, reproduced on www.jeandelville.org.
54. Delville's painting had given Scriabin the idea of writing his *Poem of Fire*, and Delville designed the cover of the score especially for his friend.
55. Kosinski, *Orpheus in Nineteenth-Century Symbolism*, p. 8. Kosinski also mentions amongst those similarities a parallel between Orpheus in Hades and Christ's harrowing of hell, as well as one between Orphic cults and Christianity.

PART IV

The Many Faces of Prometheus

The different facets Prometheus took at the turn of the nineteenth century derive, to a variable extent, from the different traits the Prometheus myth gained during its history and evolution. This explains why, in my 'typology', certain aspects of Symbolism or certain characteristics of the Promethean symbol that I previously examined will appear as partial criteria within its structure. The original traits of Prometheus's persona ('Prometheus the fire-giver', 'Prometheus the rebel', and 'Prometheus *plasticator*') will still be perceptible, even if on a symbolic level. Similarly, the religious borders that gave shape to the Symbolist map of Europe, as evoked in the previous chapter, will clearly appear in the artistic works that I shall analyse to determine Prometheus's various features at the turn of the century. Even as a symbol, Prometheus still derives from the combination of those historical and cultural elements that form part of the constitution of myths.

Among the different faces of Prometheus, I shall distinguish a vitalist Titan, who essentially developed in Germany and in the countries that were culturally associated with it. I shall also consider the mask Prometheus took, especially in England, where there was a fertile intermingling with the Pygmalion myth deriving from the original Prometheus *plasticator*. However, before observing these two facets of the Prometheus prism, I shall return for the last time to the Christianised Prometheus, to explore the way in which Symbolist artists, notably Gustave Moreau, pushed the association between Prometheus and Jesus Christ to its limit, and used it to illustrate the Symbolist *désenchantement*.

CHAPTER 1

Gustave Moreau,
Prometheus and Jesus Christ

Gustave Moreau used the subject of Prometheus several times, and his famous paintings undoubtedly played an important part in the parallel drawn between Prometheus and Jesus Christ during the *fin de siècle* period. The examination of his pictures related to the Titan provide a key to understanding the specificity as well as the value of the Symbolist association between both figures. Moreover, the fact that he repeatedly used Prometheus as a source of inspiration, with different focuses, meant that Moreau thoroughly explored the significance of Prometheus within the Symbolist debate.

If we consider all Moreau's works on the Prometheus theme, we perceive a subtle use of the superimposed figure of Jesus Christ, a process through which Symbolist concerns seem to emerge. From an aesthetic point of view, Moreau paved the way for other Symbolist artists. His most famous painting of Prometheus dates from 1868, and is entitled *Prométhée*[1] (Fig. IV.1.1). The painting was first exhibited at the 1869 Salon in Paris, but it was not a great success, remaining unsold in Moreau's studio. In some respects, such a treatment of the Titan might have seemed adventurous at that time. The pictorial tradition of portraying Prometheus's punishment, especially in France, was to emphasize Prometheus's unbearable suffering, since the main focus on the Prometheus myth before the turn of the nineteenth century was on the chastisement of rebellion, from a theological and political perspective. After the striking paintings of Titian and Rubens highlighting the horror of his punishment, Prometheus was usually depicted lying on his rock, contorted with pain. The revolution introduced by Shelley and Goethe in the interpretation of the myth had not yet reached the pictorial world. Interestingly enough, the main depictions of Prometheus during the first half of the nineteenth century were executed by academic painters in search of great historical or mythical subjects, and not by avant-garde artists who might have projected a new perception of Prometheus onto the canvas. Thus, French artists like Pradier, Lehmann and Ribot made paintings on the subject of *Prometheus Bound*, using and reusing the focus that had been adopted to represent him since Titian and Rubens. Although Moreau himself used sketches of Pradier's sculpture of Prometheus[2] with his legs bent, he nevertheless chose to represent Prometheus in an upright, conquering position. Ignoring the vulture which devours his liver, Prometheus's piercing eyes stare into the distance,[3]

FIG. IV.I.I. Gustave Moreau, *Prométhée*, Musée Gustave Moreau, Paris.
© RMN-Grand Palais / René-Gabriel Ojéda

as a reminder of the etymology of his name ('foresight'). Like most of Moreau's characters, his *Prométhée,* both because of his posture and because of his athletic build, has the quality of a sculpture from Ancient Greece.[4] As a reminiscence of Hesiod, Prometheus is bound to a column. At his feet, we can see another dead vulture, which underlines his power as well as the prospect of his liberation.

However, the most striking feature of Gustave Moreau's *Prométhée* lies in his likeness to Jesus Christ. Moreau originally was inspired not by Shelley, Goethe or Byron, but by Joseph de Maistre, whose writings put forward the idea that Prometheus was a prefiguration of Jesus Christ. Such an interpretation of the pagan figure is elaborated upon in de Maistre's ninth dialogue of *Soirées de Saint-Pétersbourg* (1821), of which Moreau had a copy in his library. In a smaller version of *Prométhée* entitled *Prométhée Enchaîné,*[5] executed by Moreau in 1869, the painter inscribed in gold letters at the bottom of the canvas Prometheus's famous words from *Prometheus Bound*'s opening scene, also quoted in Joseph de Maistre's work: VIDETE QUANTA PATIOR A DEO DEUS.[6] The choice of quotation seems deliberate, since the same words could have been pronounced by Jesus Christ himself when he felt abandoned by God. And indeed, Moreau's treatment of Prometheus emphasizes all the similarities that might exist between the two characters. Moreau depicts Prometheus with a bleeding forehead, a feature normally confined to depictions of Christ. Even though the Titan, in the final painting, is suffused with light, notably because of a small symbolic flame surmounting his brow, his head is not haloed. However, in sketches for *Prométhée,* this element of the painting was less allusive: in a drawing from 1868 which is of the same size as the final painting, it is haloed. Similarly, in a very small sketch,[7] Prometheus's 'holiness' is suggested by the wings of the vulture, whose position produces the clear impression that they belong to Prometheus. These designs were eventually discarded by Moreau in the painting he exhibited at the 1869 Salon, but Prometheus's features, which undoubtedly follow the traditional depiction of Jesus Christ, are enough to draw a parallel between the Christian and the pagan figures. Although the literary association between Prometheus and Jesus Christ had already been exploited in the 1860s, such a comparison was not commonplace in the pictorial field during that period.

This association is repeated fruitfully in other works by Gustave Moreau. In a letter dated 19 October 1868, Moreau evokes the weight of guilt that invariably seems to be the burden of mankind. Writing to a friend, he mentions 'the poetical traditions, which all situate at the beginning of mankind a golden age from which man is rejected because of his own fault. Do I have to remind you of this first revolt, symbolized by Prometheus?'.[8] Although Gustave Moreau came from a Catholic family, and therefore from a Judeo-Christian background, the reference he chooses to illustrate original sin is that of Prometheus, not of the Bible. This confirms what we have seen earlier when examining the Symbolist crisis of faith and the rejection of established religions. In order to build Symbolist syncretism, Greek myths and 'exotic imports' were substituted for the main cults. Moreau's letter, in terms of cultural references, is particularly revealing, as to illustrate his point the painter quotes Plato, whose idealism was so dear to the hearts of Symbolist artists. Moreau continues: 'Talking about the moral human failing, he [Plato] says that: "One has to blame the creator rather than the creature. Lord God of gods, seeing the human beings subjected to the generation had lost (or destroyed) in them the inestimable gift, determined to subject them to a treatment that would both punish and regenerate them." Eventually, he says this remarkable thing: "Nature and the abilities of Man have been changed and corrupted within him as early as his birth".'[9] Two important points emerge from this letter. Firstly, the fact that from a cultural point of view, the values we previously attributed to Symbolism are also Moreau's own, even if, chronologically, he appears as a precursor. Secondly, his depiction of Prometheus is unconventional, in the sense that his interpretation of the Titan operates on a symbolic level. Moreau here chooses Prometheus to epitomize mankind, which also allows him to give an instance of where the punishment for original sin against the gods is faced, not borne as a burden. To borrow Nietzsche's words again, Gustave Moreau, with his *Prométhée*, gives 'active sin' as an example, which also appears as a first step against the human feeling of guilt.

Moreau's treatment of the subject reflects the turning-point initiated by Shelley and Goethe. By portraying Prometheus, Moreau attempts to represent the dawn of a new golden age, in which man would recognize that his responsibility is not involved in original sin. His painting may symbolize the 'regeneration' of man, as quoted from Plato. Moreau clearly indicated the symbolic value he intended to give to his painting: 'the figure of a man of sacrifice and thought at grips, in life, with the torments and attacks of brutishness, and base matter'.[10] The Promethean figure used by Moreau appears as the synthesis of the different symbols he took on, as a rebel, as the bearer of the fire of knowledge and Reason, and, most of all, as the figurehead of Symbolist idealism against materialism. Surprisingly, art critics such as de Ponmartin did not view the work as the expression of a new conception of Prometheus, seeing instead a faithful illustration of Aeschylus's *Prometheus Bound*: 'It is the first time that I am shown the Prometheus I had dreamt of: the wounded forehead, the chest bleeding, but with a serene face, because he is in possession of the gods' secrets, and because he knows that his immortal idea will survive to all those perishable divinities. A landscape of a great and austere beauty frames this scene worthy of Aeschylus'.[11] Théophile Gautier, however, immediately understood the focus of Gustave Moreau's *Prométhée*. He wrote: 'M. Gustave Moreau has not given his Prometheus the colossal proportions of Aeschylus's *Prometheus Bound*. He is not a Titan. He is a man to whom it seems to us that the artist intended to lend some likeness with Jesus Christ, of whom, according to a few Fathers of the Church, he is the type and object of the pagan prediction.'[12] Gautier identifies the specificity of Gustave Moreau's painting, which is the parallel drawn between Prometheus and Jesus Christ. And the need that Gautier feels to trace the origin of such a parallel in history is also revealing of the fact that in France, at the end of the 1860s, the treatment of Prometheus as a Christianized character, in the pictorial field, was not common. But Gustave Moreau went even further in his interpretation of the Titan. *Prométhée* was only the first of a series of paintings on the subject of Prometheus, and Moreau would make use of all the power the Promethean symbol could offer to a Symbolist sensitivity.

Pierre-Louis Mathieu, in his complete edition of Gustave Moreau's paintings, notes that 'the two paintings he [Moreau] showed in 1869, *Prometheus* and *Jupiter and Europa* mark a backward step as compared with [...] more personal works [...]. They were carefully considered, highly finished pictures, designed for the salon, with all that implies of the artificial and conventional in the composition'.[13] Considering the originality of Gustave Moreau's treatment of Prometheus as opposed to previous French works of art based on the same subject, we have to disagree with Pierre-Louis Mathieu's statement on the 'artificial and conventional' aspect of the painting. Moreover, he seems to imply that Moreau chose great mythical subjects in order to find favour with the jury. This may have been partly the case with *Jupiter and Europa*, but Gustave Moreau's repeated depiction of Prometheus, after 1869, suggest that the Titan represented much more to him than an academic subject, and that, far from it, Prometheus would have been, to him, one of the most personal subjects. In that, he belonged with a few other figures and scenes that haunt his works, Salome, Oedipus, and the Pietà being the most obvious. However, Prometheus also had a particular value within Moreau's work. More than a decade after the 1869 Salon, Moreau painted the subject again,[14] in a particularly interesting context. This painting bears the same title as the 1868 original, and appears as a variation of it. Moreau executed his new *Prométhée*[15] between 1880–1885 as a gift for his friend Charles Ephrussi. The dimensions of Ephrussi's painting (18 × 11 cm), and the fact that Gustave Moreau chose watercolour, cast a new light on the composition of *Prométhée*. Although Moreau abandoned the 'privileged academic features' (the large dimensions and use of oil on canvas), the composition of *Prométhée* remained the same. This choice alone is enough to prove that in Moreau's eyes, more than a decade after the 1869 Salon, *Prométhée* represented more than a perfectly executed painting fulfilling all the requirements of the 'Academy'. Moreover, the inscription on the back is a clear indication of the value Moreau attributed to the small watercolour. The autograph letter pasted onto the back of the frame reads as follows: 'My dear Monsieur Ephrussi, Will you make me very happy and show me once again all your kind sympathy so often shown before? Place on your wall this small reminder of me. It will tell you always, however feebly, of the deep esteem and great affection that I have borne towards you.' It may be that Ephrussi himself asked Moreau to paint a reproduction of *Prométhée* for him, and that he therefore chose the subject of the painting. A second hypothesis would be that Moreau knew how much Ephrussi liked the original *Prometheus* and that he decided to paint a small version of it to please his friend. However, Moreau's autograph letter leads us to believe that Prometheus was not a commission at all, but simply a present from the painter to the collector, and he states clearly that he would like the painting to be seen by his friend as a 'small reminder of [him]'. He chose to give it to his friend as representative of both his art and himself. Having said that, it seems impossible to agree with Pierre-Louis Mathieu that the choice of Prometheus as a subject was purely strategic. To push the analysis of Moreau's letter further, we might even venture the idea that there was some sort of identification between Moreau and Prometheus. However, if such relation existed in the mind of the painter, it had nothing to do with the sort of identification that united Victor Hugo and the

Titan. The association between the French poet and Prometheus was mainly based on the heroism and greatness of character of the Greek figure, which particularly appealed to Hugo. In Moreau's case, and through his Symbolist sensitivity, the image of Prometheus was perceived on a different level, which gave shape to the various treatments of the Titan accomplished by the painter, as well as to the special connection between himself and his subject.

After the 1868 *Prométhée*, the identification with Jesus Christ increased. The athletic build of Prometheus in the original painting disappeared in later depictions of the same scene, the result of which was that, from being 'Christ-like', Prometheus became a proper avatar of Jesus Christ. The way in which he was depicted combined all the features of the traditional representation of Jesus Christ in Western Europe. But Moreau pushed further than Shelley in literature the consequences of such an association between the pagan and Christian characters. It is often said that in terms of artistic trends, the pictorial arts are usually the last to reflect such movements. But Moreau did more than illustrate what the greatest European poets had written at the turn of the century, even if he was one of the first painters in Europe to take their work into account. An unfinished painting, *Prométhée Foudroyé* [*Prometheus struck by lightning*],[16] executed not long after the 1868 *Prométhée*, contains the key to the Symbolist association between Jesus Christ and Prometheus.

The composition of the painting is entirely different from the various versions of *Prométhée* examined earlier. The setting is the same as in *Prométhée*, and Prometheus is still at the centre of the painting, but he is no longer in the foreground, and is encompassed in a wider view. This time, Moreau adopted a pyramidal composition similar to that of his famous *Jupiter and Semele*. At his feet and on the lower part of Prometheus's rock are ten lamenting Oceanids. Such an organization of the painting has the advantage of displaying a hierarchy, both spatial and symbolic. The godlike figure is in the upper part of the composition, and the only element above him, in the literal as well as the figurative sense, is Jupiter's lightning, which strikes him. On the lower part of the painting, one of the Oceanids, gripping Prometheus's left leg, looks at him with adoration, while another wrings her hands in despair. Moreau had used a similar composition in other paintings, but the organization of space within this picture also recalls the traditional depiction of the deposition of Jesus Christ, a reference that must undoubtedly be taken into account when examining *Prométhée Foudroyé*. The ten creatures on the sides of Prometheus's rock recall the Marys and Mary Magdalene at the foot of the Cross. Even if the setting and landscape are the same as in *Prométhée*, some of Prometheus's features have been altered. He no longer sits on his rock, but rests his body vertically on it, as if it were a cross. His right knee is bent, which emphasizes the posture of Jesus Christ himself on the cross. What most strikingly links Prometheus to Christ in Moreau's painting is the Titan's face. Overwhelmed with pain and exhaustion, Prometheus cannot hold up his head, and closes his eyes. Even if we know that half of Prometheus's punishment lies in the fact that he is immortal, and that he has to bear his suffering indefinitely, Moreau gives to the Titan's face the expression of a man who, after a long agony, breathes his last. Nothing of his conquering attitude and strength is left from *Prométhée*. His martyrdom is emphasized by the fact that Prometheus's head, here again, is haloed. A few subtle elements in the composition strengthen the parallel between the two martyrs. Behind Prometheus's head, the tracing of a cross is suggested by the shape given to the vulture's wings, placed at a right angle. The interest of such a feature within the painting is twofold. Not only does it strengthen the likeness between Prometheus and Jesus Christ, through a striking visual effect: it also creates the impression that the wings belong to Prometheus himself, which gives him an angelic quality.[17] Facing the combination of those specific features, which appear as a deeply conscious and sustained evocation of Christ's Passion, the question of the value this parallel held for Moreau has to be raised.

Pierre-Louis Mathieu, understandably linking *Prométhée* and *Prométhée Foudroyé*, suggested that both are literary paintings,[18] whose aim was faithfully to transpose Aeschylus's work (or, at least, its spirit) into the pictorial field, since the end of the trilogy in which Prometheus could have been struck by Jupiter's lightning was lost. He based this interpretation on the fact that the painter chose to apply to the canvas of *Prométhée Enchaîné* the verses by Aeschylus quoted earlier. Mathieu suggests that 'in an unfinished picture in the Gustave Moreau Museum [*Prométhée Foudroyé*] it is the dénouement of the tragedy that he represents, the moment when Prometheus was struck down by lightning, "still holding the divine torch whose flame shall give light to the world".'[19] If it truly is the dénouement of Aeschylus's tragedy that Moreau attempts to depict, as Mathieu proposes, Moreau is far from what Aeschylus had intended, since, as mentioned in our first chapter, the Greek playwright probably had in mind a reconciliation between Prometheus and Zeus, based on the repentance of the Titan. However, even if in *Prométhée Foudroyé*, a victorious Zeus strikes Prometheus down by lightning (as he threatens to do in *Prometheus Bound*), Moreau's commentary on his painting lets us believe that he does not try to represent the 'moral dénouement' of Aeschylus's trilogy by depicting another punishment of Prometheus. Moreau's *Prométhée Foudroyé* probably should not be understood as a pictorial account of Aeschylus, but as a symbolic scene. This is the interpretation that Moreau's own commentary invites us to make. By noticing that Prometheus 'still [holds] the divine torch whose flame shall give light to the world', Moreau uses laudatory terms to describe the work of Prometheus, which proves that his interpretation of him is not a reading of *Prometheus Bound* focusing on the question of rebellion and punishment. In this regard, the idea that *Prométhée Foudroyé* is not a literary painting can reasonably be upheld. Moreover, if Moreau had shared such an interpretation, the interweaving of pagan and Christian elements within the painting would not have been significant.

On the other hand, the nature of the association of Jesus Christ with Prometheus is suggested in the second part of Moreau's commentary, when he mentions that '[Prometheus's] flame shall give light to the world'. The light Moreau refers to is entirely symbolic. We have already frequently suggested what Prometheus's flame might represent on a symbolic level: the awakening of conscience, human feelings, but also the mastery of sciences, and the development of knowledge. We also briefly mentioned the fact that many positivists, from the first half of the nineteenth century, adopted Prometheus as an allegory of the omnipotence of sciences, and, consequently, of man.[20] However, these are certainly not the figurative meanings that we have to lend to Moreau's words. According to the Positivists, the nineteenth century, with its extraordinary scientific developments, was a century of accomplishments. In contrast, Moreau's use of the future tense (the divine torch whose flame will give light to the world) appears enigmatic. The Positivist Prometheus was not a seer nor a prophet, but a set allegory of the triumph of man. If we now consider the way in which Prometheus is represented by Moreau in *Prométhée Foudroyé*, weakened and exhausted by his perpetual suffering, no sign of such triumph can be perceived. Hence the problematic aspect of Moreau's words of hope. However, in this matter, the omnipresent reference to Jesus Christ is enlightening.

Both Jesus Christ and Prometheus sacrifice themselves for mankind, clinging to their love for humanity, and to their conviction that men are worth such a gesture. And we might assume that Moreau brings together Prometheus and Jesus Christ to emphasize their human side — which to a large extent leads them to martyrdom — in order to represent the aspirations of mankind. The fact that both Christ and Prometheus are the symbols of a new potential world order might explain why Moreau, in some way, identifies with Prometheus, since a new world order would primarily be the fruit of artistic creation. However, Moreau originally evoked the figure of the Titan in his notes in order to define the weight of the original burden. Thus, the combination of a scene of crucifixion and Prometheus's punishment in *Prométhée* is significant. The sacrifices of Jesus Christ and Prometheus result from their unconditional love for mankind, but are also justified by their faith in the potential of humanity. Jesus Christ expiates men's sin in the hope of regeneration, and Prometheus endures his punishment in the knowledge that a new era will come.

What Moreau seems to signify in *Prométhée Foudroyé* is the uncertain worthiness of mankind, which therefore questions the possibility of a new world order, of the Symbolist ideal set against materialism or 'vile matter', as Moreau himself put it. In *Prométhée Foudroyé* Prometheus still holds the torch, but the expression on his face seems to show that it is the end of his battle. And this questioning remains suspended, like Jupiter's lightning, which symbolizes the clinging of men to old sets of values, by fear of becoming their own creators. Prometheus, associated with Jesus Christ, would therefore embody the possibility of the realization of the Symbolist ideal, the power of artistic creation, but also the acknowledgement of its very impotence. The evolution of the treatment of Prometheus in Moreau's paintings allows us to grasp the meaning of the current association between Jesus Christ and the Titan. During the *fin de siècle* in France, the Christianization of Prometheus was just a means to an end. The basis of the parallel between the Christian and the pagan figures, for Symbolist artists, must be understood on another level, which is that both of them, through their sacrifice, embody the aspirations of mankind, and the hope for a new world. But in the difficult context of the late nineteenth century, in which Symbolist idealism clashed with the reality of industrial society, the synthesis between Prometheus and Jesus Christ is also emblematic of the *désenchantement* and, to a certain extent, of the impotence of the Symbolist artist. However, this mask of Prometheus was only one amongst many. In England and in Germany, where the shock of the rise of the industrial society was perceived as less brutal, or at least was not felt so deeply, the representations of Prometheus took other forms.

Notes to Chapter 1

1. Gustave Moreau, *Prométhée*, 1868, oil on canvas, 205 × 122 cm, Musée Gustave Moreau, Paris

2. James Pradier, *Prometheus*, exhibited 1827 (Paris Salon), Louvre. It was for many years in the jardin des Tuileries.

3. Gustave Moreau himself described his *Prométhée* with the following words: 'Like the pilot watching from the ship's prow, he gazes at the icy spaces in the distance, sounding all the horizons and smiling in his dream, while the blood flows from his side, under the thirsty beak of the ever insatiable vulture' (in the catalogue of the Gustave Moreau Museum, N° 196).

4. Gustave Moreau also made a wax statuette of Prometheus, represented in the same position as in this painting.

5. Gustave Moreau, *Prométhée Enchaîné*, 1869, oil on canvas, 46 × 29 cm, private collection.

6. 'See what I, a god, suffer at the hands of God!'.

7. Gustave Moreau, *Studies for Déjanire et Prométhée*, c. 1868, brown ink on tracing paper, Musée Gustave Moreau, Paris.

8. Quoted in Geneviève Lacambre, *Gustave Moreau: 1826–1898* (Paris: Réunion des Musées Nationaux, 1998), p. 99.

9. Lacambre, *Gustave Moreau*, p. 100.

10. In the archives of the Musée Gustave Moreau, Holland-bound notebook, p. 73.

11. *L'Univers Illustré* (Paris), 8 May 1869.

12. *L'Illustration* (Paris), 15 May 1869.

13. Pierre-Louis Mathieu, *Gustave Moreau: Complete Edition of the Finished Paintings, Watercolours and Drawings* (Oxford: Phaidon, 1977), p. 104.

14. Moreau also repainted the upper left part of the original 1868 Prometheus in 1880.

15. Gustave Moreau, *Prometheus* (1880–1885), watercolour with white and gold highlights, 18 × 11 cm, private collection.

16. Gustave Moreau, *Prométhée Foudroyé*, c. 1869, oil on canvas, 260 x 137 cm, Musée Gustave Moreau.

17. As mentioned earlier, Moreau had already considered using that effect in *Prométhée*, but only decided to use it in *Prométhée Foudroyé*, which, in the perspective of an association between him and Christianity, might tend to prove that symbolically, according to Moreau, the association between the two characters is not entirely complete before the final punishment of Prometheus.

18. Gustave Moreau's reputation as a 'literary painter' is not necessarily justified.

19. Mathieu, *Moreau, Complete Edition*, p. 106.

20. Pierre Albouy *Mythes et mythologies dans la littérature française* (Paris: Armand Colin, Paris, 1969), p. 161, puts forward the idea that Ballanche initiated what Albouy calls 'the St-Simonian fortune' of Prometheus: 'The Titan becomes the hero of progress, which makes of man the master of the earth, the sea, and the sky'.

CHAPTER 2

The Vitalist Prometheus

As mentioned in the previous section, when attempting to draw a Symbolist map of Europe, common aesthetic features were found to depend greatly on the particular nature of the crises Symbolists went through. This pattern encompassed cultural as well as geographical specificities, and it is therefore not surprising that the Prometheus of Germanic artists was quite different from the Belgian and French one. Yet there were many points of contact between Symbolist artists of various nationalities, and generalizations are not always helpful. The German artist Anselm Feuerbach, for example, who lived in Antwerp, Paris, Rome, and Venice, amongst other cities, painted Prometheus in a Christianized way. His monumental painting, part of the ceiling frescoes commissioned in 1874 for the auditorium of the new academy building in Vienna, shows Prometheus in a manner which presents many similarities with Rubens.[1] But, as with Moreau's *Prométhée Foudroyé*, the pictorial use made by Feuerbach of the Oceanids in *Der gefesselte Prometheus, von den Okeaniden beklagt [Prometheus Bound, Lamented by the Oceanids]*[2] produces a strong parallel between the mythological characters and the Marys at the foot of the Cross. This allowed Manfred Krüger to name Feuerbach's painting of Prometheus a 'Vor-Bild Christi',[3] a 'model of Christ'. The 'Christianization' of Prometheus was therefore not strictly limited to Belgium and France. However, Jesus Christ was often depicted in Germany at the end of the nineteenth century[4] (by the Beuron School and Franz von Stuck, for example), but, generally speaking, there was no cross-fertilization there between Jesus Christ and the Prometheus myth.

Let us now consider the treatment of Prometheus by German–speaking artists at the end of the nineteenth century, and the nature of their defining vitalism.

Towards a Golden Age

Two important elements of the Reich must be taken into account here in order to understand why the idealism of German-speaking Symbolist artists was very often expressed through the imagery of a form of Greco-Roman golden age. The first is the cultural and political context of countries that had been part of Germany during the last quarter of the nineteenth century. The second is the great importance of the two German philosophers Friedrich Nietzsche and, to a lesser extent, Karl Marx. As far as history is concerned, the creation of the German Reich was accompanied by a deep cultural identity crisis. All German people were concerned, inasmuch as this creation initiated many structural changes: liberalism, industrialism and prosperity arose, together with the effects that they had on Symbolist minds through Europe. But to that general background was added the fact that regional idiosyncrasies tended to fade out in favour of the great German Reich. The sense of dislocation at the origin of Symbolism was therefore very strong for German or former German artists like Arnold Böcklin. However, even if they felt that their cultural identity had disintegrated, those artists retained the same points of reference. The philosophy of Nietzsche was an inspiration for them. The fact that many of them created works devoted to Nietzsche is certainly not fortuitous. Very often, the way in which they treated subjects, or their choice of subject, was inspired by Nietzsche. One of the specific features of Germanic Symbolist artists is that they did not turn towards syncretism in order to resolve their spiritual crisis. They put their faith in man and his power, following the ideas of Nietzsche, as well as those of Marx. Because the faith of Germanic Symbolist artists was directed towards man and not towards substitutes for God, the expression of their idealism took a special form. As if to address the cultural crisis they were going through, and to go back to their roots, they often turned towards Nordic or Greek myths to depict a form of golden age, or, to borrow the words of Simon Reynolds,[5] inspired by a painting by Thomas Eakins,[5] of Arcadia.[6]

Germanic Symbolist artists from the 1870s until the end of the century often expressed their idealism in the form of a green, luxurious landscape, in which men — often naked — enjoyed simple pleasures. These artists were following a long German tradition, epitomized by Romantic artists such as Caspar David Friedrich, of using landscape to reflect man's state of mind. Germanic Symbolist artists also made symbolic use of the landscape, if in a slightly different manner. They did not attempt to depict a state of mind, usually arising from a confrontation with a sublime eternal landscape, at the origin of Romantic angst. The landscape in their compositions appeared as the sign of a symbiotic alliance with man. The Symbolist arcadia thus created was a sort of Eden without religious connotations, a new golden age. In this context, one can assume that the use that they made of myths was based on their cyclical power, an aspect which will be important when considering the Germanic interpretation of the Prometheus myth. Although we have based our study of the Titanic figure on the idea that the evolution of the Prometheus myth throughout the nineteenth century was a linear historical evolution of its various patterns, which eventually led to Prometheus becoming a symbol, the fact that Germanic painters used the cyclical, and therefore timeless, aspect of myths to retreat into their specific idealism is not incompatible with what he had become at that stage.

In representative 'Arcadian' works by the most important Germanic Symbolist artists, such as *Liebespaar vor Buschwerk* [*Lovers in front of a Shrubbery*],[7] *Altrömische Weinschenke* [*A Tavern in Ancient Rome*],[8] *Liebesfrühling* [*The Spring of Love*],[9] by Arnold Böcklin, *Abend* [*Evening*],[10] by Max Klinger, and the great majority of the works executed by Hans von Marées and Ludwig von Hofmann, what marks out the scenes depicted is perfect, unthreatened harmony, in which the beauty of unspoilt Nature is echoed by the perfection of young bodies. It goes without saying that, because of its intrinsic violence, the Prometheus myth, whatever its interpretation, could not be pictorially treated in such an 'Arcadian' way. However, painters for whom Arcadia played an important part, like Böcklin and Max Klinger, also painted works on Prometheus, which entitles us to wonder whether a link can be established between the mythological character and the idealized golden age of Arcadia.

Although the Germanic treatment of the Prometheus myth stood out aesthetically, it did not differ greatly from other European countries from a symbolic perspective. Germanic Symbolist artists favoured myths partly because they could be extracted from history, as well as to convey the idea of a terrestrial paradise without conjuring up religion, but it appears that the choice of Prometheus as a subject was not governed by the same intention. As far as French and Belgian paintings were concerned, the Symbolist fore-world was almost always depicted as something towards which Symbolist artists had to strive, even if such idealism, facing the tangible industrial and materialistic world, was doomed. The paintings that represented this abstraction had a dreamlike as well as nostalgic quality. We have suggested that Prometheus, through his act of resistance, symbolized the possibility for man to enter the Symbolist fore-world. Germanic Symbolist Arcadian paintings differ from these inasmuch as their fore-world was not depicted as a dream, but with a strong vitalism. Such a distinctive pattern might be explained by the fact that, whereas French and Belgian painters mainly felt their faith (in the broad meaning of the term) crumble, Goethe, followed by Marx and Nietzsche, had established a faith in man. Hence, one could assume, the unchallenged energy arising from Arcadian paintings, which express this new faith. Prometheus, in this context, had for Germanic Symbolist artists the same value as for Nietzsche, and — through a different philosophical development — Marx. Prometheus's rebellion represented the awakening of mankind, and the discovery of their own power, which led Prometheus himself to become the symbol of the rebirth of man, as well as the model of this new generation of active men. Prometheus was a subject dear to the hearts of Germanic painters inasmuch as he symbolized the condition of existence, and the origin of Arcadia. However, depending on the features that the Symbolist fore-world might have, the treatment of the Prometheus subject took various aesthetic forms, which we now have to examine in detail with three major works by Arnold Böcklin, Max Klinger, and Rudolf Jettmar.

Variations on the Rebirth of Man

Arnold Böcklin's Prometheus

The relationship between man and Nature in Arcadian paintings is also strikingly present in Arnold Böcklin's *Prometheus* (Fig.IV.2.1),[11] even though we can certainly not talk of a symbiotic relationship between the Titan and the landscape. Henry Thode, in 1905, said of Böcklin's work: 'In [his] paintings we can see two different worlds merge into one. We have become acquainted with them — the one represents the pictorial ideal of modern landscape, the other the sculptural ideal of classical man. He is incorporated into a landscape which corresponds to the

FIG. IV.2.I. Arnold Böcklin, *Prometheus*, 1882,
Collezione Barilla d'Arte Moderna, Parma. Photo: akg-images

need of modern man to see himself mirrored in nature'.[12] This comment perfectly describes Böcklin's Arcadian paintings, and it also highlights what is at stake in *Prometheus*. In this composition, it looks as if the Titan is attempting to free himself from Böcklin's atmospheric landscape. Prometheus seems to be fighting against matter. The Swiss painter chose to give Prometheus his proper Titanic dimension, so that he appears to be part of the rocky mountains to which he is bound. Such an impression is emphasized by the way in which the light is represented in the painting, filtering through clouds, and only brightening up a few elements of the composition. Because of this, it is even more difficult to distinguish Prometheus from the mountain. Moreover, the Titan is viewed from below, and blends into the cloudy sky, which, again, accentuates the impression that he belongs to the mountain. Elements from the original myth are not depicted by Böcklin, which changes our focus on the painting. Even though Prometheus is represented as bound to his rock, the vulture/eagle is not present in Böcklin's picture. Such a choice can be justified by the assumption that the painter wanted to emphasize the symbol within Prometheus, more than the myth itself. By trying to liberate himself from the unity he forms with the chaotic landscape, it looks as if Böcklin chose to represent, through that particular image of Prometheus, the symbolic rebirth of man.

In creating an atmospheric landscape in which the elements are shown in a tortured way that reflects Prometheus's struggle, Böcklin gave a cosmogonic quality to his mysterious scenery. The raging sea, the purple clouds, and the beams of sun which break through the sky give the general impression that something is in gestation. All these elements act within the paintings as various harmonies which work towards creating a deeply evocative and symbolic image. Böcklin's *Prometheus*, in this respect, appears as quintessentially Symbolist, and meets the requirements that he himself had set for an accomplished painting. In 1897, he said that 'a painting should tell something and give the person looking at it food for thought just as much as poetry does, and convey to him an impression as does a piece of music'.[13] It is striking to consider how Prometheus, like a piece of music, grips the viewer with its immediacy. Such an impression is strengthened by the fact that Prometheus is given the gigantic size that was attributed to him in original accounts of the myth. And, for this reason, the painting is also strangely reminiscent of Greek creation myths, those occurring before the time of the Olympian gods.[14] Perhaps the pictorial power of *Prometheus* lies in the fact that the struggle of the Titan, above all, appears as the expectation of a fundamental event. Prometheus's very convulsion has the intensity of a birth, although the liberation here is of a symbolic nature. The landscape, which reflects the Titan's torment, is transforming itself. The enigmatic aspect of the scene created by Böcklin comes from its timelessness, in the sense that a cosmogony is involved. The treatment of the natural elements, and, most of all, of the light, which seems to be about to reveal an essential mystery, gives a chaotic aspect to the painting. Böcklin's painting, in that respect, could be perceived as a primeval, original scene, the essence of which is the Titan's liberation. *Prometheus* depicts his birth as a free being. By liberating himself from the matter of the rocky mountain, he also symbolically allows self-awareness to expand. In that, *Prometheus* could be seen as the strong pictorial expression of one of the major ideas that developed in German philosophy at that time. In Marx's work, man, through his action on matter, frees himself from it and gains self-awareness. In Böcklin's painting, because of the link between the landscape and Prometheus's struggle, the Titan seems to be about to rise to a new life, and a new world. It is in this respect that the scene could be considered as the original scene preceding, in Germanic Symbolist thought, the Arcadian world. The justification of Prometheus's fight would be the foundation of an ideal realm in which men, freed from the tyranny of matter and all it represents, enjoy perfect harmony with a landscape reminiscent of the golden age. The immediacy of the scene's symbolism presents a close affinity to the musical medium, a model that Max Klinger drew on more explicitly and with great originality in his treatment of Prometheus.

Max Klinger's Brahms Fantasy (Op. XII)

Music, as part of the great idea of the *Gesamtkunstwerk*, was key to the work of Max Klinger, who mastered the art of drawing in the Germanic world in the 1870s. Max Schmid wrote of him: 'He loves an aphoristic Nietzschean style; or, put in musical terms, to state a theme, preceded by a prelude, which he then subjects to manifolds variations, interrupts with digressions, and finally brings to a close, usually with a grand crescendo but sometimes with a soft diminuendo'.[15] A passion for music as a model art appeared very early in Klinger's career as an artist, when he applied traditional musical classification to his works, like Whistler before him. He characterized his early *Etched Sketches* (1879) as *Opus I*, and carried on using that system until his death in 1920. Klinger, a gifted musician, was greatly inspired by Richard Wagner, who showed him the direction art should take with the concept of the *Gesamtkunstwerk*. This was the case even though the artist was part of a circle of friends that included Robert Schumann, and, most important of all, Johannes Brahms, who did not pursue Symbolism in art. In a way, it is equally surprising to consider that Max Klinger, who was so much attracted to the concept of *Gesamtkunstwerk*, essentially expressed himself through graphic art. Nevertheless, the accomplishment of the total work of art, in his mind, seemed to rely on a musical achievement through visual art, and he succeeded in his ambition.

Of all Klinger's works, his cycle on the Prometheus theme is the most closely associated with music, both by its title and its content. The cycle, entitled *Brahms Fantasy (Opus XII)*,[16] appears as a dialogue between Klinger's engravings and five songs, and the *Schicksalslied (Song of Destiny)* Op. 54 for chorus and orchestra by Brahms. The musical pieces illustrated by Klinger were composed between 1868 and 1882, and Klinger started work on his cycle in 1885. Five copies of the resulting album were produced in 1894, followed by a second edition of 150. Out of the eight full plates included in the album, combining the techniques of etching, aquatint, mezzotint and engraving, seven are directly linked to the Prometheus myth:

— Pagina XV *Evocation*
— Pagina XVI *Titanen* [*Titans*]
— Pagina XVII *Nacht* [*Night*]
— Pagina XVIII *Raub des Lichtes* [*The Theft of Fire*]
— Pagina XIX *Fest (Reigen)* [*Feast (Roundel)*]

Evocation (Fig. IV.2.2),[17] which is also one of the most famous prints by Klinger, sets the tone, atmosphere, as well as the significance of the entire cycle. Schmid described it as the 'prelude' to the cycle.

On a balcony overlooking the sea, a man, dressed in modern style, plays the piano in a flamboyant manner, and turns in astonishment towards a figure invoked by the music, a naked woman, who, as Rolf Günther puts it, is 'a personification of nature, playing a huge harp. Her gown and mask have fallen away to reveal nature unveiled, pure, as being the source of all art'.[18] That representation is particularly interesting, since such a conception of nature was at the centre of the Symbolist understanding of the world. We mentioned in a previous chapter that the theories of Symbolism on philosophy and art were remarkably influenced by the myths, legends, and religion of the Far East.[19] And one image in particular became central in Symbolist poetry, especially in France: that of Maya, the Hindu goddess of illusion, who was also the embodiment of nature.[20] The most interesting aspect of this figure is that she was represented with a veil. We can then understand why that figure appealed so much to Symbolist artists, since it symbolically conveyed both the idea that the immediate, material world was nothing but an illusion, and the belief that the truth was in an ideal fore-world. The image of Maya, named as such or not, spread to a large extent in Europe through all artistic fields, and *Evocation* is one depiction of her, associated with other symbols dear to the Symbolists' hearts. In the background, over the sea, the sky is dominated, almost like a watermark, by Titans, who, as Günther notes, 'symbolize the threatening forces of nature'.[21] However, Prometheus cannot be identified amongst them. They are treated as symbols in Klinger's composition, and the value he gives to the figure of Prometheus within the cycle is of a different nature. It is not delivered through the immediacy of a symbolic image, as in Böcklin's *Prometheus*. There is a linearity that has to be followed in the *Brahms Fantasy* to understand the meaning of the treatment of the Prometheus subject. One could perhaps venture to say that the final harmony has to be heard to apprehend the value of the cycle. It is probably here that the originality of Klinger's treatment of the Prometheus myth lies. The cycle can *a priori* appear as the partial account of the original myth, inasmuch as Prometheus is never represented on his own in it. However, because of *Evocation*, we cannot ignore the fact that Klinger attempted to — and succeeded in — giving a general symbolic and Symbolist quality to his *Brahms Fantasy*. Through the conjuring up of Maya and the power of music, the sea and other forces of nature are stirred as if by magic, which directs the general interpretation of the *Brahms Fantasy* cycle.

The following four plates appear as more literal illustrations of the myth. In *Titanen*,[22] the Titans are shown fighting against the Olympian gods, and being defeated by them. Their sunburnt skin and rudimentary weapons contrast with the bows of the Olympian gods that occupy the upper right part of the composition, bathed in light. In *Nacht*,[23] it is Prometheus's turn to stand out from the shadows in the company of Athena on a cloud in the top left corner, no doubt discussing the

Fig. IV.2.2. Max Klinger, *Evocation*, 1894,
courtesy Davison Art Collection Center, Wesleyan University.
Photographer: John Wareham

Fig. IV.2.3. Max Klinger, *Entführung des Prometheus*, 1894,
courtesy Davison Art Collection Center, Wesleyan University.
Photographer: John Wareham

Fig. IV.2.4. Max Klinger, *Der befreite Prometheus*, 1894,
courtesy Davison Art Collection Center, Wesleyan University.
Photographer: John Wareham

theft of fire. The glow that surrounds them, symbolizing wisdom, foretells his gift
to mankind. In the rest of the composition, the chaotic shapes of gigantic ancestral
creatures appear as a homage to Goya. In *Raub des Lichtes*,[24] Prometheus descends
from the sky with fire, in a pose very close to that of Bacchus in Titian's *Bacchus and
Ariadne*,[25] whilst naked men gather around him. *Fest (Reigen)*[26] contrasts with the
other prints of the cycle in that it shows an Olympian feast in idyllic settings.

In *Entführung des Prometheus* (Fig. IV.2.3),[27] Klinger depicts Hermes and Zeus's
eagle above the sea, carrying Prometheus towards the rock to which he will be
bound. As Rolf Günther puts it, the 'image [is] suffused with an almost surrealist
atmosphere'.[28] The flying group formed by Hermes, the eagle and Prometheus,
whose face is hidden in his arms, creates a striking image, whose movement is
strengthened by the general composition of the engraving. Klinger plays on shadows
and on the contrast of black and white to increase the impression of speed. The two
men and the bird, who leads the party with his penetrating beak, are positioned
in a conic way (Hermes leaning forward) which contrasts with a second inverted
cone of light created by the clouds and their reflection on the sea. The fasces of
this cone of light originate from the seashore on the left of the work. *The Abduction
of Prometheus* has to be viewed in the light of the entire cycle, and especially that
of the last engraving in the cycle in order to understand all its implications in the
perspective of Klinger's interpretation of the Prometheus myth.

In the penultimate print, *Opfer*,[29] men at the early stages of civilization are
prostrate in front of Zeus, whose wrath they attempt to appease with the sacrifice
of an ox.

In *Der befreite Prometheus* (Fig. IV.2.4),[30] the invincible Hercules has just freed
Prometheus from his torment. The Titan, in the centre of the composition, has his
head in his hands, crying with relief, and sits on the rock as if to recover slowly
from his endless martyrdom. Hercules, with his bow, stands back on the right of the
foreground, and looks at Prometheus with a smile. In this depiction of Prometheus's
liberation, the conqueror is Hercules, not the Titan himself, who appears to be
broken. In the background, on the left, Oceanids and sea creatures are looking in a
bewildered way at the free Titan, probably amazed by Hercules's exploit. It would
be wrong to say that in this cycle, Prometheus symbolizes the rebirth of man, the
focus of the *Brahms Fantasy* clearly being Hercules's glorious gesture. It is surprising
that there is no depiction of the punishment of the Titan. The absence of such
work and the special focus and perspective of the drawings provide a key to the
interpretation of the *Brahms Fantasy*.

The Titan, as such, is not the conqueror of a new world or the instigator of a new
era for mankind, but, because he is freed by Hercules, his liberation foretells new
times for men. Klinger was a great admirer of Nietzsche, and there is little doubt
that the *Brahms Fantasy* refers to *The Birth of Tragedy*. As we noted earlier, *Evocation*
puts the focus of the cycle on the power of music, and it is certainly not fortuitous
that Nietzsche, in *The Birth of Tragedy*, concludes his pages on Prometheus by saying:
'What power was it that freed Prometheus from his vultures and transformed the
myth into a vehicle of Dionysian wisdom? It is the Heraclean power of music'.[31] For
Nietzsche, Prometheus was out of the Apollonian order, which is embodied by Zeus

in the myth. For this reason, he appears as a threatening force, and therefore has to be punished. Quoting Goethe, Nietzsche interprets the value of the Prometheus figure by saying that 'The immeasurable suffering of the bold "individual" on the one hand and the divine predicament and intimation of a twilight of the gods on the other, the way the power of these two worlds of suffering compels a reconciliation, a metaphysical union'.[32] In Nietzsche's thought as well as in the *Brahms Fantasy*, this occurs through the Heracleian musical power. The antagonism between the Apollonian order and Prometheus is represented throughout the cycle and the twilight of the gods, crowned by the musical liberation, is already announced by *Evocation*, in which the forces of nature are smouldering. The *Brahms Fantasy* is the depiction of the glory of the Heracleian force, but, above all, of the omnipotent power of music. The cycle appears as a *mise en abyme* of the aim of Symbolism, which is to reach the harmony of the ideal fore-world (here inaugurated by Prometheus's liberation by Hercules) through a pure medium of which music is the model. We could therefore conclude by saying that Prometheus, for Klinger, is an instrument, being part of a set of symbols that tends towards the rebirth of man in a world where the main orders are reconciled. Brahms, in gratitude, wrote to Klinger: 'I see the music [and] the beautiful words to go with it and now I am elevated even further by your magnificent illustrations. Looking at them I can really feel the eternal continuation of the sound of music. You seem to express even more powerfully all that I longed for yet was unable to say; being similarly enigmatic and allusive. Sometimes I envy your ability to be more "precise" graphically than I could ever be [with my music], then again, I am glad that I don't need to aim for these goals. When it comes down to it, however, I do believe that all art is related in many ways and speaks the same language'.[33] Although Rudolf Jettmar's life as an artist was influenced by music as well as the art of Böcklin, his two different interpretations of Prometheus also prove to be an original treatment of the myth.

Rudolf Jettmar's two Prometheuses

The link Rudolf Jettmar established between music and fine art is not as apparent in his work as in Max Klinger's, but it is nonetheless at the very origin of his art. This is why, before examining his actual etchings executed on the Prometheus theme, it may be fruitful to consider first how Rudolf Jettmar apprehended myths and music. Indeed, as Hans von Hofstaetter put it, the Austrian artist, 'gifted, as he was, for both arts, [...] was undecided between music and painting for a long time. As a matter of fact, he never did make that decision: although he became a painter and etcher, he also remained captured by music throughout his life. At the time of his death he was an honorary member of the Vienna Academy of Fine Arts and also an honorary member of the Vienna Philharmonic Orchestra. It is in this double membership that the two poles of his life find their expression'.[34] Jettmar associated music and graphic art in his conception of art, which explains why he did not use music as a reference, or as a model to strive towards. It was at the root of his work. The two dominant streaks in his oeuvre were landscape and mythology, which, for him, were musical traits. Hofstaetter points out that 'the recurrent themes' that we find in Jettmar's work are mythological figures, amongst whom are Phaedon, Prometheus, and, most of all, Hercules: 'they have a particular appeal to musical people, because they hear in a way from within these paintings and etchings the music that inspired their creator'.[35] This can be literally true of Prometheus, inasmuch as many of the greater composers were inspired by the Titan and his various literary treatments. However, we probably have to understand that point in a more general way. Those mythological figures were linked to music because of what they embodied. Indeed, here, we can concur with Hofstaetter, who put forward the idea that Jettmar shared with the Romanticists the conception that music stemmed from myths,[36] since the artist perceived in music the expression of a godlike and immortal power. However, unlike many artists, particularly Romantic ones, he did not see the faceless Christian God behind the great mystery of music, but the Greek gods from ancient mythology. It seems that for Jettmar the cosmic power of myths was inseparable from that of music in its immaterial rendition of the elemental and mysterious forces of the world.

His first etching on the Prometheus theme is entitled *Die Befreiung des Prometheus* [*Prometheus Unbound*][37] and was executed in 1910. The influence of Klinger, whom Jettmar admired greatly, can be felt. However, although there are similarities between the art of Klinger and that of Jettmar, the latter attributed a greater, symbolic importance, to light and shadow in his etchings, an aspect especially striking in *Die Befreiung des Prometheus*.

The opposition between black and white in this print is intensified by an opposition between the left and right parts of the etching, separated in the exact middle of the composition by Prometheus's body. On the left side is the rock to which Prometheus is bound. Its contours on the bottom left corner stand out from the dark. In the upper and opposite part of this section are Hercules and Prometheus, on a promontory with a vertical slope. Both men are surrounded by light, Hercules kneeling behind Prometheus in order to kill the vulture — situated at the top right corner of the composition — with his bow. Prometheus, his head held up and pressed against Hercules's leg, faces his tormentor. His body, however, threatens to fall into the abyss, and his exhaustion is perceptible in the movement of his hands and the fact that he cannot hold his head himself. In the right section of the work, we can barely make out in the darkness the level of the sea and the raptor that dominates it.

Because of the clear opposition between light and darkness, the function Jettmar attributes to the use of black and white in his composition is apparent. Hercules and Prometheus are on the side of the light, which seems to spread in the direction of the vulture — as the arrow that is about to kill it flies through the air — whereas in the right part of the composition, everything is in darkness. This gives a Manichean value to Jettmar's etching, and shows vividly the clash between the bright rebellion of Prometheus and the dark, doomed world of Zeus and the Olympian gods. The fact that the balance of *Die Befreiung des Prometheus* relies on two 'schematic' oppositions — that of the use of black and white and that of the equal division of the composition from left to right — could have produced a rather flat work. However, Jettmar's drawing is deeply atmospheric, and the way in which

Prometheus is depicted plays an essential role in this achievement. The lower part of his body is dangling in the abyss, which symbolically shows that he has to endure the punishment of Zeus and his ruling, submitted to his fate. But keeping in mind that the lights reflect Manicheism and the two contrasted world orders, the fact that Prometheus is partly in the darkness of the void also gives a sense of his belonging to divinity and to mankind. However, the most striking feature of the way in which Prometheus is represented by Jettmar lies in what his body expresses, thus exposed and abandoned to the power of the vulture. His muscles are relaxed, not convulsed. Only the twitching of his right hand is an indication of his suffering, and of the fact that keeping his head beside Hercules's left leg is an intense effort. Nevertheless, his head accompanies the movement Hercules executes to kill the vulture, and he stares defiantly at his torturer. Even though he submits to his punishment, knowing its outcome, Prometheus does not surrender and still defies the Olympian gods.

Through symbolic use of the etching technique, and the emphasis of the power of music in the person of Hercules, Klinger's *Brahms Fantasy* and Jettmar's *Die Befreiung des Prometheus* present similarities in their approach to Symbolism. Both used Greek mythology in their work to conjure up the idea of a totality inextricably linked to the primordial power of music, so dear to the hearts of Symbolists.

Six years after the completion of *Die Befreiung des Prometheus*, in 1916, Jettmar undertook a second etching on the Prometheus theme, thus creating a diptych. However, as Hofstaetter put it, 'the second volet does not have the elemental power of the previous one'.[38] Jettmar had a five-year break in his career as an artist, during which he taught art at the Akademie der Bildenden Künste in Vienna, and the first important work that he completed when he started etching again was this rather academic composition. Interestingly enough, it is entitled *Prometheus bringt den Menschen das Feuer* [*Prometheus Brings Fire to Men*],[39] and refers to an earlier episode of the myth, the Titan's original gift of fire to mankind.

In the composition of his etching, which derives heavily from Klinger's *Raub des Lichtes*, Jettmar's symbolic value of the contrast between black and white is not as strong as in *Die Befreiung des Prometheus*. If Prometheus is surrounded by light in the second etching, it is because of Zeus's lightning, which slants from the sky, and whose power lifts up Prometheus's draped cloth. He stands on the highest point of the rock, forming the centre of the composition with Zeus's lightning. At his feet, primitive men and women — some of them clearly in despair, like the isolated prostrate figure at the bottom right corner of the etching — are squatting. A group of men on the left unsuccessfully attempt to build a fire, and they turn, half-scared, half-stunned, towards Prometheus. Jettmar thus gives a faithful depiction of the original account of the myth, without really emphasizing the symbol within Prometheus, although this scene was most probably inspired by Goethe's fragment. Such a contrast between *Die Befreiung des Prometheus* and *Prometheus bringt den Menschen das Feuer* probably casts light on two important points: Jettmar's return to a more conventional representation of Greek mythology following his time at the Academy of Fine Arts, and the fact that by 1916, the tangible reality of the war had overtaken the Symbolist ideals and conceptions. However, if we go back a few decades, and leave the continent in order to return to England, we shall see that

Prometheus, in a perhaps unexpected guise, was still stimulating the imagination and creativity of many English artists.

Notes to Chapter 2

1. Such homage is not surprising given the fact that Feuerbach studied and copied Rubens assiduously in the Munich Pinakothek.
2. Anselm Feuerbach, *Der gefesselte Prometheus, von den Okeaniden beklagt*, 1879, oil on canvas, oval, 220 × 375 cm, Akademie der Bildenden Künste, Vienna.
3. Manfred Krüger, *Wandlungen des Tragischen* (Stuttgart: Drama und Initiation, 1973), p. 52.
4. German representations of Jesus Christ challenged the traditional religious depictions, adopting new angles. See Hans H. Hofstätter, 'Faith and Damnation', in *Kingdom of the Soul: Symbolist Art in Germany 1870–1920*, ed. by Ingrid Ehrhardt and Simon Reynolds (Munich: Prestel, 2000), pp. 131–41.
5. Thomas Eakins, *Arcadia*, c. 1880, Metropolitan Museum of Art, New York.
6. Simon Reynolds, 'The Longing for Arcadia', in *Kingdom of the Soul: Symbolist Art in Germany 1870–1920*, pp. 53–59. According to Reynolds, 'Goethe's classicism was no more than the first faltering step to a German Arcadia' (p. 53).
7. Arnold Böcklin, *Liebespaar vor Buschwerk*, c. 1864, tempera on canvas, 74 × 98 cm, Kunsthaus, Zurich.
8. Arnold Böcklin, *Altrömische Weinschenke*, 1867–68, oil on canvas, 65 × 96.5 cm, Staatliche Kunsthalle, Karlsruhe.
9. Arnold Böcklin, *Liebesfrühling*, 1868, oil on canvas, 220 × 136 cm, Städtische Kunstsammlung, Darmstadt.
10. Max Klinger, *Abend*, 1882, Hessisches Landesmuseum, Darmstadt.
11. Arnold Böcklin, *Prometheus*, 1882, oil on canvas, 116 × 150 cm, Collezione Barilla d'Arte Moderna, Parma.
12. Quoted by Hans Dollinger, *Böcklin* (Munich: Bruckmann, 1975), p. 33.
13. Hans Dollinger, *Böcklin* (Munich: Bruckmann, 1975), p. 12.
14. William Vaughan, in *Kingdom of the Soul: Symbolist Art in Germany 1870–1920*, p. 89, mentions that 'In forging his own image of Prometheus bound to the rock, Böcklin is believed to have been influenced by a classical wall painting of Tityus, a giant in Greek mythology who suffered a similar fate', to which he adds the 'image of Prometheus [...] also bears a similarity to that of the blinded Cyclops in Turner's famous scene from Homer, *Ulysses Deriding Polyphemus*'. These remarks are particularly interesting if we take into account that Prometheus, as depicted by Böcklin, has an original mythological quality which allows the symbolism of the scene to develop fully.
15. Max Schmid, *Max Klinger*, 5th edn (Leipzig: Bielefeld, 1926), p. 1.
16. Max Klinger, *Brahms Fantasy (opus XII)*, 1890–94.
17. Max Klinger, *Evocation*, 1894, etching, aquatint, mezzotint, engraving, sheet 36.2 × 43.2 cm, plate 29.2 × 35.7 cm.
18. *Kingdom of the Soul: Symbolist Art in Germany 1870–1920*, p. 218.
19. We notably mentioned the importance of Schopenhauer in the import of those 'exotic' philosophies, ideas, and symbols.
20. The poet Leconte de Lisle, in France, was the first to invoke that figure, along with that of Brahma, in his *Poèmes Antiques* (1852).
21. *Kingdom of the Soul: Symbolist Art in Germany 1870–1920*, p. 218.
22. Max Klinger, *Titanen*, 1894, etching, engraving and mezzotint, sheet, 36.2 × 43.2 cm, plate, 27.7 cm × 35.8 cm
23. Max Klinger, *Nacht*, 1894, etching and aquatint, sheet, 36.2 × 43.2 cm, plate, 27.8 cm × 38.2 cm.
24. Max Klinger, *Raub des Lichtes*, 1894, etching and mezzotint, sheet, 36.2 × 43.2 cm, plate, 29.2 × 35.8 cm.
25. Titian, *Bacchus and Ariadne*, 1520–23, oil on canvas, 176.5 × 191 cm, National Gallery, London.
26. Max Klinger, *Fest [Reigen]*, 1894, etching, engraving and aquatint, sheet, 36.2 × 43.2 cm, plate, 25 × 36.1 cm.

27. Max Klinger, *Entführung des Prometheus*, 1894, etching, aquatint, engraving, 27.8 × 38.2 cm.

28. *Kingdom of the Soul: Symbolist Art in Germany 1870–1920*, p. 219.

29. Max Klinger, *Opfer*, 1894, etching, soft ground etching and engraving, sheet, 36.2 × 43.2 cm, plate, 27.8 × 36.3 cm.

30. Max Klinger, *Der Befreite Prometheus*, 1894, etching, aquatint, mezzotint, engraving, 27.6 × 36.2 cm.

31. Friedrich Nietzsche, *The Birth of Tragedy*, trans., with commentary, by Walter Kaufmann (New York: Vintage Books, 1967), p. 75.

32. Ibid. p. 70.

33. For the original German text, see Scheffler, p. 144.

34. Hans H. von Hofstaetter, *Rudolf Jettmar: Monographie* (Vienna: Tusch, 1984), p. 55.

35. Ibid., p. 55.

36. 'Jettmar ist damit der musikalischen Kunstanschauung der Romantik verpflichtet, die ihre Grundlagen letztlich aus der Antike herleitet, in der die Musik mythischen Ursprungs war; die Anwesenheit der Götter in der Musik bewirkt ihre besondere Macht', Hofstaetter, p. 1.

37. Rudolf Jettmar, *Die Befreiung des Prometheus*, 1910, etching and dry-point, 60.1 × 79.7 cm, private collection.

38. Hofstaetter, *Rudolf Jettmar*, p. 49. My translation.

39. Rudolf Jettmar, *Prometheus bringt den Menschen das Feuer*, 1916, 54 × 74.8 cm, private collection.

The Cross-Fertilization of the Prometheus Myth by the Pygmalion Myth

As we have seen in an earlier chapter on Balzac, the Prometheus myth was closely associated in his mind with the Pygmalion myth. However, such a parallel was even more striking on the other side of the Channel. Whereas for Balzac, Prometheus and Pygmalion appear almost exchangeable, in England, Prometheus, despite his fame and popularity at the beginning of the nineteenth century, was generally replaced by Pygmalion.[1] We have already examined two notable exceptions in works by Briton Rivière, in relation to Prometheus's association to Christ, and by G. F. Watts. William Blake Richmond, who had worked in Rome, devoted two canvases to Prometheus. The first, a gigantic *Prometheus Bound*, was exhibited in 1874 at the Royal Academy of Arts. Although it was favourably received by critics, it failed to sell, and Richmond presented it to the Birmingham Museum and Art Gallery. It was later de-accessioned, and unfortunately no visual records of the painting survive, which makes it difficult to gauge it in relation to Symbolist aesthetics.[2] In 1882, the artist explored the theme again in *The Release of Prometheus by Hercules* [Fig. IV.3.1].[3]

The painting anticipates Klinger's treatment of the same theme in his *Brahms Fantasy* (Op. XII) in that Hercules is the glorious, victorious figure in the painting, while Prometheus is represented as a broken man. Helen Lascelles described the painting as follows: 'Hercules, poised on a rock in strong relief against the sky, with life and energy in every line of his virile body, is shooting a last arrow at the vanquished eagle, whose presence is indicated by a feather floating down. Prometheus, a no less fine figure, but cramped from his bonds, lies in an uneasy attitude on the rock below, as if half fearing to rise lest his deliverance should not be really accomplished.'[4]

Apart from this rare appearance in British art, Prometheus disappeared almost entirely from the pictorial field, whereas Pygmalion suddenly became a favourite subject.[5] This substitution is not fortuitous, since Pygmalion, by the second half of the nineteenth century, became a double of Prometheus, as we shall argue. To consider the importance the Pygmalion myth took in Victorian society, the grounds on which the cross-fertilization of Prometheus and Pygmalion occurred

Fig. iv.3.1. William Blake Richmond, *The Release of Prometheus by Hercules*, 1882,
Wigan Metropolitan Borough Council, Courtesy of the Witt Library

will be briefly examined. When did the 'contamination' of the two myths begin, in which elements of the myths did it take root, and how did its nature evolve?

The Cross-Fertilization Process

The Pygmalion myth dates from later than the Prometheus myth, and finds its origin in an account by Ovid that relates the story of a Cypriot sculptor, Pygmalion, who despised women and their company. However, he sculpted a lifelike woman in ivory so perfect that he fell in love with it, to the point that he offered the statue presents, dressed it up, and eventually took it to bed. He prayed to Venus for his creature to come to life, and his wish was granted: a kiss from him made her human. *A priori*, such an account seems to be rather far from the original Prometheus myth.

We might assume that the confusion between Pygmalion and Prometheus has its roots in the fact that both characters were represented as sculptors. However, the reason for the contamination of the Prometheus myth appears to be subtler, if we consider its historical context, and to structure itself around several elements. The representation of Prometheus as a sculptor — as used by Balzac — is almost incidental to the evolution of the myth. As late as Plato's *Protagoras*, Prometheus forms men from clay, which allowed the *plasticator* side of his persona to develop. The origins of the protean aspect of the Titan derive from the fact that his story is above all a creation myth, on a human scale, which explains why the figure of the sculptor is just an avatar of the figure of Prometheus within its evolution. However, the cross-fertilization of the myth by that of Pygmalion certainly occurred, and we have to examine the circumstances which brought it about. Nonetheless, it is essentially from the fourth century AD that the identification of Prometheus with a sculptor took on considerable significance. At that time, it was important to transpose the metaphorical level of the sculptor's image (as Creator) to a literal level. It was essential to the Church Fathers, working within a euhemeristic perspective. As explained earlier, according to this theory, Prometheus was neither a god nor a Titan, but a skilled sculptor elevated by mankind to the rank of a divinity. This image was easier to handle than that of Prometheus as a prefiguration of Jesus Christ: the figure of the Titan as a rebel was a dangerous one to transpose into a Christian context. The image of Prometheus as a sculptor, however, met all the criteria of euhemeristic transposition, and it was accordingly widely developed.

Euhemerism had another important impact on the Prometheus myth, as it emphasized the importance of Pandora, soon to be confused with Galatea. Pandora has always been associated with her Christian counterpart, Eve, but with the difference that her ignorance and clumsiness result in the loss of the golden age. Her growing importance in a euhemeristic perspective became the main source of the contamination of the Prometheus myth by that of Pygmalion. In the most ancient myths, she was sent by Jupiter to punish men for Prometheus's crime: originally, she was not his creature. However, given the identification of the Titan with a sculptor modelling mankind, it did not take long for Pandora to appear in myths as the creation of Prometheus himself, and therefore to be identified with Galatea.

As Raymond Trousson explains, in many accounts (one of the most important being *Eccos de la Musa Trasmontana o Prometheo. Fabula Alegorica*, an anonymous Spanish poem of the seventeenth century), she is formed from clay, like other men.[6] In the same century, the theme of the Creator's love for his creature started to develop. Such a topic was absent from Renaissance versions, and thus gave the Prometheus myth a new orientation. *La Estatua de Prometeo*, by Calderón (probably written in 1669 and published in 1677), was an essential element in this evolution. The significance and symbolism of this play is rather complex, and it is not our purpose to analyse it here, but two elements are worthy of note: firstly, the fact that Prometheus is represented as a sculptor modelling a statue of the goddess Minerva; secondly, the fact that the goddess helps Prometheus to steal a sunbeam, thanks to which the statue comes to life. The parallels between Pygmalion and Prometheus on the one hand, and Minerva and Venus on the other are obviously striking, and the symbol of fire in the process of the animation of matter is crucial in the contamination of the two myths.

However, the value of the animation of matter in each myth once again takes on a different significance. The fact that Minerva replaces Venus is certainly not a fortuitous element in the Prometheus myth. Indeed, the appearance of this goddess in the myth is not exclusive to Calderón. Houdar de la Motte's *Prométhée* (1753), and Aumale de Corsenville's *Pandore* (1789) — in which Prometheus marries Pandora with Minerva's agreement — amongst numerous other works of the same period, make use of the same theme. Such an inspiration derives from Boccaccio, Boccaccio himself being inspired by Servius and Fulgentius. In chapter XLIV of the fourth book of *La Estatua de Prometeo*, in a chapter entitled 'De Prometheo Japeti Filio, qui fecit Pandoram et genuit Ysidem et Deucalionem',[7] Minerva, admiring the statue Prometheus has just modelled, asks him to follow her to Olympus, where he will find a useful present for his creature. Prometheus agrees and, observing that everything in Heaven is animated by fire, steals a spark from the Sun's chariot wheel to give to mankind. In Boccaccio's work, Prometheus appears as the spiritual creator of mankind, as *plasmator animi*. He gives man a conscience, and intelligence. It is through this gift, symbolized by fire, that he becomes the benefactor of men. Athena/Minerva, goddess of wisdom, supports Prometheus when he steals fire from the gods, a rebellion against the power of her own father. Using the figure of the goddess in such a way means that Wisdom is recruited to the rebel's side. Prometheus's love for men is represented as righteous, pure, wise and disinterested. In Goethe's 1773 *Prometheus*, Minerva was identified by critics,[8] and possibly rightly so, with Prometheus himself. On a symbolic level, Minerva stands for wisdom, which is one of the main attributes of Prometheus the fore-thinker. This would explain why Prometheus and Minerva could be seen as one soul.

In the Pygmalion myth, though the gift of life is symbolized by the same element, fire, the animation of matter which follows is of a different nature. The intervention of Venus is required, since she is the divinity of love and beauty, not of altruistic love. We could therefore assume that, if she is central in the Pygmalion myth, it is because the sculptor's love is somewhat selfish, and also because, without her intervention, which is motivated by a form of vanity, the statue would never come to life. On the contrary, in the Prometheus myth, Minerva's intercession takes the form of an assent. Pygmalion wants his statue to come to life for his own happiness, and his creation is to a large extent a reflection of himself. In spite of numerous similarities between the Pygmalion and Prometheus myths, the sculptor himself is close to the figure of Narcissus. The metaphor of fire understood as the flame of passion is part of the amorous casuistry in the myth of Pygmalion, as opposed to the Promethean flame, where what is at stake is the flame of knowledge, technology, and progress. Therefore, even if, on a literal level, the Prometheus and Pygmalion myths intertwine, they require a different type of interpretation.

A new development occurred during the nineteenth century. The metaphor of fire as creation led to Prometheus becoming the type of the (rebellious) artist amongst Romantic artists, as analysed earlier. Nonetheless, even if the Prometheus myth, for the past centuries, had frequently been cross-fertilized by the Pygmalion myth, both of them had preserved their separate identities. They never entirely merged, and in the nineteenth century both had equal success, probably for similar reasons. An examination of the social context will help us find the cause of this intertwining. Robert Upstone notes, 'The Pygmalion myth [...] touched male fears about women and their changing social status through access to education and the world outside the home'.[9] Upstone goes on to explain that the Pygmalion account was reassuring for men, inasmuch as Pygmalion is the creator as well as owner of his ideal spouse. He concludes that such a story 'mirrors the dynamics of Victorian marital relations, or stereotyped male expectations of how they should be. Pygmalion was a reflection of himself, and also an act of sexless creation not requiring sex, linking further to male fear of women'.[10] Gail Marshall, who interestingly argues that both the professional and personal history of Victorian actresses were defined by the Pygmalion and Galatea myth, and by the way in which they negotiated with the sculptural metaphor, stresses that 'there is little distinction in any of the nineteenth-century Pygmalion poems between the "statue" as animate and as inanimate female object, and crucially, coming to life offers no access to a language with which to express a dissenting sensitivity.'[11] A specific historical and sociological context might explain the 'revival' of the Pygmalion myth. The Prometheus myth certainly aroused a similar interest during the same period, but in this case, the interest was structured around the rebellious aspect of the Titan. It is not on this level of interpretation that we have to look for a clarification of the link between the two myths at that time. Nevertheless, if we take into account the nature of the works on Pygmalion which introduce elements of the Prometheus story at that stage, we may find the key to the intertwining of the two myths. This intermingling essentially occurred in the 1880s, and the main work which should be examined in order to define the circumstances under which it took place is the twelve-volume verse cycle by the sculptor Thomas Woolner, entitled *Pygmalion* (1881).[12]

The Construction of the Double: Thomas Woolner

Thomas Woolner's interest in Pygmalion is not surprising, as this artist, who was part of the Brotherhood of Pre-Raphaelites,[13] was the only sculptor in the group. The first obvious double to take into account is the identification between Pygmalion and his model. The sculptor manages to reach the climax of his art by giving life to his own creation. However, it is not on that 'double' in particular that we are going to concentrate, but on the fact that a strong and continuous link is established between Prometheus and Pygmalion in Woolner's eponymous cycle.

In the second chapter of *Pygmalion*, entitled 'Pygmalion's work', Woolner mentions Prometheus as one of the main subjects to be executed by the sculptor, along with Venus, Dionysus and Zeus. In the description of the panel Pygmalion intends to realize on the Titan, Woolner devotes 94 lines to Prometheus himself, but he is a recurrent figure in the rest of the chapter, where he appears as a link between the various mythological figures, as well as in the entire cycle. One of the most interesting aspects of the way in which Woolner deals with the figure of Prometheus is that he seems to be looking for exhaustiveness in his account of the Titan's acts, and qualities. From the beginning of the passage devoted to Prometheus, Woolner evokes the double nature of Prometheus, both godlike and human:

> Prometheus lived not wholly God nor man,[14]

He then mentions, probably thanks to a remembrance of Goethe, the close association existing between himself and Athena. This is particularly fruitful, since the cross-fertilization between the Prometheus myth and the Pygmalion myth often stems from the similarity between the couples Pygmalion/Venus and Prometheus/Athena. It is thanks to the nature of such a close relationship that creatures are brought to life: literally speaking with Pygmalion's creation (here called Hebe, not Galatea), and figuratively with men, who are awoken to civilization. However, it is only with the help of Venus that Pygmalion's wish is fulfilled, and it is only with the help of Athena that Prometheus can bring fire to mankind:

> Not love of man, but from deep love
> Of him Prometheus she her promise gave
> Of counsel: promised he should snatch the fire
> From torch of Eros, thunderbolt of Zeus,
> Or from the car of Helios seize a spark.[15]

This example allows us to consider the way in which Woolner, in terms of mythology, attempts to encompass all the existing variations given of the Prometheus myth in his work, by enumerating the many possible sources from which Prometheus might have stolen fire in order to give it to mankind.

Another important feature attributed to Prometheus in *Pygmalion* is the fact that he does not appear as a rebel against Zeus, and least of all as a trickster, two elements that we might have expected, given that Woolner undertook to synthesize the numerous strata of the myth. In the following passage, devoted to Zeus, Woolner mentions that Prometheus helped Zeus fight the Titans, because, as a fore-thinker, he has 'seen the Giants' doom/ And hoped by serving the Olympian Gods/ To claim for wage a spark of Heaven's fire'.[16] In his poem, Woolner emphasizes the idea that Prometheus is above all the benefactor of mankind. It is said of Prometheus that:

> But for his pigmies, who fast multiplied,
> And waxed in force with every watched-for chance;
> He was invincibly resolved to win
> The vital spark by which alone they might
> Be lifted from the brutes[17]

It is almost reluctantly, and only inspired by his love for mankind, that Prometheus commits the crime for which he will be severely punished. Woolner 'shaded off' the rebellious and conqueror aspect of Prometheus, a feature which, as mentioned earlier, was one of the main elements of divergence between the Prometheus and the Pygmalion myths.

Although Woolner tried to give an account of all the variations on the Prometheus myth, one major aspect of the myth and of Prometheus's persona itself is missing. I am here referring to Prometheus *plasticator*, Prometheus giving shape and life to mankind, who is not evoked until the very end of the poem. One could therefore assume that Woolner omitted that side of Prometheus precisely to avoid any confusion or any contamination between Pygmalion and Prometheus. However, even before examining the ending of the poem, we have to reject such a hypothesis and examine more closely the lexical field and metaphors of fire and creation-making within the poem, inasmuch as it elaborates a tight network between Prometheus and Pygmalion, which already casts light on Woolner's 'omission'.

From the fourth book, a clear parallel is established between the sculptor and Prometheus:

> Longed not Prometheus for the fire of heaven
> Wherewith to solace miserable man,
> More vehemently than sought Pygmalion
> The spark to flash his Hebe into life[18]

The 'spark' here attributed to Pygmalion is noteworthy, since this word is a recurrent one in the passages on Prometheus quoted above. Their mutual quest to bring their 'beloved' to life, metaphorically or not, is thus clearly established in this parallel. In the same book, and perhaps even more importantly, after Pygmalion's prayer to Venus to give life to his statue, he receives the following response:

> [...] Men cannot,
> In earthly state handle pure truth and fire,
> The means of Gods, and still remain unscorched.
> But you are strong; the prize shines bright in view,
> Cost what it may a pathway must be cleared.
> And if you forward press unfalteringly,
> Pallas Athena may beside you march.[19]

Here again, although not named as such, Prometheus is clearly evoked, through the themes of the theft of fire, punishment, and, most of all, his special relationship with Pallas Athena. The mention of the goddess could be interpreted in two ways, since Pygmalion's prayer is addressed to Venus, and not to Athena. Either it is simply implied, here, that the relationship uniting Prometheus and Athena is a model to be followed by Pygmalion and Venus, or a subtle superimposition of the Pygmalion on the Prometheus myth can be perceived, based on the blurring of the goddess's identity.

The comparison between Prometheus and Pygmalion goes even further in the seventh book, when Pygmalion, reflecting on his art, wonders why the art of generations of sculptors remained static and 'lifeless' in Ancient Greece, because of the process of imitation:

> Till Daedalus with new Promethean fire,
> Carving the stubborn blocks of wood and stone
> To limbs detached, gave to his images
> The air of will and motion! Rude, uncouth
> They were. But they had life, the breath of Gods![20]

This passage is particularly fascinating, as the adjective 'Promethean', for the first time in *Pygmalion*, evolves naturally to become applied to the sculptural field. What Daedalus managed to do symbolically thanks to Promethean fire, that is to give 'life', 'the breath of Gods', to his statues, is now recalled by Woolner in anticipation of what Pygmalion will achieve with the help of Venus. The network of correspondences and associations between Pygmalion and Prometheus in Woolner's cycle is getting tighter and tighter. However, the establishment of such links is made even clearer in the conclusion of Book XI (at the end of which the miracle has just been accomplished), where the figure of Prometheus, again, is conjured up by Woolner, who seems to invite us to a reading *a posteriori* of *Pygmalion*, in the light of the now unveiled parallel established between the sculptor and the Titan.

> The minstrels unto gaping crowds forth poured
> In floods Pygmalion's almighty deeds,
> The doing which had taken ten long lives;
> Achilles not more brave, Alcides strong;
> And a moot question if Prometheus self,
> Or even Hephaestus could have wrought a form
> That breathed a sweeter life than Hebe's smile.[21]

That conclusive and crucial passage is the only one in *Pygmalion* to allude to Prometheus as *plasticator*. Given that Woolner had devoted a long part of his fourth book to Prometheus, being very careful and minute in the restitution of the various versions of the myth, we must assume that Woolner ingeniously structured *Pygmalion* in order to build progressively an association, and even a superimposition of Prometheus and Pygmalion. The intertwining metaphors and images, combined with the superimposition of the couples formed by Pygmalion and Venus on the one hand, and Prometheus and Athena on the other, results in the identification of both characters. Woolner's cycle is particularly remarkable for its consciously established association between Pygmalion and Prometheus, which is not simply the result of the long evolution of myths. Woolner clearly states here that Pygmalion is one of Prometheus's masks, but the choice of that mask requires interpretation.

As a sculptor, Woolner was undoubtedly drawn towards that figure. However, his choice is probably deeper, and shared with other artists from his generation, who were not necessarily sculptors. As an artist, and for various reasons, the mask of Pygmalion probably appealed more to him than that of Prometheus.

First of all, choosing Pygmalion for an artist possibly meant rejecting the rebellious side of the Titan. We mentioned that Woolner shaded off that aspect. Although Prometheus's love of mankind and creation-making powers had all the characteristics to seduce the Aesthetes, the violence bound to his rebellion, on the other hand, did not necessarily appeal to them. At the very least, it might have been slightly opposed to their chief focus, the ideal of Beauty, which leads us to the second and most important reason for their interest in Pygmalion. That mask allowed them to stand for their own selves as artists. Pygmalion was entirely human, which favoured the identification with him, but, at the same time, his creation-making power, directed towards Beauty, matched that of Prometheus in its ability to generate life, an ideal which was even more vivid for Symbolist artists. In this connection, their art was striving towards an ideal realm whose existence relied on that possibility. Eventually, the Pygmalion myth became a reflection of the narcissism of the artist, the figure of Narcissus being also extremely popular with Symbolists. All of these elements might explain why so many works of art based on Pygmalion flourished in England during the second half of the nineteenth century. The most famous remains Edward Burne-Jones's *Pygmalion Series*,[22] but we might also cite *The Wife of Pygmalion, A Translation from the Greek*,[23] by George Frederic Watts, John Tenniel's *Pygmalion and the Image*,[24] and Ernest Normand's *Pygmalion and Galatea*.[25]

The figure of Prometheus can also be seen in the works of these artists, or of other artists of this generation, who were inspired by the figure of Pandora. She was, of course, inextricably linked to the myth of Prometheus *plasticator*. An interest in her certainly stemmed from a larger fascination for the type of the femme fatale, but we cannot ignore the fact that the appeal of Pygmalion, of Galatea, and of Pandora at the same historical period, when Prometheus virtually disappeared from English artistic works, made the Titan conspicuous by his absence. This is another element suggesting the superimposition of Pygmalion and Prometheus. Harry Bates's sculpture *Pandora*[26] is particularly remarkable in this regard, as the mixed media in which she is represented seems to embody the likeness between the first woman and Galatea, the two creatures being formed from the mineral element. Pandora here appears like Galatea before she comes to life.

In a different medium, John William Waterhouse's *Pandora*[27] and Dante Gabriel Rossetti's chalk drawing bearing the same title[28] are probably the most famous works of that period on the subject. Lawrence Alma-Tadema's small diploma picture for the Royal Watercolour Society, another *Pandora*,[29] is also worth mentioning for its graceful quality. It could be said of the construction of such a network of references and of the special focus on Pygmalion, seen as a mask of Prometheus, that the artists decided to draw on the pure Symbolism of the Prometheus myth, while fading out its essential dynamic and, to some extent, violent dimension.[30] In the Victorian context, the figure of Prometheus might also have faded out because he represented a strong male figure, at a time when the figure of the femme fatale, perceived as castrating, was predominant. The Pygmalion myth, on the contrary, objectified the woman, and in this respect, was most reassuring. It was also a way of using Prometheus as a mere symbol (paradoxically, by hiding him), and of extracting the myth from the Titan. This leads us to the final Symbolist mask of Prometheus, which is also the accomplishment and fulfilment of the Titan as a symbol.

Notes to Chapter 3

1. Following Byron's ode and Shelley's *Prometheus Unbound*, there were very few treatments of the Prometheus subject. However, George Augustus Simcox, in 1867, attempted to write the third part of Aeschylus' trilogy, and James Robinson Planché wrote a parody of the relationship between Pandora and Prometheus, entitled *Olympic revels, or Prometheus and Pandora, a burletta* (1831), which adapted George Coman's *The Sun Poker*. Another popular treatment of the myth on stage was Robert Reece's *Prometheus; or, the Man on the Rock!* In the 1860s. The burlesque tradition of the Prometheus myth, which is outside the bounds of this book, was thoroughly examined by Edith Hall and Fiona Macintosh, *Greek Tragedy and the British Theatre* (Oxford: Oxford University Press, 2005). If we now consider the second part of the nineteenth century, apart from the original paintings by Briton Rivière and G. F. Watts, and William Blake Richmond mentioned earlier, the most important work on the subject was certainly Robert Bridges' *Prometheus the Firegiver: A Mask in the Greek Manner* (London: George Bell and Sons, 1883), in which Bridges portrays Prometheus as a noble rebel overthrowing the tyrannical Zeus.

2. The critic of the *Pall Mall Gazette*, however, gave the following description of the work on 2 May 1874: 'Upon a sharp cape of rock that juts into the lurid sky out of a sea of sinister calm, the figure of Prometheus is outstretched[...]And we may also note now the way in which the work is enriched by the suggestive management of its accessories, by the presence of the wild birds that fly silently and curiously around, by the ominous stillness in the sea and sky and by the sombre harmony of colour'.

3. William Blake Richmond, *The Release of Prometheus by Hercules*, 1882, oil on canvas, Wigan Metropolitan Borough Council. The canvas is so badly damaged that it probably cannot be restored.

4. Helen Lascelles, *The Art Annual*, 1902, p. 17.

5. Cf. Essaka Joshua, *Pygmalion and Galatea: the History of a Narrative in English Literature* (Aldershot: Ashgate, 2001), and Gail Marshall, *Actresses on the Victorian Stage: Feminine Performance and the Galatea Myth* (Cambridge: Cambridge University Press, 1998).

6. Trousson, pp. 210–12.

7. 'On Japet's Son Prometheus, who made Pandora, and begat Ydid and Deucalion'.

8. Karl Kérényi, *Prometheus*, p. 16; H. Düntzer, *Goethes Prometheus und Pandora*, 1874, p. 37. The passage that Trousson quotes to concur with Düntzer's comment on the relationship between Prometheus and Minerva ('Minerva and Prometheus appears as the mirror of the artist's soul') is the following:

> Und du bist meinem Geist,
> Was er sich selbst ist.

9. Robert Upstone, 'The Artist's Studio', in *Exposed: The Victorian Nude*, ed. by Alison Smith (London: Tate Publishing, 2001), pp. 186–87.

10. Ibid. pp. 186–87.

11. Marshall, *Actresses on the Victorian Stage*, p. 22.

12. Thomas Woolner, *Pygmalion* (London: Macmillan, 1881).

13. Along with Dante Gabriel Rossetti, William Michael Rossetti, John Everett Millais, William Holman Hunt, James Collinson and Frederic George Stephens. The Pre-Raphaelite Brotherhood was founded in 1848.

14. Thomas Woolner, *Pygmalion*, p. 24.
15. Ibid., p. 27.
16. Ibid., p. 31.
17. Ibid., pp. 31–32.
18. Ibid., p. 52.
19. Ibid., p. 72.
20. Ibid., p. 105.
21. Ibid., p. 173.
22. Sir Edward Burne-Jones, *The Pygmalion Series* (1868–1870), *The Heart Desires*, 99 × 76.3 cm; *The Hand Refrains*, 98.7 × 76.3 cm; *The Godhead Fires*, 143.7 × 116.8 cm; *The Soul Attains*, 99.4 × 76.6 cm, oil on canvas, Birmingham Museums and Art Gallery. There is also another set in a private collection.
23. George Frederic Watts, *The Wife of Pygmalion, A Translation from the Greek* (1868), oil on canvas, 67.3 × 53.3 cm, The Farringdon Collection Trust, Buscot Park, Oxfordshire.
24. John Tenniel, *Pygmalion and the Image*, 1878, watercolour on paper, 58.4 × 36.5 cm, Victoria and Albert Museum, London.
25. Ernest Normand, *Pygmalion and Galatea*, 1886, oil on canvas, 152.5 × 121cm, Atkinson Art Gallery, Southport Arts and Cultural Services, Sefton M.B.C.
26. Harry Bates, *Pandora*, c.1890, marble, ivory, bronze and gilt, 94 × 50.8 × 73.7 cm, Tate Britain.
27. John William Waterhouse, *Pandora*, 1896, oil on canvas, 152 × 91 cm, private collection.
28. Dante Gabriel Rossetti, *Study for Pandora*, 1869, chalk on paper, Faringdon Collection Trust, Buscot Park, Oxfordshire, UK.
29. Lawrence Alma-Tadema, *Pandora*, 1881, watercolour, 26 × 24.3 cm, Royal Watercolour Society, London.
30. Some critics found William Blake Richmond's 1882 *Prometheus* too effeminate. See Alison Smith, *The Victorian Nude* (Manchester: Manchester University Press, 1996), p. 182.

CHAPTER 4

Prometheus and the
Total Work of Art

For Symbolist artists, at different levels, the figure of Prometheus was a reflection of their spiritual concerns. He reflected their spiritual crisis, which explains the importance of a christianized Prometheus, onto which they could transfer their need for the Absolute. But more broadly, he also reflected their spiritual aspirations: considering any of Prometheus's masks previously examined, the essence of the fascination for the Titan revolved around his creative power. And this fascination did not exclusively hinge on those features inherited from the original figure of Prometheus *plasticator*. I am alluding to a larger symbolic power thanks to which the Titan entailed the possibility of a new world order, of a new golden age, through cosmic regeneration.

For artists, the creative power of Prometheus obviously led to his use as a mirror (sometimes distorting, if we think of Pygmalion) which reflected themselves during the process of creation. Within the Symbolist context of Art for Art's sake, such a *mise en abyme* could not be avoided. However, the use of Prometheus as a symbol went even further at the very end of the nineteenth century, since he became a key figure in the attempt to achieve the great dream of the total artwork, named *Gesamtkunstwerk* by Richard Wagner. The term refers to an ideal form of art which would fully integrate drama, art, poetry, and, most of all, music — whose immateriality is already linked to the sacred — into a spectacle much greater than the sum of its parts. It was more than a union, or a gathering of different arts: the magnificent dream of Symbolist artists was that of an organic fusion. According to Wagner, the link uniting all arts had been lost, and, in their isolation, they had been corrupted. In this respect, Aeschylean drama, as (supposedly) played in Ancient Greece was given as a model of such achievement. This model was surely a hypothetical one, since, even now, there are still many uncertainties about the way in which Aeschylus's dramas were performed. But the dream went further than this idealization, because the *Gesamtkunstwerk* concentrated all the aspirations of the Symbolists. Their conception of the total artwork exceeded even the rather strict definition given by Wagner, who applied the term mainly to the operatic genre. The *Gesamtkunstwerk*, because of its totality, became inextricably linked in the Symbolist mind to the synaesthetic ideal, and to correspondences, through which the Symbolist fore-world could be reached. In this respect, aspirations turned towards that concept, the achievement of which would also be the fulfilment of Symbolism, the accomplishment of the ideal. Given the significance of the total work of art for Symbolists, they were bound to turn towards the figure of Prometheus in order to try and achieve it.

Firstly, the figure of Prometheus had supposedly allowed Aeschylus to conjure up a striking and beguiling artistic expression, so that a reference or homage to the Greek playwright was probably perceived as a way of following in his footsteps. Secondly, and more widely, the *Gesamtkunstwerk,* to Symbolist artists, relied on a mysterious and sacred creative alchemy, very close indeed to a cosmogony, which Prometheus, as a symbol, embodied.

For the final generation of Symbolists, the concepts of synaesthesia and correspondences took a different significance than for the first Symbolists. It became more than an ideal, in the sense that various scientific theories from the very end of the nineteenth century gave what might be termed positivist grounds to what were then considered by the majority of people to be Symbolist dreams. The apparition of such theories dramatically changed the inflection of the interpretation of the figure of Prometheus. Those deriving from Thomas Young's theory of light were the most important. As opposed to Isaac Newton's theory that light was a stream of particles, Young proposed that light was a wave motion, and that the colour was determined by its wavelength. Moreover, since he believed that wave motions had to be carried by a material medium, the existence of an 'æther' filling the entire universe had to be assumed. Young's discovery had incredible repercussions on the theory of synaesthesia and its artistic use. At the end of the century, scientists put forward the theory that the vibrations of sound and light were very similar, which resulted in the idea that the seven colours of the spectrum and the seven notes of the European scale were in fact two different aspects of the same vibration field. This led Alexander Wallace Rimington 'to deal with colour in a new way, and to place its production under as easy and complete control as the production of sound in music',[1] by creating and patenting his famous Colour Organ in 1893. Synaesthesia, and its consequences for Symbolists, thus found a rational explanation and application. We shall see how they were used in late Symbolist attempts to create total artworks.

Another essential new element introduced with Symbolism at the dawn of the twentieth century was theosophy, notably the doctrine formulated by Helena Blavatsky. To a certain extent, it pushed the Symbolist credo to the extreme, and encompassed the new perception of the cosmos as a gigantic field of unknown and mysterious vibrations with unlimited possibilities. Theosophy distinguished the ephemeral from the imperishable in man, and relied on the idea that man had a permanent and essential transpersonal conscience, involved in a slow spiritual awakening. An important theosophical idea was that matter and spirit were not antagonistic, but part of the same superior unity, and the aim of the always evolving human conscience was eventually to be reunited with the absolute source. As we shall now see through the work of František Kupka and Alexander Scriabin, they were very much influenced by those new ideas, and Prometheus, as the awakener of conscience, remained a central figure for the late Symbolists, and was even strengthened as such.

Totality, Vibration Field, and Prometheus (František Kupka)

František Kupka had an original personal philosophy, and he brought this originality to his various interpretations of Prometheus. But what we call originality, some would call contradiction. His personality had a strong spiritual side, which culminated in his interest in occultism,[2] but at the same time, he claimed to be a rationalist, and put forward scientific explanations for all the phenomena he experienced, however esoteric. Such a tendency was probably due to the fact that he was strongly influenced by theosophy, which in theory was a fusion between science, religion and philosophy. It is particularly clear in his book entitled *La Création dans les arts plastiques*,[3] in which he never names theosophy as such, but claims that 'the artist is the conductor of the specific state of the nervous system which entails or establishes the telepathic communications and [...] taps the wave of an idea which is — as we say — "in the air".'[4] This sounds very much like the application of the principles of theosophy to the artistic field. Kupka started writing *La Création dans les arts plastiques* from 1910, but did not publish it in Czechoslovakia until 1923, when he wanted to abandon mysticism in favour of materialism. His book is the perfect reflection of this transitional period. An even better reflection is his treatment of Prometheus, which intervened during that crucial period in his life, from an aesthetic and philosophical point of view.

His first treatment of Prometheus was not the result of a spontaneous choice, since it was a commission, but he felt a strong affinity with his subject, and soon used it 'for his own art' to achieve personal artistic goals. From 1905 to 1909, Kupka, like his friend and compatriot Alfons Mucha, made a living out of various illustrations. This is how the publisher Auguste Blaizot came to commission illustrations from Kupka for a luxury edition of Aeschylus's *Prometheus Bound*. Kupka was not entirely free to treat the Prometheus subject as he wanted, as his illustrations had to be faithful to the general spirit of the play, and accurate in matching its different scenes. Kupka therefore opted for an archaic style deprived of perspective and highly decorative. Such a style recalled in many respects the art of ancient Egypt. However, the biggest influence to be felt in Kupka's 18 etchings and aquatints in black and orange was without doubt that of the Viennese Secessionist movement, with its flat treatment of space, extreme stylization, decorative patterns, and its interest in frescoes.[5] This is not surprising, since Kupka lived and studied in Vienna between 1892 and 1894, but it is intriguing in the sense that, when he arrived in Paris in 1896, he had decided to keep his distance from mysticism and from the inclination for metaphysics that he had inherited from the Viennese culture, and which he associated with Symbolism. By doing so, he wanted to apply French pictorial theories to his own art,[6] and to favour the depiction of nudes, or scenes of nature. Settling in Paris, for him, also meant adopting a French style. Margit Rowell, examining the role of Prometheus in Kupka's art and discussing how he was influenced by the Vienna Secession, put forward the idea that 'this reaffirmation of the value of those pictorial beginnings, in the context of his personal activity, was going to free him in return from his obsession with the contemporary French avant-gardes (fauvism, cubism), with their formal theories and with their practices'.[7] The Prometheus subject allowed

Kupka to free himself both from the Viennese aesthetic — by reaching a climax in this mode of expression — and from French dictates, by retaining only what was quintessential from those two sources of inspiration. In other words, his works on Prometheus allowed him to find his own style, an emancipation which led him to abstraction from 1912. Rowell goes on say that 'eventually, the quick evolution towards abstraction which was going to follow would make the synthesis of both: it would transpose his observation of the forces of nature onto the canvas (understood, in the French sense, as structure, colour, movement) in radically flat bi-dimensional images, while still expressing a cosmic and symbolic vision'.[8] In order to have a clear understanding of what the Prometheus treatment brought to his work, we have to examine the free, personal vision of the Titan in his *Prométhée bleu et rouge* (Fig. IV.4.1).[9]

Dating from 1909–10, *Prométhée bleu et rouge* demonstrates a very personal style, and the depiction of nature around the figure of Prometheus clearly points out a peculiar conception of the cosmos. A preliminary sketch from the Meda Mladek collection[10] demonstrates the way in which his conception of the landscape evolved. In this study, as Marcella Lista put it, 'a sort of luminous aura surrounds the titan in concentric waves, in the manner of the 'thought forms' of occultist iconography'.[11] Lista refers here to the occultist idea that thoughts are real things, even though they are difficult to identify, given that we cannot perceive the actual image of the thought, but the image of the effect caused by its accompanying vibrations in ethereal matter. Kupka's choice of such patterns around Prometheus may therefore be revealing of the remaining influence of occultism and mysticism in his art. However, in the final version of *Prométhée bleu et rouge*, the figuration of vibrations is enlarged to the landscape and is altogether different, appearing as a reflection of his interest in materialism and the synaesthetic application of Thomas Young's theories to art. Vertical yellow and blue waving lines seem to irradiate from the landscape and the earth. Such graphic patterns undoubtedly represent the cosmos rhythms, and can already be found in the illustrations of *Prometheus Bound*, notably in that of the Oceanids' song. Kupka's Prometheus, in the middle of the painting, has a physical appearance very close to Jean Delville's *Prométhée*. Extremely muscular, he does not show any sign of martyrdom. He is shown holding firmly a gigantic flower still rooted in the ground. With his conquering look, his left hand on his hip, the Titan looks as if he has a symbiotic relationship with nature, and at the same time, as if he is its master. It is not surprising if we consider that Kupka expressed the idea that 'the example of organic coherence in the surrounding world offers itself, at hand, to any painter, any sculptor. May they create as logically as nature does!'.[12] This indication, together with the definition that he gave of the artist in his *Création dans les arts plastiques,* enables one to assume that some sort of identification with Prometheus was at stake here.

A crucial aspect of *Prométhée bleu et rouge* resides in the choice of these colours. Theosophical circles were extremely interested in the colour spectrum understood as vibrations. They perceived in red the colour of sheer matter, and in blue, the other end of the spectrum, that of spirit, or ether. Prometheus would thus appear as the synthesis between matter and spirit, and as the cosmogonic symbol par

Fig. IV.4.1. František Kupka, *Prométhée bleu et rouge*, 1909–1910,
Narodni Gallery, Prague. Photo: akg / De Agostini Pic.Lib.
© ADAGP, Paris and DACS, London 2012.

excellence. Another important element concerning the place of the theory of vibrations in Kupka's art is the fact that — commenting on the gymnastic exercises that he executed naked in his garden in the morning — he explained that 'his entire body [was] penetrated by lights and perfumes', and went on to say: 'I thus live marvellous moments, adorned with nuances being poured from the chromatic keyboard of Titans'.[13] With those words, Kupka sustained a possible identification with Prometheus, and in describing the 'chromatic keyboard of Titans' underlined the importance of a synaesthetic conception of the cosmos guaranteed by universal cosmic vibrations. According to Marcella Lista, Kupka was inspired by the theories of Elisée Reclus: 'the identification of the artist with Prometheus is [...] an answer to the interrogation phrased by Reclus at the end of the chapter "Progress" of *The Earth and its Inhabitants*: "Who will determine limits to the power of man, whereas he will benefit from a perfect harmony with the immense mechanism of nature, and all of his vibrations will be measured by the course of the stars" '.[14]

The influence of Reclus was going in the same direction as another major source of inspiration for Kupka in his interpretation of Prometheus: that of Lucien Dhuys, who wrote the preface to Blaizot's edition of *Prometheus Bound*. Dhuys himself made an original interpretation of the Prometheus myth, putting forward the idea that the Titan was the embodiment of a decisive period in Ancient Greece, which could be compared with the turning point between the Old and New Testaments. Dhuys explained that the cruel and unfair reign of the Olympian gods is challenged by Prometheus, who introduces the possibility of a change in the balance of the Universal forces, therefore announcing the final victory of man over destiny. The emphasis Dhuys put on the cosmic power of Prometheus had a great impact on Kupka's own understanding of the Titan. What is particularly interesting is the fact that Dhuys named his personal philosophy, based on the power of the human spirit, 'Orphism', a philosophy which shared many principles with the philosophy that Kupka developed at that time. Dhuys stated that 'the orphic magus [who] [...] was teaching the evolution of natural forces emerged from the primordial chaos, slowly organised to create, in their last effort, the man in whom their conscience had arisen. In this regard, Orphism was unveiling the power of the spirit first oppressed by matter, and which, through a free return, and exalted by a strange force, was taming the matter that had created it'.[15] Such a philosophy is close to that developed in Elisée Reclus's *The Earth and its Inhabitants*,[16] in which he famously stated that 'Man is Nature becoming aware of itself'. This soon became one of Kupka's principles. Even if the conception of Prometheus evolved because of the development of such ideas, it is fascinating to see that, in spite of that, the duo Prometheus-Orpheus re-emerged at the end of the period we are interested in. It is now time to examine another work of art, which was also influenced by similar philosophies, but in which the principle of synaesthesia was concretely applied to a total artwork.

Beyond the Gesamtkunstwerk: *Prometheus, the Poem of Fire* (Op. 60)

Alexander Scriabin toured and travelled extensively outside Russia, and became part of Symbolist circles in London, Paris, Switzerland, and above all, Brussels. This allowed him to collect and make a certain number of Symbolist ideas his own, and even to push them to the extreme. Scriabin was truly a strange character, whose ego matched his ambition, outsoaring boundaries between arts. As a composer, he still remains a marginal figure, inasmuch as he was deeply influenced by his peculiar philosophy, and by other forms of art. As James Baker put it, 'he came increasingly under the influence of diverse aesthetic, philosophical, and mystical doctrines which impelled him toward an artistic vision of unprecedented grandiosity'.[17] His great early fascination was with Nietzsche, but, from 1905, his interests expanded. He became intimate with Jean Delville, who designed the frontispiece of the *Prometheus* score, and also got involved in the theosophical circles of Annie Besant and Madame Blavatsky,[18] whose influence eventually led him to write mystical poems, entitled *Promethean Fantasies*.[19] Scriabin was fascinated by Wagner's conception of the *Gesamtkunstwerk*. However, his own view of what the total work of art had to achieve was even wider than Wagner's. Wagner saw the *Gesamtkunstwerk* as a fusion, a synthesis between all the arts, but did not mention the principle of synaesthesia, which Scriabin considered to be crucial. Like Swedenborg, Charles Baudelaire, and Arthur Rimbaud,[20] Scriabin could not conceive of reaching the absolute of the total artwork without relying on correspondences and synaesthesia, the sensory keys to the Symbolist fore-world.

Prometheus, the Poem of Fire (Op. 60), was his last complete work, but when he died in 1915, aged 43, Scriabin was working on a colossal multimedia composition entitled the *Mysterium*, through which he was convinced mankind would transcendentally unite. Scriabin intended the *Mysterium* to incorporate a gigantic orchestra, dancers, a choir, a colour and an olfactory keyboard, poetry, and, last but not least, bells suspended from clouds (zeppelins). The seven-day-long work was to be performed in an amphitheatre built for the purpose in the foothills of the Himalayas, in symbiosis with the elements: the preludes were to accompany sunrises, the codas sunsets, flames erupting accordingly, and perfumes varying depending on the music. Scriabin conceived his work as some sort of experience mankind had to undergo before the ultimate cosmic regeneration.[21] From the description of how he intended his *Mysterium* to be performed, we can see that he pushed the Symbolist fascination for synaesthesia to its limit. Interestingly enough, when he started composing *Prometheus, the Poem of Fire*, he believed that the work he was working on was the *Mysterium* in question, but he soon realized that it was too early to achieve his full vision. Nevertheless, the concept of the *Mysterium* left its trace on *Prometheus*. We could assume that, for Scriabin also, the last step, or the threshold leading to the total artwork was the figure of Prometheus, which integrated that of the creator, of the great one who was sacrificed, and of the first (new/super) man. Because *Prometheus* was composed at the end of his life, it was steeped in Scriabin's system of thought. Some might say that the greatness of this work largely relied on his egomania and theosophical delirium. Whatever was at its root, it is undeniably a unique musical piece, and this is also true from an 'art-crossing' point of view. Osbert Sitwell, George Bernard Shaw, and John Singer Sargent, who all attended the Premiere of *Prometheus* in 1914 in London, were in awe of Scriabin's unique creation.

Although Scriabin emulated Chopin at the beginning of his career as a composer, his style evolved dramatically over time and through the developing of his theosophical and Symbolist ideas. This resulted in a personal, peerless compositional style and atonality. However, perhaps because Scriabin's persona and work were inseparable, the passage to atonality came gradually and naturally, and was completely integrated in his musical expression. In his last orchestral works, he developed an obsessive fascination for a mystic chord, named the Promethean chord (C, F♯, B♭, E, A, and D), which, not surprisingly, is at the heart of *Prometheus*.[22] Its particular sonority resides in the association of two fourths, one pure and one augmented, with the tritone (also famously named *diabolus in musica*). Hugh Macdonald says of this chord that 'mystic is not a bad epithet, especially with its unintentional suggestion of mist, since the harmony seems to float motionless, despite heaving and fluttering and recurrent attempts to animate this timeless music'.[23] In spite of its title, *Prometheus, the Poem of Fire* is very far from being a symphonic poem, and it would be pointless to try and find a precise narrative about Prometheus within the musical piece. However, the piece is very atmospheric, and we know from Scriabin himself that the aspect of Prometheus he was interested in was the relationship of the Titan with mankind, and the fact that he elevated them from their bestial level by offering them the flame of knowledge. Given the aim of Scriabin's *Mysterium*, we might reasonably assume that he identified with Prometheus, since he himself wanted to bring back mankind to spiritual harmony through cosmic regeneration. In our analysis of *Prometheus*, we shall rely on the Eulenburg edition,[24] with an introduction by Faubion Bowers which methodically states what symbolism Scriabin imputed to his music.

Scriabin had a peculiarly mathematical way of structuring his works, but unfortunately, he never explained what his proceedings were. Even though *Prometheus* has a complex internal structure, its general form is tripartite.[25] The most fundamental aspect of the piece is probably its orchestration, which contributes greatly to the atmosphere of Prometheus as well as to its Symbolism. The piece was written for a large orchestra of quadruple woodwind, eight horns, five trumpets, percussion (including a tam-tam), strings, piano, organ, and a wordless chorus. At the opening of the work, in the introduction to the piece, only the woodwind, strings, percussion and brass can be heard, forming the famous mystic chord,[26] representing original chaos. After the statement of the main theme ('Creative Principle') by the horns, open fourths played by muted trumpets (bars 21–25) symbolize Prometheus's gift of Fire, while at bar 22, a solo trumpet plays the 'theme of Will'. From that bar until the end of their intervention, bar 25, 'the muted trumpets repeat their spur to action and their seesaw symbolizes the descent of spirit into matter followed by the ascent of earth into heaven or the soul into after-life'.[27] Thus, in this introduction, the main themes of the work, together with the elemental and symbolic forces which are at the heart of the piece, are already presented, and the different instruments or parts of the orchestra are attributed a symbolic function.

The exposition starts at bar 26 with the 'Dawn of consciousness' theme, first given by the flutes and horns. At bar 30 the piano enters, which represents Man, as opposed to the orchestra, which represents the Cosmos. From bar 99 ('Avec Délice'),[28] Bowers suggests that 'Scriabin's eroticism appears',[29] an assumption confirmed at bar 105 with the indication 'avec un intence [sic] désir'.[30] Bowers continues: 'trills suggest sexual ecstasy, ravishment, pleasure and delight — in this instance Man's self-discovery'.[31] The piano, representing Man, plays the 'Creative Principle' theme at bar 131, in a significantly symbolic way. Moreover, the theme is given a perfect fourth higher, in order to highlight that 'Matter has ascended into Spirit'.[32] From then on, the 'Creative Principle' theme is revealingly renamed 'Ego' by Scriabin. At bar 146, the atmosphere of 'softness' becomes 'sourd[e], menaçant[e]',[33] when two trumpets play a perfect fourth 'which says *ya yesm* (I am)'.[34] Thus, thanks to the gift of Fire, Man goes from self-discovery and inarticulate ecstasy to the affirmation of this new-found identity.

In the development, starting at bar 193, Scriabin essentially exploits this new motif, in order to explore and express the new horizon open to Man thanks to such a discovery. From bar 235, Scriabin evokes his 'conquering of fears through defiance',[35] which, at bar 355, leads to Man's victory, 'over himself and God through action, activity, self-discovery, experience and mystical ritual, which is celebrated with 'Dance of Life' theme, exposed by the piano at bar 393.

Finally the chorus enters in an apotheosis to start the Coda (bar 449). Man, who so far had been represented as an abstraction, because of his conquests and elaboration of civilization, is now Mankind, which allows the cosmic regeneration to take place: the 'Cosmic Dance of Atoms' starts at bar 510. Then, borrowing Scriabin's own words to describe the conclusion of his unique work, Bowers states: 'All contours of themes shatter and splinter. The world of men is dematerialised and disintegrated into the cosmic dust of Nirvana. Man's incarnated Spirit is re-released into the ether as pure disembodiment. Wind- and star-swept it is blown by solar winds and galactic orgasms of ecstasy into the blue nothingness of the void'.[36] The Symbolism at stake in *Prometheus*, with a great emphasis on the relationship between Matter and Spirit, certainly reflects the ideas of theosophy, but is also an astonishing attempt to conjure up visions.

We can see how the tripartite form of the piece serves the purpose of *Prometheus*, since it emphasizes the chronological evolution at its heart. The recapitulation appears as an apotheosis, and only then does the chorus enter, thus underlining its symbolic and programmatic value within the work. The chorus, mankind, is awoken to civilization thanks to Prometheus's gift of fire. It is particularly significant that the mystic chord resolves itself at the end of *Prometheus* in a glorious F♯ major, which is also the only triad in the *Poem of Fire*. Thus the music changes from a mystic, eternal and indefinite suspension to a clear-cut harmony representing the origin and triumph of civilization, and its essential place within temporality.

One of the most interesting aspects of Alexander Scriabin's work resides in the effective use he made of synaesthesia in his work. According to Hugh Macdonald,

Scriabin's application of that principle derives from a conversation that he had with Rimsky-Korsakov, 'finding, [...] in 1907, that they both associated colour with pitch, albeit different ones'.[37] Thus, in *Prometheus*, Scriabin used a corresponding colour for each harmony, which resulted in the following correspondences, presented by Scriabin in the form of a series of fifths, here represented in a circular way together with the meaning Scriabin imputed to them (Fig. IV.4.2).[38]

When Scriabin started composing *Prometheus*, no such device as a colour organ existed, and he never saw his vision materialize. But, by the time that the work was played in London, a *tastiera per luce* (keyboard of lights) had been conceived to fulfil his wish. As Hugh Macdonald explained, 'the music is in two parts, one part giving notes (colours) that change very slowly, ten times in all, each one lasting about two minutes, The second part reflects the harmonic patterns of the music, the note (colour) corresponding to the harmonic 'tonic' at any given moment, and so it changes constantly, sometimes very rapidly',[39] which explains why the notations on the score are divided into an upper and a lower part indicating the colour base. The major issue with such a table of correspondences and with the fact that the *tastiera per luce* was altogether rather rudimentary, is that the succession of colours could not be a reflection of the rich harmonies created by Scriabin. This was increased by the fact that both B and E were pale blue, and Eb and Bb steel (only a slight variation in colour). Moreover, 'our aural perception of music is a great deal more advanced than our visual perception of colour, so that the simple reiteration of one colour every time a certain harmonic center recurs has no dynamic value compared with that of music: steel-grey on page one is the same experience as steel-grey on page ten'.[40] Leonid Sabaneev, musicologist, friend and biographer of Alexander Scriabin, wrote an account of the use of light in *Prometheus*,[41] and the Bibliothèque Nationale de France has a copy of a score belonging to Sabaneev, annotated by Scriabin in the Praga restaurant in Moscow in March 1913. This gives many indications as to what the composer intended to achieve from a lighting point of view and allows us to understand how he visualized his work and how he linked colours to certain atmospheres (instead of tempi, Scriabin used poetical French terms describing atmospheres or moods), but Sabaneev's score is not really enlightening regarding the synaesthetic value of *The Poem of Fire*.

However, one element is particularly striking in relation to the association of the symbolism of music and colours. According to Scriabin's indications, the work finishes in bright blue, a colour which represents the triumph of mankind. The bright blue of creativity, symbolically conquered by Man after his self-discovery (the 'Creative Principle' is renamed 'ego' when this appropriation takes place), overcomes the red colour that had remained dominant in the development of the tripartite form, precisely when the 'I am' played on the piano struggles against the rest of the orchestra (the Cosmos). Given that the work starts with the mystic chord, whose mystery largely relies on its fundamental tritone C-F♯, and concludes in a frank F♯ major, we can put forward the idea that the synthesis of light, colour and music had a symbolic value. Red, the colour of the Will and elemental forces, is eventually overcome by blue, the colour of mankind and civilization, and Spirit, a fundamental opposition of primary colours already seen in František Kupka's

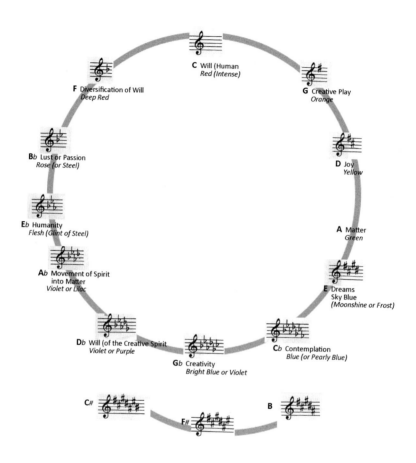

FIG. IV.4.2 Scriabin's Correspondences

works on Prometheus. Even if the synaesthesia perceived by Scriabin was originally relying on his individual perception, it appears that his symbolic and art-crossing vision had a striking consistency.

Alexander Scriabin's dream of a total work of art, more than the dream of a fusion between different arts and the production of a symbiotic effect, revealed an ambition to create a fusion between the artwork and the world. Through the tangible application of the principle of synaesthesia to a work of art, associated with the figure of Prometheus, the Titan took on a new symbolic significance. With the import of scientific theories deriving from the theory of vibrations, the existence of correspondences and synaesthesia seemed to be given a valid proof, and the cosmic regeneration dreamt of by the Symbolists then appeared as a real possibility. An unexpected reconciliation between two antagonistic interpretations of Prometheus was thus witnessed. The materialistic, positivist image of the Titan, representing the unlimited power of science — which dominated during the twentieth century and which still prevails — was brought together with the Symbolist one, inherited from Romanticism, for which Prometheus was, above all, an embodiment of idealism and spirituality. With the Symbolists' improbable and somewhat fanciful appropriation of scientific theories, the Symbolist crisis was soothed through a reconciliation with the spirit of modernity. That, together with the crude and vivid reality of the First World War, soon turned the page on Symbolism.

Notes to Chapter 4

1. A. B. Klein, *Colour Music, the Art of Light* (London: Lockwood, 1930), p. 258.
2. František Kupka, before his arrival in France, was a medium.
3. František Kupka, *La Création dans les arts plastiques* (Paris: Cercle d'art, 1989).
4. Ibid., p. 209.
5. Gustav Klimt, in this respect, is the most obvious reference.
6. His works anterior to 1905 are notably influenced by Impressionism.
7. Margit Rowell, 'Le Prométhée de Kupka', in *František Kupka 1871–1957 ou l'invention d'une abstraction* (Paris Musées: Musée d'art moderne de la ville de Paris, 1990), p. 25.
8. Ibid., p. 25.
9. František Kupka, *Prométhée bleu et rouge* (1909–1910), watercolour on paper, 32.1 × 29.3 cm, Narodni Gallery, Prague.
10. František Kupka, *Study for Prométhée bleu et rouge*, 1908–09, pastel on paper, Meda Mladek Collection, Prague.
11. Marcella Lista, 'Le rêve de Prométhée: art total et environnements synesthésiques aux origines de l'abstraction', in *Aux origines de l'abstraction, 1800–1914* (Paris: Réunion des musées nationaux, 2003), p. 217. My translation. This article was published not long before the PhD on which this book is based was submitted, and similar conclusions are shared on the value of Prometheus for late Symbolism.
12. Quoted in Miroslav Lamač 'Un Univers nouveau', in *František Kupka: 1871–1957 ou l'invention d'une abstraction* (Paris: Musée d'art moderne de la ville de Paris, Paris Musées, 1990), p. 10.
13. Kupka, *La Création dans les arts plastiques*, p. 136.
14. Marcella Lista, 'Le rêve de Prométhée: art total et environnements synesthésiques aux origines de l'abstraction', p. 217.
15. Quoted in Margit Rowell, 'Le Prométhée de Kupka', p. 28.
16. Elisée Reclus, *The Earth and Its Inhabitants* (New York: D. Appleton and Company, 1882–95).
17. James M. Baker, *The Music of Alexander Scriabin* (New Haven and London: Yale University Press, 1986), p. vii.

18. Scriabin never became a member of the Theosophical Society, but he attended several meetings in Switzerland.

19. One of his most notorious works, *The Poem of Ecstasy*, derives from one of his own 'literal' poems.

20. In the sonnet 'Voyelles'.

21. Scriabin left 72 pages of sketches for an introductory composition (known as *Prefatory Action*) whose aim was to prepare mankind for the *Mysterium* and the ensuing Apocalypse. The fragments of the piece were assembled by Alexander Nemtin, who attempted to re-create it. The resulting piece was played by the pianist Alexei Lubimov under the conductors Cyril Kondrashin in Moscow and Vladimir Ashkenazy in Berlin in 1996.

22. The mystic chord first appeared in the middle of Scriabin's *Fifth Sonata*.

23. Hugh Macdonald, *Skryabin* (Oxford: Oxford University Press, 1978), p. 55.

24. Alexander Scriabin, *Prometheus or the Poem of Fire* (op. 60) (London: Eulenburg, 1980).

25. For a full musical analysis of the *Poem of Fire*, see Baker, *The Music of Alexander Scriabin*, pp. 235–67.

26. The mystic chord never appears as a melodic motif.

27. Faubion Bowers's introduction to Alexander Scriabin, *Prometheus, the Poem of Fire* (London: Eulenburg, 1980), p. III.

28. 'With delight'.

29. Indeed, ecstasy, according to Scriabin, was one of the keys to cosmic regeneration, and he often compared the relationship of his audience with his music as an act of love, understood as a form of trance.

30. 'With intense desire'.

31. Faubion Bowers's introduction to the score, p. IV.

32. Ibid., p. IV.

33. 'muffled, threatening'.

34. Faubion Bowers's introduction to the score, p. IV.

35. Ibid., p. IV.

36. Ibid., p. IV.

37. Hugh Macdonald, *Skryabin*, p. 56.

38. Alexander Scriabin, *Prometheus, the Poem of Fire* (London: Eulenburg, 1980), p. 1.

39. Hugh Macdonald, *Skryabin*, p. 57.

40. Ibid., p. 56.

41. Interestingly, it was published under the title '*Prometheus* von Skrjabin', in Kandinsky's *Almanach der Blaue Reiter* (Munich: Piper, 1912). Kandinsky himself translated the article from the Russian.

CONCLUSION

In conclusion, I shall examine a monumental work on Prometheus published in 1922, which serves as a description both of what happened to the mythological figure after Symbolism, and of the fortune of Symbolism itself. Written by Elémir Bourges, it was the work of a lifetime. Bourges spent almost 30 years working on his gigantic poem, which is influenced by Symbolism, but goes beyond it and beyond the boundaries of this book. However, it offers some valuable insights into Symbolism. At the beginning of *La Nef*, Prometheus, full of optimism, awaits his deliverance, and announces that, when it comes, a cosmogony and a new world will soon arise. But the Symbolist dream does not come true. The void left by Zeus in the world after he is overthrown gives way to despair and horror. Prometheus's flame is extinguished, and his son, the new man, is blind. The tone of *La Nef* is pessimistic, probably because of the death of Bourges's beloved daughter, and, more obviously, because of the experience of the First World War, but nonetheless Bourges chose the figure of the Titan to express what he saw as the failure of Symbolism, and the fact that its idealistic fore-world was doomed. *La Nef*, through Prometheus, illustrates that the hopes of Symbolism were a delusion. Harley Granville Barker, in *The Madras House*,[1] also chose the figure of Prometheus to express the failure of a retreat into art. Prometheus, in any case, was the key to that world, thanks to his creative power and/or his sacrifice. In the works of Scriabin and Kupka examined in the previous chapter, the suffering of the Titan was no longer emphasized. He was a triumphant figure, and Symbolism appeared as a path towards modernism.

Thus, from being a trickster, as in Hesiod, and from being responsible for the evils endured by mankind, Prometheus became a positive figure on which hopes relied. The first step towards this new perception of Prometheus was *Prometheus Bound*, even though this sole surviving element of the trilogy was surely not intended as a glorification of Prometheus against Zeus. Aeschylus's work almost certainly ended with a reconciliation between the Titan and Zeus. The decisive moment in the history of the Prometheus myth occurred with Goethe and the *Sturm und Drang*, when Prometheus became a man, or at least the archetype of man. Artists became fascinated with the double origin of Prometheus, both man and god, and for the first time in the history of the myth, they started considering the relationship between Prometheus and the beneficiaries of his sacrifice, mankind. From then on, he was no longer a mythical character as such: no more was he a god fighting another god, and the notion of hubris, which had always been essential in the understanding of the myth, started to fade in favour of the heroism of Prometheus's act. The notion of guilt disappeared. Prometheus became the champion of mankind, the voice of the oppressed against an arbitrary and capricious power. Even more importantly,

Prometheus claims his own creative power, his ability to create from inner forms (which is also the aesthetic credo of the *Sturm und Drang*), rather than to imitate Creation itself. From a myth, Prometheus becomes a symbol of freedom: freedom from guilt, and freedom in creation. Despite a revival of interest in his figure during the Renaissance, the real glory was engendered by Goethe's ode and developed during the nineteenth century.

The talent and power of Goethe's expression and new translations of *Prometheus Bound* allowed the European societies of the time to measure and project themselves on the Prometheus myth, which seemed to give shape to their concerns in a perfect way. It seems that, after being in the shadows since the seventeenth century, the Prometheus myth was ready to be considered in a new light. Goethe allowed Prometheus's voice to be heard, and to become a human symbol, the harbinger of mankind. Goethe first inspired some of the most famous musicians of his time: Schubert and, indirectly, Beethoven. Romanticism soon adopted the Prometheus figure: in an ode, Byron made of the benefactor of mankind a Romantic hero and model, ready to push his sacrifice to its limits, 'making death a victory'. However, after Goethe, it is surely Percy Bysshe Shelley's *Prometheus Unbound* which had the strongest impact on the evolution of the Prometheus figure, and had a decisive influence on the way in which Symbolist artists later interpreted him. Shelley was the first to explore the full extent of Prometheus's creative power, a power relying on the Word, and entailing a cosmogony. The fortune of Prometheus as the key to a new world was born, and was soon widely developed. In France, the use of the Prometheus figure adopted a different angle, since the creative power of the Titan caused a direct association with the figure of the artist. Such an approach was not new. Piero di Cosimo had already made of Prometheus the representation of the artist, but it took new dimensions from Romanticism, especially with Victor Hugo, who almost obsessively established a parallel between Prometheus and himself as a poet. Hugo also projected on the figure of the Titan that of the outlaw, with which he largely identified. Honoré de Balzac used Prometheus as a model for the artist, but for different reasons. Prometheus, according to him, was the symbol of the artist because of his creative power, and his ability to give life to his creations. Balzac's own aesthetic ideals were therefore projected onto Prometheus, since his ultimate aim in the *Comédie Humaine* was to create a tangible society, and to be God in relation to his own characters. Prometheus thus increasingly appeared as the symbol for an alternative world, but a world which would be governed by mankind, thanks to their newly accepted creative power. In the case of Hugo and Balzac, this alternative world was a metaphor for the work of art. Balzac's interpretation of Prometheus as the representation of an aesthetic credo was already cross-fertilized with the Pygmalion myth, and the heirs of Romanticism, the Symbolist artists, would fully explore that parallel.

There was no real breaking-point between Romanticism and Symbolism, which appeared as a further exploration of the Romantic concerns, but a major factor shaped the state of mind of Symbolism, and gave an even greater impetus to the interpretations of Prometheus. The general crisis of faith at the heart of Symbolism resulted in the elaboration of a complex syncretism which appeared as a spiritual substitute for the lost faith of Symbolist artists. This crisis was more or less intense across Europe, according to the various political and religious contexts, and the way in which the industrial revolution had developed. In France and Belgium, where the religious factor played an important role within Symbolism, the double nature of Prometheus, both human and godlike, was crucial. Even though Symbolist artists rejected Christianity, they had an incredible thirst for spirituality, and Prometheus was soon identified with Jesus Christ, with whom he shared a human side. Jesus Christ was still glorified by Symbolist artists, but only in specific passages of the Bible, like the episode in the Garden of Gethsemane, when he appears as a man abandoned by God. In this respect, Prometheus was an ideal figure for Symbolism: like Jesus Christ, he loved mankind, and was part of it. He had sacrificed himself for it, but at the same time, he was not linked to the notion of human guilt, and, most of all, he was a pagan figure. This, combined with the fact that he was an image of the artist offering an alternative vision of the world, soon made of Prometheus a key Symbolist figure. Orpheus, for different reasons, was also associated with Jesus Christ, and was an iconic representation of the artist.

In the German Reich, the religious concerns were not as strong as the issue of cultural and political unification, and the focus on Prometheus was influenced by the interpretations of philosophers such as Marx, and more importantly Nietzsche, who was a truly Symbolist philosopher. The two men both saw in Prometheus the figure of a conqueror freed from the gods, ignorant of the notion of guilt, and who therefore had unlimited creative power. Even though Marx and Nietzsche had different philosophies and systems of thought, both emphasized in the Titan the representation of Man freed from his own chimeras, endowed with the power of self-awareness, and facing boundless possibilities. There again, in a very different context, Prometheus was at the centre of an alternative world or realm, that of mankind. Thus, even when Prometheus was depicted enduring his horrendous punishment, Symbolist painters such as Gustave Moreau and Arnold Böcklin either represented the Titan with a determined look, his eyes clearly turned towards a new world, or surrounded by an atmospheric landscape announcing a new cosmogony. There was surely an identification of Symbolist artists with Prometheus, fighting base matter, and therefore the world they despised. Such a focus on the myth was particularly clear in England, where Symbolism was on the side of Aestheticism, and where Prometheus, through a *mise en abyme*, appeared under the mask of the artist Pygmalion. However, Prometheus's symbolic value was deeper, since within Symbolist syncretism, he was the key to the ideal fore-world, the Symbolist ultimate goal. Unlike artists from the previous generation, such as Balzac or Hugo, the alternative world Prometheus represented was not only a metaphor for artistic creation. Interestingly, whereas some Symbolist artists, especially in France and Belgium, turned towards the godlike side of Prometheus to satisfy their thirst for spirituality, German-speaking artists turned rather towards his human side to dream of Arcadia.

Prometheus thus gradually became associated with what, according to Symbolists, also led to this ideal realm, namely correspondences and synaesthesia. Klinger's cycle on Prometheus, *Brahms Fantasy*, was based on this idea. But when Symbolism was later enriched with the discovery of new theories, notably that of vibration fields and Theosophy, the fore-world was seen in a new light, correspondences being suddenly understood as tangible and rational facts. Concurrently, Prometheus took on an even greater importance. Until then, he had embodied an alternative vision of the world: linked to an idealist world order, he had represented the possibility of a new cosmos, opposed to the materialistic reality entailed by the Industrial Revolution. However, at the beginning of the twentieth century, the allegory of Prometheus representing omnipotent science and the until then antagonistic Symbolist interpretations of the Titan surprisingly coincided. In fact, 'scientific' theories seemed to justify and fulfil the Symbolists' idealistic aspirations. The works of Kupka and Scriabin show the concentration of Symbolist faith and ideals in the figure of Prometheus, who became the embodiment of a pure human form, taming the forces of matter and who, by doing so, appropriates the world. This had tremendous consequences for the interpretation of Prometheus, as well as for Symbolist dreams. The issue was no longer to access the ideal fore-world, but to shape and create the world in the image of the Ideal. Prometheus thus became a symbol of the reconciliation between artists and the world, and proved to be a key to resolve the crisis of faith. The Symbolists modelled and projected their aspirations onto the Prometheus symbol, a prism filtering both the image of the Symbolist artist and their vision of the world. The protean Prometheus, Symbolist figure par excellence, thus led to Modernism.

Note to the Conclusion

1. Harley Granville Barker, *The Madras House* (London: Eyre Methuen Ltd, 1910, 1925), pp. 128–29; 152–53.

BIBLIOGRAPHY

I. Texts and Translations

AESCHYLUS, *Prometheus Bound*, trans. by Phillip Vellacott (New York: Penguin Classics, 1961)

—— *Prometheus Bound*, ed. by Mark Griffith (Cambridge: Cambridge University Press, 1983)

AESOP, *The Complete Fables*, trans. by Olivia and Robert Temple (Penguin Classics, 1998)

APOLLODORUS, *The Library of Greek Mythology*, trans. by Robin Hard (Oxford, New York: Oxford University Press, 1997)

Babrius and Phaedrus, ed. and trans. by Ben Edwin Berry (Cambridge, MA: Harvard University Press, 1965)

BACON, FRANCIS, *De Sapientia Veterum Liber*, in *The Works*, ed. by J. Spedding, R. L. Ellis, and D. D. Heath (London, 1889–92)

BALZAC, HONORÉ DE, *La Comédie humaine* (Paris: Gallimard, Bibliothèque de la Pléiade, 1951–59)

—— *Cousin Betty,* trans. by James Waring (London: J. M. Dent, 1897)

—— *The Unknown Masterpiece*, trans. by Ellen Marriage (London: J. M. Dent, 1896)

BARMBY, JOHN GOODWYN, *The Promethean: or Communist Apostle* (1842)

BOCCACCIO, GIOVANNI, *Genealogia deorum gentilium libri*, ed. by V. Romano (Bari: Laterza, 1951)

BOURGES, ELÉMIR, *La Nef* (Paris: Stock, 1904, 1922)

BRIDGES, ROBERT, *Prometheus the Firegiver* (London: George Bell and Sons, 1884)

BROWNING, ELIZABETH BARRETT, *The Poetical Works with Two Prose Essays* (London: Oxford University Press, 1951)

BYRON, GEORGE GORDON N. (6th Baron), *Ode to Napoleon Buonaparte* (London: John Murray, 1814)

—— *Selected Poetry*, ed. with an introduction and Notes by Jerome J. Mc Gann (Oxford, New York: Oxford University Press, 1994)

—— *Byron's Letters and Journals*, ed. by Leslie A. Marchand, vol. 5: 'So Late into the Night' (London, John Murray, 1976)

—— *Lord Byron, The Major Works*, ed. by Jerome J. McGann (Oxford: Oxford University Press, 1986, 2000)

—— *Lord Byron, The Complete Poetical Works*, vol. 4, ed. by Jerome McGann (Oxford Clarendon Press, 1986, 1992)

CALDERÓN DE LA BARCA, PEDRO, *Obras completas*, ed. by A. Valbuena Briones, vol. I: *La Estatua de Prometeo* (Madrid: Aguilar, 1959)

CESAROTTI, M., *Prometeo legato, tragedia trasportata in versi Italiani* (Padua, 1754)

CHAPMAN, GEORGE, *The Poems of George Chapman*, ed. by Phyllis Brooks Bartlett (New York: Russell & Russell, 1962)

ERASMUS, DESIDERIUS, *Adagia, id est: Proverbiorum, paroemiarum et parabolarum omnium, quae apud Graecos, Latinos, Hebraeos, Arabos, etc. in usu fuerunt* ([Frankfurt a. M.]: Typis Wechelianis, Sumptibus Joannis Pressii, 1643)

EURIPIDES, *Ion* (Oxford: Oxford University Press, 1954)

FICINO, MARSILIO, *Marsilii Ficini, philosophi Platonici, medici atque theologii, omnium praestantissimi, opera...* (Basel, 1561)

FULGENTIUS, *Fabii Planciadis Fulgentii V.C. Opera*, ed. by Rudolf Helm (Leipzig, 1898; repr. Stuttgart, 1970)

GOETHE, JOHANN WOLFANG VON, *Early Verse Drama and Prose Plays*, ed. by Cyrus Hamlin and Frank Ryder, trans. by Robert M. Browning, Michael Hamburger, Cyrus Hamlin, and frank Ryder (New York: Suhrkamp, 1988)

——*Werke, 5: Aus Meinem Leben; Dichtung und Warheit* (Munich: Winkler, 1973)

The Auto-biography of Goethe. Truth and Poetry: from my own life, trans. by the Rev. A. J. W. Morrison, M.A. (London: Henry G. Bohn, 1849), p. 38

——*Selected Poems*, ed. by Christopher Middleton, trans. by Michael Hamburger (Princeton: Princeton University Press, 1983)

GRANVILLE BARKER, HARLEY, *The Madras House* (London: Eyre Methuen, 1910, 1925)

HESIOD, *Theogony* and *Work and Days*, trans. by M. L. West (Oxford: Oxford University Press, 2008)

HOBBES, THOMAS, *Man and Citizen: 'De Homine' and 'De Cive'*, ed. by Bernard Gert, trans. by C. T. Wood and T. S. K. Scott-Craig (Indianapolis: Hackett, 1991)

HOMER, *The Odyssey*, trans. by Walter Shewring (Oxford: Oxford World's Classics, 1998)

HORACE, *Odes*, 2 vols, ed., trans., and with an introduction by David West (Oxford: Clarendon Press, 1995, 1998)

HUGO, VICTOR, *Odes et Ballades*, ed. by Pierre Albouy (Paris: Gallimard, 1964)

——*Dieu (L'Océan d'en haut).* (Paris: Nizet, 1960)

——*Œuvres poétiques complètes*, ed. by Francis Bouvet (Paris: Pauvert, 1961)

——*Toute la Lyre* (Paris: Nelson, 1916)

——*Selected Poems of Victor Hugo: A Bilingual Edition*, trans. by E. H. and A. M. Blackmore (Chicago: University of Chicago Press, 2001)

HYGINUS, *De Astronomia* (Michigan: University of Michigan Press, 1998)

JUVENAL, *Satires, with the satires of Persius*, with an English translation by William Gifford, rev. and annotated by John Warrington, introduction by H. J. Rose (London: Dent Dutton, 1954)

LE FRANC DE POMPIGNAN, J. J., *Tragédies* (Paris, 1770)

LUCIAN OF SAMOSATA, *Works*, with an English translation by K. Kilburn (London: Heinemann; New York, Macmillan, 1959)

MENANDER, *Works*, ed. and trans. by W. G. Arnott (Cambridge, MA: Harvard University Press, 2000)

MONTI, VICENZO, *Poemetti mitologici* (Turin: Unione Tipografico-Editrice Torinese, undated)

MORELL, T. *Aischulou Prometheus Desmotes. Cum Stanleiana versione, scholiis ... amplissimisque ... notis; quibus suas adjecit, necnon scholia de metro, ac Anglicanam interpretationem* (London, 1773)

OVID, *Metamorphoses*, trans. by A. D. Melville, with an introduction and notes by E. J. Kenney (Oxford: Oxford University Press, 1986)

PÉLADAN, JOSÉPHIN, *La Prométhéide* (Paris: Chamuel, 1895)

PICO DELLA MIRANDOLA, GIOVANNI, *De Hominis dignitate Heptaplus de ente et uno, e scritti vari*, ed. by Eugenio Garin, vol. I (Florence: Edizione Nazionale dei Classici del Pensiero italiano, 1942)

PHILEMON, *Fragmenta*, trans. by F. Dübner (Paris: Didot, not dated)

PHILODEMUS, *On Piety*, ed. with translation and commentary by Dirk Obbink (Oxford: Clarendon Press, 1996)

PINDAR, *Complete Works*, ed. and trans. by William H. Race (Cambridge, MA: Harvard University Press, 1997)

Plato, *Complete Works*, ed. by John Cooper and D. S. Hutchinson (Indianapolis: Hackett, 1997)

——*Protagoras*, trans. by C. C. W. Taylor (Oxford: Oxford University Press, 2009)

Pomponazzi, Pietro, *Libri quinque de fato, de libero arbitrio et de pradestinatione*, ed. by R. Lemay (Padua: Antenore, 2011)

Potter, Robert, *The Tragedies of Aeschylus* (Norwich, 1777)

Quinet, Edgar, *Prométhée* (Paris, 1838)

Shelley, Percy Bysshe, *Shelley's Poetry and Prose*, selected and ed. by Donald H. Reiman and Sharon B. Powers (New York, London: Norton, 1977)

Tertullian, *Apology; De Spectaculis*, trans. by T. R. Glover (London: Heinemann, 1966)

——*Ante-Nicene Christian Library*, vol. VII, trans. by Peter Holmes (Edinburgh: T. & T. Clark, 1868)

Vasari, Giorgio, *The Lives of the Artists*, trans. by Julia and Peter Bondanella (Oxford: Oxford University Press, 1998)

Villani, Filippo, *Le vite d'uomini illustri fiorentini*, annotated by Count Giammaria Mazzuchelli (Venice: Academico della Crusca, Pasquali, 1747)

Voltaire, *Œuvres Complètes*, vol. 18C: *Pandore*, ed. by Ulla Kölving and others (Oxford: Voltaire Foundation, 1968)

Woolner, Thomas, *Pygmalion* (London: Macmillan, 1881)

II. References

IIa. Literature

Adams, H. P, *Karl Marx in his Earlier Writings* (London: Allen and Unwin, 1940)

Albouy, Pierre, *Mythes et mythologies dans la littérature française* (Paris: Armand Colin, 1969)

Bachelard, Gaston, *Psychoanalysis of Fire* (Boston: Beacon Press, 1964)

Baudelaire, Charles, *Intimate Journals*, trans. by Christopher Isherwood (Mineola, NY: Dover, 2006)

Boyd, James, *Notes to Goethe's Poems*, vol. I (1749–1786). (Oxford: Blackwell, 1944)

Burkert, Walter, *The Orientalising Revolution*, new edn (Cambridge, MA: Harvard University Press, 1995)

Butler, B. M., *Byron and Goethe, Analysis of a Passion* (London: Bowes and Bowes, 1956)

Carré, J. M., *Goethe en Angleterre*, 2nd edn (Paris: Etude de Littérature Comparée, 1920)

Carlyle, Thomas, *Sartor Resartus*, ed. by Kerry McSweeney and Peter Sabor (Oxford: Oxford Paperbacks, 2000)

Černý, Václav, *Essai sur le titanisme dans la poésie romantique occidentale entre 1815 et 1850* (Prague, 1935)

La Cravache parisienne, 16 June 1888

Day, Martin, *The Many Meanings of the Myth* (Lanham: University Press of America, 1984)

Delcourt, Marie, *Héphaistos ou la légende du magicien* (Paris: Université de Liège-Belles Lettres, 1957)

Dietz, Karl-Martin, *Metamorphosen des Geistes, I: Prometheus- Vom göttlichen zum menschlichen Wissen* (Stuttgart: Freies Geistesleben, 1989)

Le Don Quichotte, Paris, 22 juillet 1876

Dorra, Henri, *Symbolist Art Theories: a Critical Anthology* (London: University of California Press, 1994)

Dougherty, Carol, *Prometheus* (London: Routledge, 2005)

Duchemin, Jacqueline, *Prométhée, histoire du mythe, de ses origines orientales à ses incarnations modernes* (Paris: Les Belles Lettres, 2000)

DUMÉZIL, GEORGES, *Le Festin d'immortalité* (Paris, 1924)

ELIADE, MIRCEA, *Images and Symbols*, trans. by Philip Mairet (London: Harvill Press, 1952, 1961)

——*Myths, Dreams, and Mysteries*, trans. by Philip Mairet (London: Collins, 1968)

——*The Quest: History and Meaning in Religion* (Chicago and London: University of Chicago Press, 1969)

Esthétique du Symbolisme (Brussels: Palais des Académies, 1962)

FONTENELLE, *De l'origine des fables* (Paris: Alcan, 1932)

FRAZER, J. G., *The Myths of the Origin of Fire* (London, 1930)

FRONTISI-DUCROUX, FRANÇOISE, *Dédale: mythologie de l'artisan en Grèce ancienne* (Paris: F. Maspero, 1975)

FRYE, NORTHROP, *A Study of English Romanticism* (Brighton: Harvester Press, 1968)

GAUNT, WILLIAM, *The Aesthetic Adventure* (London, Jonathan Cape, 1945)

GIDE, ANDRÉ, *Romans, récits et soties. Œuvres lyriques*, ed. by Maurice Nadeau (Paris: Gallimard, Bibliothèque de la Pléiade, 1958)

GRABO, CARL, *Prometheus Unbound: an Interpretation* (Chapel Hill: University of North Carolina Press, 1935)

GRAPPIN, PIERRE, *La Théorie du génie dans le préclassicisme allemand* (Paris: PUF, 1952)

GRAUBY, FRANÇOISE, *La Création mythique à l'époque du Symbolisme: Histoire, analyse et interprétation des mythes fondamentaux du Symbolisme* (Paris: Nizet, 1994)

GRIFFITH, MARK, *The Authenticity of the Prometheus Bound* (Cambridge: Cambridge University Press, 1977)

GRIMAL, P., *Mythologies de la Méditerranée au Gange* (Paris: Larousse, 1963)

HALL, EDITH, and FIONA MACINTOSH, *Greek Tragedy and the British Theatre, 1660–1914* (New York, Oxford: Oxford University Press, 2005)

HARDWICK, LORNA and EVA PARISINOU, *Translating Words, Translating Culture* (Bristol: Bristol Classical Press, 2000)

HEILBRUN, FRANÇOISE, *Victor Hugo: Photographies de l'exil* (Paris: Réunion des musées nationaux, 1998)

HERINGTON, C. J., *The Author of the Prometheus Bound* (Austin: University of Texas Press, 1970)

HINDLE, MAURICE, *Mary Shelley's Frankenstein* (London: Penguin, 1994)

HOLMES, RICHARD, *Prometheus²: The Two Shelleys and Romantic Science*, lecture given on 27 October 2011 at the School of Advanced Studies, London

L'Illustration, Paris, 15 May 1869

JENKYNS, RICHARD, *The Victorians and Ancient Greece* (Oxford: Blackwell, 1980)

JOSHUA, ESSAKA, *Pygmalion and Galatea: the History of a Narrative in English Literature* (Aldershot: Ashgate, 2001)

JUNG, CARL GUSTAV, KARL KÉRÉNYI, and PAUL RADIN, *Le Fripon divin*, trans. by Arthur Reiss (Geneva: Georg, 1958)

KAUFMANN, WALTER (ed. and trans.), *The Portable Nietzsche* (New York: Viking Press, 1954)

KÉRÉNYI, KARL, *Prometheus, Albae Vigiliae* (Zurich: N.F., 1946)

——*Mythologie des grecs* (Paris: Payot, 1952)

KNIGHT, A. H. J., *Some Aspects of the Life and Work of Nietzsche, and particularly of His Connection with Greek Literature and Thought* (New York: Russell and Russell, 1933, 1967)

KOSINSKI, DOROTHY, *Orpheus in Nineteenth Century Symbolism* (London: U.M.I Research Press, 1989)

KRÜGER, MANFRED, *Wandlungen des Tragischen* (Stuttgart: Drama und Initiation, 1973)

LECLERQ, CATHERINE, *Prométhée et le Golem* (Brussels: La Lettre volée, 2000)

LECOURT, DOMINIQUE, *Prométhée, Faust, Frankenstein, fondements imaginaires de l'éthique* (Paris: Livre de poche, 1996)

LEHMANN, A. G., *The Symbolist Aesthetic in France 1885–1895* (Oxford: Blackwell, 1950, 1968)

LÉVI-STRAUSS, CLAUDE, *Myth and Meaning* (London: Routledge, 1978)

LICHTENBERGER, H., *Pandore. Goethe* (Strasbourg: Faculté des Lettres de l'Université de Strasbourg, booklet 57, 1932)

LUCAS, DONALD WILLIAM, *The Greek Tragic Poets,* 2nd edn (London: Cohen and West, 1959)

McGUINNESS, PATRICK, PETER COOKE and DEE REYNOLDS, *Symbolism, Decadence and fin de siècle* (Exeter: University of Exeter Press, 2000)

MARCHAL, BERTRAND, *Lire le Symbolisme* (Paris: Dunod, 1993)

——*Lecture de Mallarmé* (Paris: Corti, 1985)

MARSHALL, GAIL, *Actresses on the Victorian Stage: Feminine Performance and the Galatea Myth* (Cambridge: Cambridge University Press, 1998)

MARX, KARL, and FRIEDRICH ENGELS, *Collected Works*, vol. I (London: Lawrence and Wishart, 1975–2004)

MAUROIS, ANDRÉ, *Prométhée, ou la vie de Balzac* (Paris: Hachette, 1965)

MICHAUD, GUY, *Message poétique du Symbolisme* (Paris: Nizet, 1961)

——*Le Symbolisme tel qu'en lui-même* (Paris: Nizet, 1994)

MILLER, JOHN HILLIS, *Versions of Pygmalion* (Cambridge, MA: Harvard University Press, 1990)

MOCKEL, A., *Propos de littérature* (Paris, 1894), republished in *Esthétique du Symbolisme* (Brussels: Palais des Académies, 1962)

MORÉAS, JEAN, 'Manifeste du Symbolisme' *Le Figaro*, 18 September 1886, pp. 1–2

MORICE, CHARLES, *La Littérature de tout-à-l'heure* (Paris, 1889)

MORRIS, WILLIAM, *The Earthly Paradise*, 4 vols (London: Longmans, Green and Co., 1904)

NIETZSCHE, FRIEDRICH, *The Birth of Tragedy*, trans. with commentary by Walter Kaufmann (New York: Vintage Books, 1967)

——*The Will to Power*, trans. by Walter Kaufmann and R. J. Hollingdale, ed. by Walter Kaufmann (New York: Vintage Books, 1968)

——*The Gay Science*, trans. with commentary by Walter Kaufmann (New York: Vintage Books, 1974)

NORWOOD, G., *Greek Tragedy*, 4th edn (London: Methuen, 1948)

PAPE, WALTER, *1870/71–1989/90 German Unifications and the Change of Literary Discourse* (Berlin, New York: de Gruyter, 1993)

PANOFSKY, DORA and ERWIN, *Pandora's Box: The Changing Aspects of a Mythical Symbol* (New York: Bollinger Foundation, 1962)

PENCAK, WILLIAM, 'Lyres against the Law', *Legal Studies Forum*, 23.3 (1999), 293–314

RÉATTU, JACQUES, *Sous le signe de la Révolution* (Paris: Musée de la Révolution Française, Actes Sud, 2000)

RECLUS, ELISÉE, *The Earth and Its Inhabitants* (New York: D. Appleton and Company, 1882–95)

RENUCCI, PAUL, *L'Aventure de l'humanisme européen au Moyen Age (XIVème-XVème siècle).* (Paris: Les Belles Lettres, 1953)

REYNOLDS, MARGARET, *The Sappho History* (Basingstoke: Palgrave Macmillan, 2003)

——*The Sappho Companion* (London: Chatto and Windus, 2000)

RIBOT, THÉODULE, *La Philosophie de Schopenhauer* (Paris: Alcan, 1874)

ROBB, GRAHAM, *Victor Hugo* (New York: W. W. Norton, 1997)

SAINT-VICTOR, PAUL DE, *Les Deux masques*, 3 vols (Paris, 1880, 1894)

SATO, TOMOKO, and LIONEL LAMBOURNE (eds), *The Wilde Years* (London: Barbican Centre, 2000)

SCEPI, HENRI, *Les Complaintes de Jules Laforgue* (Paris: Gallimard, 2000)

SCHILLER, FRIEDRICH, *Wereke: Nationalausgabe*, XX: *Über die Ästhetische Erziehung des Menschen in einer Reihe von Briefen* (Weimar, 1962)

SCHURÉ, EDOUARD, *Le Drame musical*, 2 vols (Paris: Didier, 1886)

SCHWAB, R., *La vie d'Elémir Bourges* (Paris: Stock, 1948)

SÉCHAN, LOUIS, *Le Mythe de Prométhée* (Paris: PUF, 1951, repr. 1985)

——*Pandora, l'Eve grecque* (Paris: Bulletin de l'Association Guillaume Budé, XXIII, 1929)

SHELLEY, MARY, *The Poetical Works of Percy Bysshe Shelley* (London: Edward Moxon, 1839)

SWEDENBORG, EMANUEL, *The New Jerusalem* (The Swedenborg Association, 1997)

SYMONS, ARTHUR, *The Symbolist Movement in Literature* (London, William Heinemann, 1899)

THOMAS, L., *Bourges et la Nef* (Paris: Mercure de France, 1920)

THORSLEV, PETER L. JR., *The Byronic Hero, Types and Prototypes* (Minneapolis: University of Minnesota Press, 1962)

TROUSSON, RAYMOND, *Le Thème de Prométhée dans la littérature européenne* (Geneva: Droz, 1964, repr. 2001)

L'Univers illustré, Paris, 8 May 1869

VALÉRY, PAUL, *Lettres à quelques-uns* (Paris: Gallimard, 1952)

——*Œuvres*, ed. by J. Hytier (Paris: Gallimard, Bibliothèque de la Pléiade, 1968)

VOLTAIRE, *Œuvres complètes*, 52 vols (Paris: Garnier, 1877–1885)

WAGNER, RICHARD, *Religion and Art*, in *Prose Works*, vol. VI, trans. by Ashton Ellis (London, 1897)

WALZEL, OSKAR, *Das Prometheussymbol von Shaftesbury zu Goethe*, in *Wortkunst*, volume VII (Munich: Hueber, 1932)

WEST, MARTIN L., *Studies in Aeschylus* (Stuttgart: Teubner, 1990)

——*The East Face of Helicon*, new edn (Oxford: Clarendon Press, 1999)

WERBLOWSKY, R. J. ZWI, *Lucifer and Prometheus, a Study of Milton's Satan* (London: Routledge, 1999)

WIELAND, CHRISTOPH MARTIN, *Beiträge zur geheimen Geschichte des menschlichen Verstandes und Herzens* and *Ueber die Von J.J.Rousseau vorgeschlagenen Versuche den Wahren Stand der Natur des Menschen*, in *Sämmtliche Werke*, 53 vols (Leipzig: Göschen, 1818–28)

WILAMOWITZ-MOELLENDORFF, ULRICH VON, *Aischylos Interpretationen* (Berlin: Weidmann, 1914)

WILDE, OSCAR, *Salomé* (London: Faber, 1989)

WOLFF, H. M., *Goethe in der Periode der Wahlverwandschaften (1802–1809).* (Berne: 1952)

WOOLNER, AMY, *Thomas Woolner, R.A. Sculptor and Poet: His Life in Letters* (London: Chapman and Hall, 1917)

WUTRICH, TIMOTHY RICHARD, *Prometheus and Faust: The Promethean Revolt in Drama from Classical Antiquity to Goethe* (Westport, CN: Greenwood, 1995)

ZIOLKOWSKI, THEODORE, *The Sin of Knowledge, Ancient Themes and Modern Variations* (Princeton: Princeton University Press, 2000)

IIb. History of Art

ARASSE, DANIEL, *Le Sujet dans le tableau* (Paris: Flammarion, 1997)

CHRISTIAN, JOHN, *The Last Romantics: The Romantic Tradition in British Art* (London: Lund Humphries, 1989)

DOLLINGER, HANS, *Böcklin* (Munich: Bruckmann, 1975)

ECKER, JORGEN, *Anselm Feuerbach: Leben und Werk* (Hirmer, 1991)

EHRARDT, INGRID and SIMON REYNOLDS (eds.), *Kingdom of the Soul, Symbolist Art in Germany 1870–1920).* (Munich: Prestel, 2000)

FACOS, MICHELLE, *Symbolist Art in Context* (University of California Press, 2006)

FRANKLIN GOULD, VERONICA (ed.), *The Vision of G. F. Watts* (London: Yale University Press, 2004)

GIBSON, MICHAEL, *Symbolism* (London: Taschen, 1995)

HOFSTAETTER, HANS VON, *Rudolf Jettmar: Monographie* (Vienna: Tusch, 1984)

Rudolf Jettmar (1869–1939): Bilder Von Hellen und Dunklen Mythen (Vienna: Museen der Stadt Wien, 1989)

JULLIAN, PHILIPPE, *Dreamers of Decadence: Symbolist Painters of the 1890s* (London: Pall Mall Press, 1971)

KEISH, CLAUDE, PETER-KLAUS SCHUSTER, and ANGELIKA WESENBERG (eds), *Spirit of an Age: Nineteenth-Century Paintings from the Nationalgalerie, Berlin* (London: National Gallery Company, 2001)

KUPKA, FRANTIŠEK, *La Création dans les arts plastiques* (Paris: Cercle d'art, 1989)

LACAMBRE, GENEVIÈVE, *Gustave Moreau: 1826–1898* (Paris: Réunion des Musées Nationaux, 1998)

LAMAČ, MIROSLAV, 'Un univers nouveau', in *František Kupka: 1871–1957 ou l'invention d'une abstraction* (Paris: Musée d'art moderne de la ville de Paris, Paris Musées, 1990)

LEHRS, MAX, 'Max Klingers "Brahms-Phantasie"', *Zeitschrift für Bildende Kunst*, 6 (1895), 113–18

Lexicon Iconographicum Mythologiae Classicae, vol. VII (Zürich: Artemis & Winkler, 1981–1999)

LISTA, MARCELLA, 'Le rêve de Prométhée: art total et environnements synesthésiques aux origines de l'abstraction', in *Aux origines de l'abstraction, 1800–1914* (Paris: Réunion des musées nationaux, 2003)

LUCIE-SMITH, EDWARD, *Symbolist Art* (London: Thames and Hudson, 1972)

MADRAZO, PEDRO DE, *Catálogo de los cuadros del Real Museo de Pintura* (Madrid, 1843)

MARTIN, JOHN RUPERT, *Rubens Before 1620* (Princeton: Princeton University Press, c. 1972)

MATHIEU, PIERRE-LOUIS, *Gustave Moreau: Complete Edition of the Finished Paintings, Watercolours and Drawings* (Oxford: Phaidon, 1977)

MYRONE, MARTIN, ed., *Gothic Nightmares: Fuseli, Blake and the Romantic Imagination* (London: Tate Publishing, 2006)

—— *Bodybuilding: Reforming Masculinities in British Art, 1750–1810* (New Haven and London: Yale University Press, 2005)

NASH, JANE C., *Veiled Images: Titian's Mythological Paintings for Philip II* (Philadephia: Art Alliance Press; London: Associated University Presses, 1985)

PALADILHE, JEAN, and JOSÉ PIERRE, *Gustave Moreau* (London: Thames and Hudson, 1972)

RAGGIO, OLGA, 'The Myth of Prometheus: Its Survival and Metamorphoses up to the Eighteenth Century', *Journal of the Warburg and Courtauld Institutes*, 21 (1958), 44–62.

RAPETTI, RODOLPHE, *Symbolism* (Paris: Flammarion, 2005)

REID, JANE DAVIDSON, *The Oxford Guide to Classical Mythology in the Arts, 1300–1990s* (New York, Oxford: Oxford University Press, 1993)

REYNOLDS, SIMON, *William Blake Richmond: An Artist's Life, 1842–1921* (Michael Russell, 1995)

ROWELL, MARGIT, 'Le Prométhée de Kupka', in *František Kupka 1871–1957 ou l'invention d'une abstraction*, (Paris Musées: Musée d'art moderne de la ville de Paris, 1990)

SCHMID, MAX, *Max Klinger*, 5th edn (Leipzig: Bielefeld, 1926)

SPOONER, S., *A Biographical History of the Fine Arts*, 4th edn, vol. II (New York: Leypoldt and Holt, 1867)

SMITH, ALISON (ed.), *Exposed: The Victorian Nude* (London: Tate Publishing, 2000)

—— *The Victorian Nude: Sexuality, Morality and Art* (Manchester: Manchester University Press, 1996)

SUIDA, WILHEM, *Titien* (Paris, 1935)

WETHEY, HAROLD E., *The Paintings of Titian*, vol. III, *The Mythological and Historical Paintings* (London: Phaidon, 1969)

IIc. Music

Baker, James M., *The Music of Alexander Scriabin* (New Haven and London: Yale University Press, 1986)

Bertagnolli, Paul, *Prometheus in Music: Representations of the Myth in the Romantic Era* (Aldershot: Ashgate, 2007)

Klein, B., *Colour Music, the Art of Light* (London: Lockwood, 1930),

Lacché, Mara, 'L'Humanisme de J. G. Herder dans la pensée esthético-musicale de F. Liszt', *Ostinato Rigore*, 18 (2001), 43–53

Liszt, Franz, *Chöre zu Herders 'Entfesseltem Prometheus'*, R. 539, 1850

——*Franz Liszts musikalische Werke. I, Für Orchester* (Farnborough: Gregg Press, 1966)

Macdonald, Hugh, *Skryabin* (London: Oxford University Press, 1978)

Schubert, Franz, *Prometheus* (1819). D674, in *Gesänge*, Band III (Frankfurt, London, New York: C. F. Peters)

Alexander Scriabin, *Prometheus, the Poem of Fire* (London: Eulenburg, 1980)

INDEX